THE EVOLUTION
OF POLITICAL SOCIETY

THE EVOLUTION
OF POLITICAL SOCIETY

An Essay in
Political Anthropology

MORTON H. FRIED
Columbia University

McGraw-Hill, Inc.

New York St. Louis San Francisco Auckland Bogotá
Caracas Lisbon London Madrid Mexico City Milan
Montreal New Delhi San Juan Singapore
Sydney Tokyo Toronto

THE EVOLUTION OF POLITICAL SOCIETY

17 18 19 20 BAH BAH 9 9 8 7 6 5 4 3

Library of Congress Catalog Card Number: 67–18129

ISBN: 0–07–553579–3

Design by Jeanette Young

For Martha,
who loves politics
but prefers it
contemporary

CONTENTS

INTRODUCTION

Oh Meliboeus, I have half a mind
To take a writing hand in politics.

—Robert Frost

There is much to be said for an introduction. It may warn you away from the rest of the book before you've really invested in it. So I will try to tell you very briefly what I go on about at greater length in the chapters. Actually, it is good for me to do so, because in some important respects this book runs against the current of present theoretical tendencies in my own field of anthropology and in that fascinating adjacent neighborhood, political science. As in much of contemporary social science, concern in these fields is concentrated on behavioral and systems analysis; the field of vision tends to be restricted to what is directly observable. Functionalism reigns, and the view is synchronic. The attempt to derive yet another set of generalizations about cultural evolution will strike many as quixotic. To talk about the evolution of polity will seem antediluvian. Yet some problems don't go away. The fact that they have not been solved by famous thinkers of the past might serve as a warning to those who come later along the path, but instead it sometimes seems to act as a goad. More seriously, changes in the conceptions and methods of the relevant fields of inquiry sometimes threaten to expunge the questions that previous thinkers struggled with in vain. The language changes, and key words are repudiated, as are "state" by the new political scientists and "tribe" in the present case. Many social scientists concerned now define the political as a ubiquitous aspect of social organization and treat it as something perduring and without determinable beginning. But linguistic shifts and even changes in the strategic concepts of social science are not enough to abolish certain key questions. Some students continue to ask how the ordering of social relations became so complex, how invidious distinctions arose among the inhabitants of a single society, how exploitation developed, and how the political state came to be. Although some illumination of parts of the answers to these questions may come from so called "behavioral" approaches, the basic questions are about evolution, and the basic answers will be evolutionary.

Because the language of political science and political anthropology is anything but standardized, the book begins with definitions. Because the gap between any and all existing nonhuman primate societies and every known human society is so great, the necessary treatment of political-like elements in primate society is placed in the definitional preamble. In a sense they are the elementary limiting conditions out of a great range of which the behavior of our ancestors emerged 2 million years ago.

The simplest human societies of which we have knowledge are those classified and described in this book as "egalitarian." In the course of Chapter 3 we make an extensive analysis of the way in which such societies are organized and how relations are maintained within them and among them. We are particularly interested in certain questions of long standing: whether or not they are associated with certain characteristic forms of economic organization, whether or not they may be spoken of as having law, and whether or not and to what degree they are warlike. The next degree of complication in the evolution of political society is identified with the appearance of ranking. The definition of ranking used in this book is a little unusual, but there are precedents for the usage here adopted. Similarly, the next level is identified with stratification, and it is clearly distinguished from ranking by a somewhat unique definition. Whereas the rank society, that is, a society with ranking but not stratification, is relatively stable, provided that it is not unbalanced by pressures emanating from more highly organized societies, the stratified society is by nature unstable. It must give way fairly rapidly to a more complex system of political organization or return to a lower level of organization, that is, revert to rank or egalitarian structure. Should it move successfully on to the higher level of organization, its form will be transmuted into that of a state. In the final chapter we briefly consider the character of the state and the means by which this form of organization takes shape. A distinction is proposed between pristine and secondary states, between states that took shape in the absence of predecessors and those that were formed because pre-existing states supplied the stimuli or the models for organization.

It is fitting that this introduction conclude with the same sentiments I expressed in an earlier article covering some of the same ground. I have been led to write this book by my ignorance of any modern attempt to link up the contributions that have been made in various subdisciplines into a more or less unified theory of the emergence of ranking, social stratification, and the state. That the theory offered here is crude, often too special, and (still) by no means documented seems less important than that it may be used as a target to attract the fire and better aim of others.

That is the end of this introduction. It puts me in mind of a story told by Machiavelli: Having been wearied by a long speech, Castruccio Castracani was asked by the orator, "Perhaps I have fatigued you by speaking so long?" To which Castruccio replied, "You have not, because I haven't listened to a word you said."

THE EVOLUTION
OF POLITICAL SOCIETY

CHAPTER 1

Concepts
and Definitions

Some scholars think definitions are poison. Trying to free political science from the blight of procrustean definitions, Arthur Bentley said, "Who likes may snip verbal definitions (like paper dolls) in his old age, when his world has gone crackly and dry" (Bentley, 1949, p. 199; I came across the remark in Easton, 1953, p. 94). Lucy Mair tells us that Bronislaw Malinowski hated definitions, and her opinion of them doesn't seem much higher. About the definition of law she regretfully remarks, "Floods of ink have been wasted on this subject" (Mair, 1962, p. 19).

Among my friends and colleagues are those who have warned that definitions are old-fashioned and tend to parochialize a discussion. I agree that infatuation with archetypes is likely to be fatal to the questing and particularly the scientific intellect. But there is an immense gulf between hypostasized ideals and the tool use of definitions.

One really discouraging thing is the realization that a great many truly brilliant people have played with the same problems and have, in the course of their work, offered many good words and definitions: so many, in fact, that the problem of meaning lies all entangled and, turning to a subject, one must often begin by telling what his words signify for him.

All these things have been said so many times before that the present writer must shudder as he repeats that the need for definition is akin to the need for tools. Basically, the test of language used for scientific expression is utility, and utility is measured, not by truth or falsity per se, but by ability to convey distinctness, similarity, identity, independence, dependence, association, and other presences or absences of relationship, all to the nicest degree.

Take the subject matter of this book. What is meant by political organization? Should it be distinguished from government and, if so, how? Can a useful distinction be made between government and social control? Between reinforcements and sanctions, customs and laws? It is simple to generate such questions, most of which have already led to discussions running into thousands of pages. It is a matter of utmost difficulty—probably impossible—to offer universally acceptable solutions. For this reason alone, it seems wise to give up the belief that definitions must be true or false; for the purposes suggested here they are better evaluated as more or less useful (*cf.* Cohen, 1935, p. 835; Seagle, 1941, pp. 3–6). In any case, the present attempt does not seek to establish a new vocabulary but only to make as clear as possible the statements and arguments that follow. However it may seem to the reader, my goal has been to avoid what one journalist has called "the arcane language of the professional . . . which aims at precision while never achieving clarity."

CULTURE, SOCIETY,
AND SOCIAL ORGANIZATION

It is often said that the scientific concept of culture is the great contribution of anthropology to our times, but Leslie A. White, reviewing Alfred Kroeber and Clyde Kluckhohn's inventory of definitions of culture, concluded that the concept of culture is so protean as to be of dubious value. Marvin Harris (1963), who is critical of the epistemological bases of many pronouncements about culture, has made an interesting attempt to place the concept of culture on an operational basis. Present purposes are better served, however, by treating culture in a way now regarded as conventional, in terms of the process by which it is transmitted, that is, through symbolic learning.

Behavioral psychologists are accustomed to dealing with learning as a phenomenon of biological level. Problems faced by cultural anthropologists, however, are quite different from those usually tackled by psychologists interested in learning theory. In some instances, where cross-fertilization has been possible, significant uses have been made of models drawn from psychology; George P. Murdock's drawing upon Clark Hull's theories is one notable illustration. In terms of the broadest posing of problems of culture, it seems profitable to make a distinction not usually applied in psychology and to differentiate three kinds of learning according to the contexts in which they occur. We may refer to them as "situational," "social," and "symbolic" learning.

Situational learning is the most widely distributed of the three and is almost synonymous with life. Certainly it is found among protists and all forms of animal life. It is the process by which an organism adopts or alters a behavioral response on the basis of experience. Presented with a stimulus, the organism establishes a response pattern, and recurrent presentations of similar stimuli elicit similar responses, sometimes with increases or decreases in reaction time as the series proceeds. Most significant about this kind of learning situation is the immediate relationship between stimulus and response, characterized by the absolute need for the organism personally to encounter the stimulus and to form its own response pattern. Creatures limited to situational learning cannot communicate, nor can they be communicated with. Situational learning by itself is and must remain solipsistic. Consequently, its capacity for aggregation is almost zero. A creature may accumulate a small number of learned responses during its lifetime, but they will be wiped out with his death.

Social learning occurs when one organism, perceiving another encounter a stimulus and emit a response, acquires that response as part of its own behavioral repertory. Social learning has limited possibilities of aggregation but represents an enormous advance over situational learning in this respect. Organisms are capable of stockpiling learned responses for situations not yet encountered. It is also possible for a certain amount of communication, often random, to take place, and some of it may carry learned responses across a generational threshold. Social learning also places an adaptive premium upon the formation of certain types of social interaction, favoring the transmission of information through transient or semipermanent population aggregates.

No organism can rely upon social learning alone. All organisms that learn socially also learn situationally. Man is one of the organisms that learns both situationally and socially. But man, as remarked before, also learns symbolically.

The crux of symbolic learning is the omission of the original situation. In situational learning the learning organism encounters and responds to a situational stimulus. In social learning the organism perceives another organism encountering and responding to the stimulus situation. In symbolic learning the stimulus situation is not present but is represented by something else—by a symbol. The symbol may be a fairly complex bit of representational behavior, but most symbols are relatively simple, highly concentrated substitutes for the originals.

Symbolic learning consequently has almost infinite possibilities for aggregation, as idea can be added to idea and as new formulations can be tried symbolically with minimal waste of time and effort. It is also supremely "time-binding," as one well-known phrase has it. The general behavior of one generation shapes and, to a great extent, determines the behavior of the next and is its raw material, apart from genetic patterns. Although something similar can occur in social learning, the difference in magnitude is so great as to constitute a genuine difference of kind.

Against this background, "culture" may be defined as the totality of conventional behavioral responses acquired primarily by symbolic learning.[1]

It may be asked, why define culture when we want to talk about political organization? It is precisely because we want to talk about political organization that we define culture: Some anthropologists and some political scientists, as well as other social scientists, have come very close to identifying the political with the cultural. Such identification is not difficult, particularly in simple societies where, as we shall see, political activities are not sharply set apart and tend to be embedded in a very generalized institutional setup. Beyond this level, some scholars have been impressed by the fact that most political norms exist, not because they are sanctioned by force, but because they are conveyed to the young in the course of growing up, as part of the process

---

[1] About the qualifying word, "primarily": Culture includes very many socially learned traits. It is quite possible that the earliest stone-working traditions, like the very ancient pebble industry, were transmitted subculturally through social learning. All modern cultures are heavily loaded with socially learned components, including kinesic and postural traits, as we have been told by Ray Birdwhistell and Gordon Hewes. That such a socially learned area should play an important role in culture does not in any way compromise the dependence of culture upon a system of symbolic learning.

of enculturation. There are also the theorists who are impressed with the integration of culture and see a shared value system as the basis of a political system. Whatever their theoretical point of departure, theorists of these persuasions end by confusing custom and law, social control and the state, and culture and political organization. Even more common is the confusion between social and political organization. Approaching this problem, we may begin with the carefully phrased definition of society offered some years ago by a group of social scientists:

A society is a group of human beings sharing a self-sufficient system of action which is capable of existing longer than the life-span of an individual, the group being recruited at least in part by the sexual reproduction of its members[2] (Aberle *et al.*, 1950, p. 101).

We need not analyze this definition, though we warn critics to read the article before raising comments. Our purposes are served by the clear distinction between society thus defined and culture as previously categorized.

If "society" refers to a group of parties, "social organization" refers to the relations that exist among the parties. By the term "social organization" we comprise the totality of patterned relations among the members of a society, the subgroups formed in the course of these relations, and the relations among these groups and their component members. As usually employed by anthropologists, the concept of social organization includes all instances of the phenomena under study and should therefore be described in terms of statistical, that is, enumerative, models. Presentations of specific social organizations should therefore be heavily descriptive, and much care should be taken to indicate ranges of variation and alternative patterns. Conversely, social structure, as usually taken by anthropologists, relates to a more abstract level and comprises analytical

---

[2] In the light of increased interest in primate ethology and nonhuman forms of grouping, it seems unwise to confine the definition to human beings.

models constructed from the data of social organization. It tends to convey the basic modal structures cf the society and pays less attention to descriptive detail—and even less to variations or alternatives. Because social structural studies tend to concentrate on modalities and on more abstract social data, it is not surprising that there should be a tendency to confuse social structure and polity. This tendency is particularly unfortunate because "social structure" refers to exactly the same sectors of culture as does "social organization." As we continue to refine our vocabulary, each subsector of social organization will have an implicit parallel in social structure.

SOCIAL CONTROL AND SANCTIONS

The universe of things designated as social organization (social structure) can be divided into a large number of categories of greater or less congruence, depending on selections of focal points or, what is perhaps the same thing, of problems. Do we wish to know how commodities enter the system, circulate, and are consumed? We differentiate economic aspects from others. Do we wish to know how members of the society, once recruited, are instructed in the ways of the society? We concentrate on education in its various guises, formal and informal. When we seek to know something about the regulation of social relationships, we realize that the sphere of regulatory activities overlaps all others, but still we can concentrate on social control.

Social control is taken to consist of all the nongenetically acquired processes by which individual and group behavior is directed along certain lines and diverted from others. There can be little argument with the observation that in all societies the single most significant complex of social-control apparatuses is to be found in the system of education, including both formal and informal means.

Given the existence of biogenetic restrictions on behavior, the process of enculturation may be viewed as the means by which specific behavioral alternatives are selected and dispersed in a population. It is precisely because the biogenetic organism possesses a wide latitude of capabilities beyond those selected in the process of education, and because that process is itself inexact, that additional mechanisms are required to retain individual and group behavioral manifestations within established boundaries. The essential device by which this goal is accomplished is the sanction, a reward or punishment used by an individual or group to lead or confine within stated channels the behavior of others.

It is useful to distinguish sanctions from reinforcements. Reinforcements, coextensive with learning, comprise the broadest grouping of directives of behavior. Including sanctions, they comprise all events that favor the adoption or extinction of modes of conduct and thus take in things that are neither social nor cultural and that may be completely fortuitous in relation to the behavior being influenced. On the other side, sanctions are distinctly social and usually cultural as well and must be consciously applied, which is to say that, during the course of their formulation or application, the party that applies them does so with awareness of the line of conduct that is to be approved or censured. Not that the sanction will necessarily accomplish its intended end or that it will have no other effects; but there must be a concept of breach or there cannot be a sanction. If a field of social action and interaction is imagined in terms of individual behavioral streams, two polar patterns may be isolated. One comprises a chain $a_1 \rightarrow a_2 \rightarrow a_3 \rightarrow a_n \rightarrow$, in which a represents any behavioral act that is in general conformity with existing sociocultural standards. These standards are known by different terms in different vocabularies: "norms," "usages," "customs," "folkways," "mores," and so on. Elements of conduct do not exactly replicate one another in what we may call a "normal" stream, but the discrepancies are small enough to be disregarded. (Actually, the amount of discrepancy tolerated is itself an important variable. Variations of limits of toleration apply to different age groups, social classes, or even to different kinds of relationships and situations.)

When the discrepancy is too large, a breach is said to have occurred, and this breach also is referred to by a variety of such terms as "deviation," "wrongful act," "tort," and "crime." In this second pattern, discovery of a breach compels an attempt at correction, the primary function of which is to restore the normal behavioral stream. It results in a different type of chain: $a_1 \rightarrow a_2 \rightarrow b \rightarrow c \rightarrow a_n$, in which b represents a breach and c its correction. Reinforcements serve to establish and maintain a normal behavioral chain, particularly in the process of enculturation. Sanctions serve as the major mechanisms for correcting breaches that have occurred. It is both obvious and important, however, that sanctions have great latent affect and that expectation of their use may lead to the avoidance of breach. One of the most common types of reinforcement is the telling of stories about sanctions, which is probably a universal cultural component.[3]

POWER AND AUTHORITY

Situations are frequently encountered in which the voice of reason counsels a particular course, but, apart from uttering the advice, no action is taken to ensure that

---

[3] Implicit in this discussion of sanction is general agreement with the position elaborated by A. R. Radcliffe-Brown (1933, pp. 531–4) in regard to positive (also called "premial") sanctions (or rewards) and negative sanctions (or punishments). The outstanding alternative is to return to John Austin, who scathingly denounced the concept of positive sanctions that had been advanced by John Locke and Jeremy Bentham. For Austin, a sanction was an *evil* that any rational creature would exert himself to avoid (Austin, 1954, pp. 16–7). Two points may be made against the Austinian position: There is good reason to believe, following developments in behavioral psychology, that positive reinforcements are more effective in a learning process and more resistant to extinction. There is also some difference in the use to which the concept of sanction is being put. For Austin, sanction had meaning essentially in the context of law; we are using the concept more broadly, and part of the difference is therefore related to a divergent view of the problem.

the course taken will be the one recommended. In Bushman
hunting the lead is usually taken by one of the men who is
considered luckier or more skilled, but no sanctions enforce
his recommendations (Thomas, 1959, p. 183). Many examples of parallel type can be given, but one small bit of
an account of a Fox Indian ceremonial sums it up. The
hero of the story had many wonderful abilities:

> He did not fail, it is said, to know everything. He even
> knew where the game animals were and continued to
> tell the hunters. "Yonder really is where you will kill
> (them)," he said to the hunters. It it said that they con-
> tinued to kill (the game) just where he mentioned to
> them. He always told the truth that way. He never, it
> is said, spoke falsely; he always told the truth (Michel-
> son, 1932, p. 25).

What is described is the use of authority without any application of sanctions. The minimal use of sanctions is probably withdrawal of company or withdrawal of reciprocity.
A simple case of the former is recited by Jane Richardson:
"Lone Wolf, a very prominent chief, and his brother-in-
law Ωpeigudl, also a topadok'i, got into a bitter fight. People
moved away and went to camp with others" (Richardson,
1940, p. 21). She added the comment, "Should the topadok'i
of a band quarrel with anyone, particularly with his own
kinsmen, his followers might impose upon him their own
supreme sanction: withdrawal of support . . ."

Withdrawal of support is a special case within the more
general area of reciprocity, which has been viewed, perhaps
most notably by Malinowski (1926), as the basis of social
organization. The importance of reciprocity in its various
forms and guises is such that more extended discussion is
required.[4] At this juncture, however, it may be provisionally

---

[4] We can agree with those who see in social reciprocity one of the
great adaptively advantageous characteristics (see Service, 1962, p.
42), noting that this feature, like others exposed to selective pressure,
may also be nonadaptive, depending on the situation. A telling point
has been made by C. R. Carpenter (1942, p. 180), who describes

accepted as a sanction with the warning that its scope and effectiveness vary to an unusual extent. At one extreme is individual withdrawal of affection or esteem, which may be expressed with exquisite subtlety and which can be called a "sanction" only at great peril to the utility of the term. At the other extreme, however, is the forced exclusion of an individual or a group from the basic reciprocal relations of society. Excommunication, particularly as it was practiced in the pronouncing of anathema on specific individuals in medieval Europe, was clearly a sanction of great potency, which was used overtly as a political weapon.

The difficulty of neatly delimiting the concept of sanction parallels the difficulty of erecting a simple hard-and-fast rule by which authority can be differentiated from power. "Authority" is taken here to refer to the ability to channel the behavior of others in the absence of the threat or use of sanctions.[5] Power is the ability to channel the behavior of others by threat or use of sanctions. Authority and power may go together or appear separately. A splendid example of authority without power is any dictionary or, more properly, the writer of any dictionary or standard reference work. It is more difficult to give an example of power without authority, for demonstration of the former is usually a prime source of the latter. Situations exist in which compliance is obtained only by continual application and in-

---

social reciprocity as a universal characteristic "from the amoeba to man" and certainly common to primates.

[5] One of the best definitions of "authority" I have come across is that of Bertrand de Jouvenal (1957, p. 29): "the faculty of gaining another man's assent." As he also sees authority as lacking the element of force and primarily as the basis for formation of voluntary associations, he is moved to comment on the obvious conflict with contemporary usage, as implied in terms like "authoritarian state." He says that "authoritarian governments" are actually those with inadequate authority, which must therefore fall back upon intimidation. As for modern usage, he claims that "this corruption of the word is of quite recent date" (p. 30). Interesting as this line of reasoning may be, it seems to avoid the reality about which we shall say much in the sequel: the inextricable association between state organization and violent intimidation.

cessant threat of sanctions, as in Nazi-occupied France. Such illustrations are tremendously complicated, however, because many of the functions of government were sustained for reasons and through mechanisms that had nothing to do with the German rulers. Also there were sectors of the indigenous communities that did respond favorably to the Nazi overlords. Though not entirely free of similar complexities, the smaller world of the prisoner-of-war camp displays clearer-cut power in the absence of authority, as we use these terms.

CUSTOM AND LAW

The purpose served by distinguishing sanctions from reinforcements and power from authority is the same as that involved in discriminating law from custom. It enables us to treat a phenomenon characterized by continuous variation in terms of polarized criteria. At the cost of qualifying detail, the analyst achieves relatively high degrees of clarity and facilitates comparison and the development of models showing process—how the phenomenon in question moves and the probabilities of different directions of movement. In the case of custom and law we wish to erect means of separating a special class of cultural events from all others. To take an example from our own society, we should like to be able to distinguish, *inter alia,* between what happens when somebody breaks wind in public and what happens when somebody passes a red light, takes someone else's purse without first obtaining permission, or kills somebody. Posing the problem in this way may conceal one of its salient features. Our society makes a drastic distinction between the first action and the other three. In other societies, however, there may not be such a sharp division, apart from the precise content of the activities mentioned.

There has tended to be a rather sharp division among social theorists respecting the evaluation of cultures. For some, all attempts at evaluation are invidious, and evaluation begins with the act of discriminating different institutional sectors of a given culture. Others raise objections at the point at which some primitive cultures are said to lack one or more of these institutional sectors. For example, if the presence of religion is made to depend upon the presence of unmitigated belief in monotheism, many cultures may be said to lack religion. By parallel processes of reasoning, there are objections to assertions that specific cultures or societies of certain levels of developmental complexity lack law or state organization. In recent years, those who view law as a universal component of culture have tended toward philosophical idealism and cultural relativism, whereas those who would restrict the appearance of law to a more rigid set of criteria have tended to be philosophical materialists favoring some theory of cultural evolution. It has not always been thus.

The study of jurisprudence has been one of many contending schools of thought, few of which survive in the sense of having active contemporary partisans. Two schools present rather neatly the essence of the conflict. The earlier, historical school was founded in the second decade of the nineteenth century by Friedrich Karl von Savigny with the appearance of the journal *Zeitschrift für geschichtliche Rechtswissenschaft*. A main thesis of historical jurisprudence is put succinctly by J. Walter Jones (1940, pp. 55–6):

> A people's law, like its language or its moral or political order, is the product of the *Volksgeist*—of something vaguely conceived to be compounded only in part of reason and primarily of intuition, custom, tradition, animal instinct, authority; or, in Maine's words, of the huge mass of opinions, beliefs, and superstitions produced by institutions and human nature reacting one upon another.

The crucial statement is the one relating law to custom. It seems clear that the work of Savigny, which fits brilliantly into the romantic development of German nationalism, does not confuse custom with legislation or with legal rules. For him the question was one of sources of law rather than of law itself, and that is why it is not surprising that he should have devoted so much of his time not to Germanic custom but to Roman law. Approximately a century later, however, a late flowering of historical jurisprudence assumed more and more often the position that the only distinction between custom and law was one of degree.

Nineteenth- and early twentieth-century jurisprudents were enthusiastic readers and users of ethnographic materials, and sometimes, as in the case of Sir Henry Maine, they made substantial original contributions as well; indeed, it should not be forgotten that Lewis Henry Morgan was a practicing lawyer and that the discipline has since drawn some of its most successful scholars from previous specialization in the law. At any rate, the close connections between jurisprudence and anthropology led to equal closeness in the development of their views of the evolution of law and political society. In those views the progression of ideas went from the identification of custom as an important source and basis for law through the holding of legislation subordinate to custom (*cf.* Jones, 1940, p. 57), finally arriving at the point at which law was figuratively swallowed by custom. A frequently cited illustration of the last position is the remark of E. Sidney Hartland (1924, p. 5), "Primitive law is in truth the totality of the customs of the tribe." This position is taken as a conscious revision of the definition offered by Austin to which we shall advert later (Hartland, 1924, p. 137).

Hartland's position, though rarely defended in terms of his work, has continued to enjoy considerable currency, if not domination of the field. Malinowski's views were similar, although expressed in totally different ways. Julius Lips took issue with Roscoe Pound and with Radcliffe-Brown for their failure to acknowledge that law is a universal rubric and declared that

. . . there is no people without fire, without language, without religion, or without law. Our social, religious, and legal concepts do not coincide with those of the primitives; what we must do is to find the correct equivalent for our modern institutions in primitive societies (Lips, 1938, p. 489; it is very interesting to compare this statement with the orientation explained by Paul Bohannan, 1957, pp. 4–6 *et passim,* which both resembles Lips' position and departs from it at significant junctures).

Marcel Mauss, whose theoretical contributions lead us to expect something grossly in harmony with Malinowski, does not disappoint. His remark is also interesting for being almost untranslatable. (If such an event can occur between two such close cultures what are the problems of "translating" concepts of legal order between traditions without a trace of common descent?) Mauss said, "Le droit comprend l'ensemble des coutumes et des lois" (Mauss, 1947, p. 110).[6]

A lengthy catalogue of similar opinions could easily be gathered. I prefer to turn, however, to E. Adamson Hoebel's criticism of Hartland for including too much in the concept of law and for failing, therefore, to state any explicit criteria of law (Hoebel, 1954, p. 21).[7] Hoebel is inclined to take a position with strong overtones of Radcliffe-Brown, hence necessarily of John Austin, when he associates legality with the application or threat of sanctions by a determinate social body (Hoebel, 1954, p. 28). Yet he wants to eat his cake and have it too. Although he excludes some customs from the province of jurisprudence, he argues that no culture lacks law or, for that matter, the state (Hoebel, 1958, pp. 467–507, especially p. 506).

---

[6] I encountered this remark in an interesting but, on this point, inconclusive article by J. P. B. de Josselin de Jong (1948, p. 71). The same problem of translation, of conveying the distinction between *le droit* and *la loi,* occurs with German; see Stanley Moore's (1960, pp. 645–6) discussion of F. Engels' use of the terms *Gesetze* and *Recht.*
[7] Compare Pospisil's criticism of Malinowski's approach to law: "The present writer objects to Malinowski's view because law is defined so broadly as to include most of the customs of a society. For this reason the theory does not lend itself to being a workable tool for the ethnographer" (1958, p. 257).

To understand better the problems raised so far, it is necessary to give a few particulars about the contributions of Austin, whose name is associated with analytical jurisprudence. Although he lectured in the first half of the nineteenth century, Austin's main influence was posthumous but widespread. Central to his notion of law, which had substantial intellectual antecedents in the work of English rationalist philosophers from Hobbes to Bentham and later was the concept of sovereignty, a paramount and determinate social locus of command with the power to enforce its directives. Austin took pains to distinguish "positive laws" from various things called "law," like natural law, laws of nature, institutional rules, and morality, within which he counted custom. The Austinian conception of law and its relation to the concept of sanction has been summarized by Edmund Robertson:

> [The word "command"] is the key to the analysis of law, and accordingly a large portion of Austin's work is occupied with the determination of its meaning. A *command* is an order issued by a superior to an inferior. It is a signification of desire distinguished by this peculiarity that "the party to whom it is directed is liable to evil from the other, in case he comply not with the desire." . . . Being liable to evil in case I comply not with the wish which you signify, I am *bound* or obliged by it, or I lie under a duty to obey it. The evil is called a *sanction,* and the command or duty is said to be *sanctioned* by the chance of incurring the evil. The three terms *command, duty* and *sanction* are thus inseparably connected (Robertson, 1911, p. 572).

It is the next step that is decisive. *Not all commands are deemed laws.* Austin gave more than one reason for this distinction, but the most important involves the requirement that commands must emanate from a determinate source. This requirement, in turn, involves several things: the existence of an independent political society with primary access to power concentrated in the hands of an individual or group, which individual or group constitutes the locus of sovereignty. For Austin discovering this locus was not difficult; he merely sought patterns of habitual obedience to a commonly recognized superior. Although monarchies or dictatorships seem to present the clearest approximations to the Austinian model, there is considerable flexibility in his formulations permitting application of his definitions and theses to all known forms of polity.[8] The most urgent matter is the discrimination of a locus of paramount political power. This power may well be shared, not only among people, but also among institutional bodies, in order to comprise mutually restraining executive, legislative, and judicial branches, but there can be completely different systems of power delegation or diffusion. Austin did not find it necessary to implicate the ideology of political systems or to inquire into legitimacy or the source of power. Admittedly, this omission has been one of the main points at which criticism of Austin has been directed. Robertson points a way out:

> We may here interpolate a doubt whether the condition of independence on the part of the head of a community is essential to the legal analysis. It seems to us that we have all the elements of a true law present when we point to a community habitually obedient to the authority of a person or a determinate body of persons, no matter what the relations of that superior may be to any external or superior power. Provided that in fact the commands of the lawgiver are those beyond which the community never looks (Robertson, 1911, p. 574) . . .

Finally, in this very brief discussion of Austinian concepts, it should be noted that the insistence upon defining law as the command of a superior to an inferior does not mean that the sovereign (whether dictator, king, or president)

---

[8] Austin used examples drawn from the government of the United States and was under no illusions about the extent of the power of the British monarch.

has to originate the substance of the command, which is to say he does not have to be its original legislator. That function may have been played in the dim past, perhaps even by some nonsovereign individual or body. The important thing is that the sovereign enforces some rule.

Returning to the definitional problem of distinguishing customs from laws, we can turn to the dictionary for usage of "custom" and identify it with any habitual or usual course of action, any established practice. "Law," on the other hand, we define in Austinian terms as a rule of conduct enforced by sanctions administered by a determinate locus of power, whether by the sovereign itself or by a surrogate.

We may pause in this context to define "deviation" as any departure from custom and "crime" as any departure from law. As further detail is given in subsequent chapters, it will be found necessary to refine these terms and to add a few others. A few major concepts remain to be introduced before the argument begins.

POLITICAL ORGANIZATION AND GOVERNMENT

Harold Lasswell's aphoristic definition of politics as "who gets what, when and how" goes to the heart of the matter but casually takes in all of economics in transit. A dictionary is helpful in suggesting that politics refers to "the theory or practice of managing affairs of public policy." Politics also refers to "the organization or action of individuals, parties, or interests that seek to control the appointment or action of those who manage the affairs of a state" (*Webster's New Collegiate Dictionary*, 1961, p. 654). Although the last phrasing has highly useful aspects, it introduces a major problem by assuming the existence of a state; one of the main problems upon which we are advancing is the emergence of the state.

Political organization is an aspect of social organization. Departing from the definition of social organization and adding elements borrowed from the previous discussion, we offer a formulation adapted to our own needs: Political organization comprises those portions of social organization that specifically relate to the individuals or groups that manage the affairs of public policy or seek to control the appointment or action of those individuals or groups.

It should be noted that the definition of political organization does not prescribe the character or severity of sanctions. Some sanctions are required to maintain even the simplest system of public policy. Probably the minimum sanctions are those mentioned earlier in the Kiowa example: Political inferiors can remove themselves from the vicinity (that is, jurisdiction) of the commander, or the commander can desert his unresponsive charges. As is well known, the latter possibility remains even in the most sophisticated systems, but opportunities for exercise of the former decline, often to the vanishing point, in the presence of the true state.

Government may be differentiated from political organization as an aspect of a larger whole and is taken here to comprise the system and apparatus of administration of the political organization and the personnel carrying out those administrative functions. As for personnel, it is obvious that, although some cultures have minimal role specialization, all must to some degree distinguish between an individual acting in a governmental role and in any other.

LEGITIMACY

One of the most central yet difficult concepts is that of legitimacy. It is frequently encountered in definitions of the state, sometimes in definitions of the political system, and sometimes in definitions of law. With regard to the last, Hoebel (1954, p. 27) declares that, "The essentials of legal coercion are general social acceptance of the application of physical power, in threat or in fact, by a privileged party, for a legitimate cause, in a legitimate way, and at a legitimate time."

S. N. Eisenstadt (1963, p. 5) similarly includes the concept of legitimacy among the things he regards as attributes of a political system: "The political system is the organization of a territorial society having the legitimate monopoly over the authorized use and regulation of force in the society." As for the definition of the state, we may turn to many commentators. The one selected is Hans Kelson, who has struggled with the problem of detaching law from all other kinds of rules and the state from all other forms of association. Kelson has written:

> The sociological description of the State as a phenomenon of domination is not complete if only the fact is established that men force other men to a certain behavior. The domination that characterizes the State claims to be legitimate and must be actually regarded as such by rulers and ruled. The domination is legitimate only if it takes place in accordance with a legal order whose validity is presupposed by the acting individuals; and this order is the legal order of the community the organ of which is the "ruler of the State" (Kelson, 1961, pp. 187–8).

What then is this principle of legitimacy? In Kelson's view it is equivalent to the accepted rules of the game: the principles of validation of the legal order of a community "in the way in which the legal order itself determines" (Kelson, 1961, p. 117).

When the concept of legitimacy, in the sense in which we are using it, is encountered in contemporary social science, it is probable that some influence of Max Weber will be discernible. For Weber, legitimacy was the endowment of a rule "with the prestige of exemplariness or obligatoriness" (Weber, 1954, p. 4; cf. the translation in Weber, 1947, p. 125, and Weber, 1962, p. 72). Along with most other commentators on this difficult subject, Weber refused to attempt to make an absolute distinction between law and custom: "But, of course, the transitions from the orientation of conduct toward an order by virtue of mere tradition or mere aim-rationality to the belief in legitimacy are indeterminate in actual life" (Weber, 1954, p. 4).

Weber classified types of legitimacy according to the means by which it was guaranteed. One of his most fundamental distinctions was between subjective guarantees— sometimes called "internalization,' in which the actor accepts authority because he believes in it, whatever the reason—and objective guarantees, which depend on expectations of reactions to one's behavior. Within this second type, Weber discussed two major variants, distinguishing convention from law.

> A system of authority will appear to be a) *conventional,* where its validity is externally guaranteed by the probability that deviation from it within a definable social group will be met with relatively general and significantly perceptible disapproval. b) Such a system of authority will be considered as *law* if it is externally guaranteed by the probability that unusual behavior will be met by physical or psychic sanctions aimed at compelling conformity or at punishing disobedience and administered by a group of men especially charged with the authority for that purpose (Weber, 1962, p. 75).

Weber leaves no doubt that the salient difference is in the requirement of a determinate locus of enforcement. Compare this view with Austin's conception, noting that his definition of law comprises three criteria:

> 1. Laws properly so called are a species of *commands* . . . (flowing) from a determinate source . . . a *determinate* rational being . . . or aggregate of rational beings. . . . (W)henever a *command* is expressed . . . one party signifies a wish that another shall do or forbear: and the latter is obnoxious to an evil which the former intends to inflict in case the wish be disregarded . . . 2. Every sanction properly so called is an eventual evil *annexed to a command* . . . purposely to enforce obedience . . . 3. Every duty properly so called supposes a *command* by which it is created (Austin, 1954, pp. 133–4).

Austin emphasizes by repetition that "every positive law, or every law strictly so called is a direct or circuitous command of a monarch or sovereign number to a person or persons in a state of subjection to its author" (1954, p. 134).

Whereas Weber was most concerned with the agents of enforcement, Austin before him sought deeper sources of law. No one would accuse Weber of mistaking the policeman's nightstick for law, but Austin's critics have assumed for a century that he placed the entire weight of his system upon the utterance of legislation. It seems unjust in view of Austin's support, among other things, of "judge-made law" (1954, p. 191). At any rate, as I hope to show later, Austin's conceptions fit very well with analyses of law and the state along lines of socioeconomic-class stratification. Curiously, for someone whose contributions to the sociological understanding of stratification have been so important, Weber's approach is less well adapted to this kind of analysis than to the currently fashionable behavioral analysis of political systems.

The last statement furnishes a means of returning the discussion to the concept of legitimacy. David Easton, a political scientist of what Heinz Eulau calls "the behavioral persuasion," quotes with approval a remark of Weber's to the effect that the idea of the state in empirical reality turns out to be "an infinity of diffuse and discrete human actions . . . and . . . relationships . . . all bound together by an idea, namely, the belief in actual or normative validity of rules and of the authority-relationships of some human beings towards others" (Easton, 1953, p. 133n., citing Shils & Finch, 1949, p. 99). Easton's own formulation is less turgid but to the same point: "A policy is authoritative (legitimate) when the people . . . consider that they must or ought to obey it" (Easton, 1953, p. 132).

Actually, when one follows even Austinian thought into this question, the answers proffered are disappointing, although certainly no more so than most of those offered in the century since he lectured. At the crux of the matter is the relationship between a government and the population it administers. Particularly in the work of theorists who themselves come from states based upon capitalist economies, there is an assumption that, in the final analysis, political power must be psychologically and sociologically validated. That is to say, the mass of the populace must obey most of the laws for some reason other than fear of punishment. In Austin's words:

> Now the permanence of every government depends on the habitual obedience which it receives from the bulk of the community. For if the bulk of the community were fully determined to destroy it, and to brave and endure the evils through which they must pass to their object, the might of the government itself, with the might of the minority attached to it, would scarcely suffice to preserve it, or even retard its subversion (Austin, 1954, p. 302).

As for the sources of habitual obedience, Austin did less well than Weber but clearly showed the way:

> Supposing that a given society were adequately instructed or enlightened, the habitual obedience to its government which was rendered by the bulk of the community, would exclusively arise from reasons bottomed in the principle of utility (Austin, 1954, p. 296) . . .

> Since every actual society is inadequately instructed or enlightened, the habitual obedience to its government which is rendered by the bulk of the community, is partly the consequence of custom: They partly pay that obedience . . . because they, and perhaps their ancestors, have been in the habit of obeying it (Austin, 1954, p. 299).

From this point Austin returns to his utilitarian orientation and offers a version of contract theory: Even the poorly instructed and unenlightened prefer to leave the "state of nature" or the dread condition of anarchy, taking refuge in organized government and thus offering themselves to a sovereign.

Legitimacy, no matter how its definition is phrased, is the means by which ideology is blended with power. Legitimacy is most clearly grasped in terms of its principal functions: to explain and justify the existence of concentrated social power wielded by a portion of the community and to offer similar support to specific social orders, that is, specific ways of apportioning and directing the flow of social power.

With our own definition of legitimacy we have moved considerably beyond the simple presentation of key terms and concepts and have plunged rather deeply into argument. It is time, therefore, to move directly into that argument. We begin with a brief survey of patterns analogous to social control among animals other than man, concentrating on the recent increase in our knowledge of primate behavior in natural environments.

CHAPTER 2

Egalitarian Society: Preliminary Considerations

Equality is a social impossibility. Despite the soundness of this generalization, there is truth in the American Negro slogan "We shall overcome!" and the inequality that the slogan challenges has begun to crumble. The paradox is a trick, of course, since the word "equality," like most of the words already discussed, has a variety of meanings; through slight degrees of difference these meanings achieve polarity. It is necessary, therefore, to begin by discarding one of the meanings: Equality need not be identity, things can be equal without being the same. Yet, even as we attempt this circumscription, we may damage our argument. In our example of the civil-rights movement in the United States, the announced ultimate goal is identity: identity of Negro and white opportunity and treatment before the law. But there are bound to be many dissimilar components. For example, achieving identity (equality) in the areas mentioned may require a transitional grant of superior treatment, of concessions to compensate for long deprivation and hasten the balancing. Equality, thus defined in action, emphasizes limited areas of identity in a field of differences.

The raw material for a society is comprised of individual organisms. Despite the remarkable efficiency of genetic replication, no two organisms, even those proceeding from a single ovum fertilized by a single sperm, are identical. Beyond this area lie broader and broader fields of divergence. In all societies of interest to us, including those of primates and various other mammals, there are finite differences of age, sex, strength, endurance, speed, visual or auditory acuity, intelligence (this alone covers a variety of phenomena usually confused), beauty, disease resistance, and so on. So standard is the probability of variation that in evolutionary theory it has been treated as an element of special significance in at least two ways: as the source of necessary flexibility, providing the reservoir of forms for adaptation, and as the basis for taking the population and not the individual as the unit. As will be seen, the latter is of particular interest because it seems to have an intimate relationship with the structure of primate social groups, which, to a high degree, are defensive constellations.

Because there can be no such thing as a society composed of exactly equal members, one may wonder that we use the term "egalitarian society." Two justifications are offered. First, the term may be understood as an ellipsis, the missing word being "relatively." Societies so designated lack formal ranking and stratification as defined later and therefore approach, although they certainly do not attain, true equality. Second, the term itself is usually somewhat programmatic and is encountered in political slogans. Though most of the words chosen in a scholarly or scientific context are valued, at least in theory, for their political neutrality, the political coloration of "egalitarian" fits our purpose rather well.

STATUS AND ROLE

The word "status" is fairly old in any meaning of interest to our argument, that is, in the significance of "social standing," even if the most extensive glosses on this usage come from relatively modern sociology. Like the word "state," status derives from a Latin form of "to stand" and is also related to the word "estate," most clearly seen in the sense of a great segment of society. The word "role," on the other hand, is relatively new although equally clear in the adaptation of its meanings. Derived from a French word referring to the part played by an actor, role has been characterized as the activity counterpart of status.

Though most of the following statements are obvious, they have been included to make certain that all important concepts used in our argument are presented.

Any given individual, even a member of the simplest known human society, certainly plays a number of roles and occupies a variety of statuses during his lifetime, usually within relatively brief time spans, that is, within the same day or hour. Among the commonest roles that one may be called on to play almost simultaneously are disciplinarian, comforter, source of emotional warmth, lover, hater, food supplier, food processor, entertainer, fighter, educator, and so on. Similarly, persons normally occupy a variety of statuses, often at the same time. While a man is "father" to A, he is "husband" to B, "son" to C and D, "son-in-law" to E and F, and so on. Also, he may be a Heron—that is, a member of the Heron clan—or a member of a lineage In the latter capacity he may be the eldest male in the senior surviving generation, hence the "leader" or "chief." He may be a member of a society that meets to sing, keep order in the camp, or play a certain kind of game. He may have a specialized job, perhaps as a shaman, the steersman of a boat, or a skilled smith. Apart from entailing special behavior, each of these roles is a status or a position in a society. There are many ways to group statuses: by similarity of content, complexity, the sex or age of their holders, and so forth. Certain ways of assorting statuses are of special interest to our argument. The first of these is the dichotomy between achieved and ascribed status. To the extent, for example, that the marital state is an achievement, and not something made inevitable by birth and survival, it shows that achieved status may be found in all societies. The significance of the distinction is rather obvious. Other things being equal, one expects societies with high proportions of ascribed status to be more set, closed, and internally less mobile than those with a lot of achieved status.

Following the example of Elman R. Service (1960; 1960a; 1962, pp. 24–5), statuses can be distinguished according to whether they shift from individual to individual, as the reference group to which they apply also shifts, or remain constant from one individual in one reference group to the next. The most common example of the former, ego-centric statuses are kinship terms. While I am "father" to my own brood I may be "uncle" to yours, if you happen to have a culture in which the so-called "lineal" terminology is employed. In other words, in no society can a man be "father" to everybody in the kinship terminology. On the other hand, if I am a priest of the Roman Catholic Church, I may have the status and designation "Father," and would be so recognized by a good portion if not the whole of my community. This designation is an example of "sociocentric" status terminology, as are such terms as "editor," "first baseman," "captain," "professor," or "President." Egocentric statuses can be endowed only with very limited social power, effective only within the limits of such a small group as the family. Even small formal groups structured about kinship or the expansion of familial principles, like small-scale lineages, have their power figures who are recognized as occupying sociocentric statuses and are identified by sociocentric terms. The matter is complicated, however, by the fact that in many societies with complex political organizations the family, however it may be defined in that culture, is deliberately endowed with strong powers.

It is commonly thought that the concept of status necessarily implies hierarchy. There is good reason for this belief: The social orders in which science has grown to the point of making explicit analyses of status are invariably organized hierarchically. Another basis for the association of status and hierarchy is the content of some of the original work on animal society that emphasized the linear dominance hierarchy. The famous work of T. Schjelderup-Ebbe on barnyard fowl contributed the notion of the pecking order. Subsequent work, however, has made four things abundantly clear. First, not all dominance series are linear: Some show marked instability, the animals shifting relative positions; others have more than one animal at particular dominance levels; still others form discontinuous series, in which an animal dominant over another may be not dominant over a third, which in turn *is* dominant over the second. Second, some animal social orders of variable duration are devoid of superiority-inferiority relationships except to the degree that the human observer projects his own values into what he sees. This kind of projection is common in writings about social insects. Third, particularly in observations of some of the primates it has been noted that over-all dominance ratings are of dubious significance, for different animals are differentially dominant in different activities. Finally, research in the past ten or twenty years has shown convincingly that dominance hierarchies, involving fighting and other forms of aggressive behavior, are much more pronounced under laboratory conditions than in nature. The main independent variables seem to be two: artificial crowding, so that many more animals are raised in a far more restricted area than would occur in a natural ecological situation; and artificial constriction of the food supply. Even where food may be adequate or more regularly available and abundant than in nature, it is usually distributed by the human attendants in a way that provides the opportunity for "monopoly," although that word with its heavy freight of economic meaning may be inappropriate.

What we may conclude from past and current research on dominance in nonhuman societies is that patterns are too divergent and variable to present a clear model applicable to human cultural evolution. The absence of a single template does not mean that the work on dominance is not relevant. It is exceptionally rewarding and continues to show promise in many as yet poorly explored areas. We are warned, however, that no simple gradient exists that justifies any conclusion about man's "real nature."

PRESTIGE

Prestige, a real and important factor in all known human societies, may be viewed as the ideological component of status. I see no way to deal with prestige in the absence of symbols, for prestige, stripped to its essentials, depends upon shared evaluations of status. The dictionary says that prestige is "the power to command admiration." Imitation is said to be the sincerest form of flattery, and to some extent it may indicate prestige; behavioral deference also reflects prestige. Both exist in the absence of symbolic systems,[1] but the main means of conveying prestige are symbolic, and of these means speech is the most important.

It is theoretically possible to have a society in which all statuses are at parity. Few if any known human societies have ever actually placed statuses at par; what they have done to create such an illusion is treated later. It must be noted, however, that all known societies do create status hierarchies; even the simplest usually have a few different statuses that do not necessarily integrate into a single overall order. We have already mentioned age as an unavoidable source of individual difference; it is a universal source of status difference as well. In many societies, of course, age is used extensively to create highly formalized categories

---

[1] See pp. 42–3, for C. R. Carpenter's nonsymbolic "prestige."

among the members; such societies usually have gradients of prestige that parallel the age-grade series. Even more widespread is the difference in prestige associated with the sexes. Most of the simplest and some of the most complex societies regard women as inferior and restrict their roles and statuses accordingly.

Our most significant point about prestige, however, is that it has no necessary connection with power, although it does have a necessary connection with authority, using both of these terms as established in the previous chapter. This does not alter the fact that a society may confer enormous power on certain prestigious statuses—which, after all, is one of the key political processes. Much remains to be said about it in the following chapters. At this juncture, however, I am much more concerned with the possibility, the reality of which I believe is subsequently illustrated, that human societies exist with statuses that are arranged in a hierarchy according to prestige but that do not endow the most vaunted statuses with any power whatever.

A DEFINITION OF EGALITARIAN SOCIETY

An egalitarian society is one in which there are as many positions of prestige in any given age-sex grade as there are persons capable of filling them. Putting that another way, an egalitarian society is characterized by the adjustment of the number of valued statuses to the number of persons with the abilities to fill them. If a particular period is rich in able persons, their number will be large, and at other times it will contract. Let it be put even more strongly. An egalitarian society does not have any means of fixing or limiting the number of persons capable of exerting power. As many persons as can wield power—whether through personal strength, influence, authority, or whatever means—can do so, and there is no necessity to draw them together to establish an order of dominance and paramountcy.

Let there be no mistake. An egalitarian society as here defined has some members who are less assertive, less successful than others. By and large, however, differences among members, apart from sex and age, tend to be ephemeral. Strength, sensory acuity, excellent performance—these strong points constitute an ideal in all simple societies; accidents, bad luck, illness—such things can put the mighty out of commission, making them temporarily dependent or ruining them altogether. Furthermore most egalitarian societies have powerful leveling mechanisms that prevent the appearance of overly wide gaps in ability among members. Even though the society may struggle to preserve its defective members, harsh environmental conditions, often met almost directly, regularly thin its ranks, particularly among the young. But the society itself has mechanisms that, given limitation of variability, produce even greater homogeneity. Think, for example, of the various means by which simple cultures identify the successful hunter. Many of the animals taken by primitive hunters are brought down through the coordinated efforts of a group of men. At the end, the creature is pierced by many projectiles or struck by many clubs. Whose blow killed it? Some societies award the kill to the first man who actually makes the hit. Others, however, make the award to the man who spotted the animal. Still others say the animal belongs to the man whose weapon struck the first blow, and that man may not have even been there, having lent the weapon to another. Although rationalizations may be offered to explain each of these procedures and others as well, true significance lies less in trying to comprehend what are, at best, merely plausible reconstructions of origins. It seems more significant to understand the phenomenon as a whole—all the techniques by which credit for bringing game to camp is randomized, spread among all the eligible men in the society.

EGALITARIAN SOCIETY
AND RECIPROCAL ECONOMY

At the heart of an egalitarian society is a fundamentally egalitarian economy. The model of such an economy approximates very well the type of economic integration that Karl Polanyi (1953, pp. 162–84) epitomized as "reciprocal." We welcome Marshall Sahlins' recent refinement of Polanyi's scheme, which includes the discrimination of three types of reciprocal economic behavior. Although they obviously overlap, they are remarkably clear and distinct in their essentials. According to him "The spectrum of reciprocities proposed for general use is defined by its extremes and mid-point" (Sahlins, 1965, pp. 147–9). This eminently logical proposal offers three models: First is the model that emphasizes "altruism" and solidarity. Called "generalized reciprocity," its main characteristic is, somewhat paradoxically, "the vagueness of the obligation to reciprocate" that follows any donation. Actually, there are serious pressures for reciprocation, but they are largely implicit, setting no equivalents or time limits, and being in the general nature of expectations that when the opportunity arises a return will be made. It is of the greatest importance to note, as does Sahlins (1965, p. 147), that the system does not require return transactions. In other words, balance is not required: Those who can, give and continue to give. It is equally true to say that those who need, take and continue to take. They may do so even if the donor fails his responsibility to give while still having things to be given. It is exceptionally difficult to talk about "theft" in such a context, and we discuss this situation and its consequences later.

The second model, entailing the relatively swift exchange of a *quid* for a *quo* is called "balanced reciprocity." The limiting case, in which the same amounts of the same kinds of things are exchanged in an on-the-spot transaction, is amply illustrated and documented (*cf.* Sahlins, 1965, p. 148). However:

> "Balanced reciprocity" may be more loosely applied to transactions which stipulate returns of commensurate worth or utility within a finite and narrow period. Much "gift-exchange," many "payments," much that goes under the ethnographic head of "trade" and plenty that is called "buying-selling" and involves "primitive money" belong in the genre of balanced reciprocity (Sahlins, 1965, p. 148).

A third model, at the farthest extreme from altruistic generalized reciprocity, is "the attempt to get something for nothing with impunity" (Sahlins, 1965, p. 148). Sahlins calls this "negative reciprocity" and describes it as the most impersonalized exchange, carried out purely for the sake of advantage.

The second and third models of reciprocity have only minor application in egalitarian societies and serve, as Sahlins has indicated, in peripheral areas of social relations, that is, in the area of "tribal" and "inter-tribal" activities (Sahlins, 1965, pp. 151–2). We use these models in turning to larger political phenomena; at this point, however, we are concerned with equality and find that it rests at the outset upon the workings and requirements of a reciprocal mode of economic integration.

A NOTE ABOUT ETHNOGRAPHY

Before going further, we offer a few remarks about the ethnographic basis of the arguments in this book.

To begin with, our relative brevity of treatment does not allow for presentation of an extended case record. Accordingly, the material presented is in the nature of illustrations and should not be confused with proof.

An alternative method sometimes used is to present general statements followed by elaborate bibliographic glossing as every recoverable instance is enumerated, not by presentation, but by furnishing the information necessary to enable the reader to retrieve the item himself. Even this technique would have been unsuitable for the present format, being more appropriate to the monograph and dissertation. That unsuitability is not the only or even the basic reason for failing to use it. It is worthwhile to raise the question of the real meaning of extended ethnographic citation.

Broad-gauged citation of ethnographic works is immediately subject to several caveats. There are obvious questions about reliability: Who made the observations and under what circumstances? Is the account primary, or has it gone through various hands? In dealing with different accounts, has the writer paid attention to time differences and accompanying differences in exposure to other cultures? How do we know that the recorded responses are representative? Who were the informants, the interpreters? Who was observed? Above all looms the question: What is an ethnographic sample? How does one count *n* studies in the same culture area but relating to different "tribes"? To such qualifying questions must be added another major problem. Most of our data come from societies that may be markedly different and certainly live in very different circumstances and environments from those of the remote past. Other things being equal, our most reliable information comes from scientifically trained ethnographers whose observations have been made in a period when hardly any society has not felt the weight of contact with a more complex society. Even if such contacts have been slight and have not resulted in massive importations of alien elements, the past centuries have featured the elimination or total incorporation of almost all primitive societies in the prime environments. Most primitive cultures that survive are found in rather inhospitable habitats (Fried, 1952, pp. 391–412). The consequences of this condition can hardly be overstated. As we show further on, one of the most important variables in the development of complex political systems is population size and density; these factors rest, in turn, upon the carrying capacity of the environment interacting, of course, with cultural features. Simple extrapolation from observations of Eskimo, Bushman, or other cultures in marginal habitats to paleolithic cultures in the Pleistocene is dangerous.

Dangerous but not impossible. Obviously, we must use the data that are available; we cannot cast information out because it is not ideal. The important thing is to know what we are working with and, to the extent that we can, to take account of probable divergences and complications. It may be comforting to reflect that other sciences have similar problems. One of the most respected is astronomy, despite the fact that the carefully exposed photograph of the night sky taken through the world's largest and most powerful lens is something of a fiction. The "stars" and other phenomena in the picture never were, are not now, and never will be in the relative positions shown.

Without pursuing this theme further, we wish at this juncture to make clear our awareness of the difficulties of using the ethnographic record. As the discussion proceeds, comments on methodological compensations designed to meet these hazards are introduced.

PRIMATE SOCIETIES

At the risk of alienating friends among zoologists and anthropologists specializing in primate ethology, I begin this section by referring to some remarks of Paul Vinogradoff, the proponent of historical jurisprudence whose work was discussed briefly in Chapter 1. Surveying some of the most important contributions to the problem of the origin and development of domestic groups, Vinogradoff came to the conclusion: "Considering the immense variety of conditions in ancient times, it is improbable that any exclusive theory will be true in all cases. . . . This being so, we shall not attempt to trace one line of normal and continuous evolution of marriage" (Vinogradoff, 1920, p. 167).

What may have been a shrewd piety about fifty years ago, when the actual field study of primates was scarcely begun, becomes a procedural necessity now that there is a reasonable, although rapidly expanding, volume of reports on the organization of the societal patterns found among different primate species. In a nutshell, variety is the rule. What is worse, the principle of phylogenetic closeness is of extremely dubious usefulness in this area.

Information is now available on the social patterns of at least nine different species of primates other than man, which was obtained by careful observation under natural or seminatural conditions, that is, where the animals range freely over extensive parcels of land. Usually the habitat is an island, for it has natural boundaries. Some of the food in such an environment is naturally available, but usually additional foods must be supplied.[2] The area occupied by the animals is large enough to permit a number of distinct social units to form without having continuous contact. In some instances the area is large enough to permit different groups to live for long periods without coming into contact.

The animals that have been observed under wild or seminatural conditions include gibbons, spider monkeys, two kinds of macaques, gorillas, baboons, howlers, langurs, and orangutans. Some of these animals live in tiny groups, for example the gibbon, reported to average about six in a group. Japanese monkeys sometimes congregate in groups of several hundred (Chance, 1961, p. 18). Sex ratios vary as widely, with the gibbon at parity and the rhesus running 5:1 in favor of females. Among some of the primates, the gibbon being most notable in this respect, mating is very stable and based upon pairs. Other primates do not seem to form mating pairs for any length of time. The rhesus

---

[2] Supplying food to the undomesticated primates is such a regular feature that the primatologist Kinji Imanishi has suggested the recognition of a stage between domestication and the wild which he calls "provisionization." The term was developed as part of an interesting vocabulary applied to the description of the ethology and social behavior of the macaques of Japan (Imanishi, 1963, p. 70).

monkeys copulate and separate, sometimes within a matter of minutes; in any case, the females copulate with at least two or three males in each breeding season (Koford, 1963, p. 150). Observation of copulation among wild gorillas has been limited to two sequences (Schaller, 1963, pp. 283–6), but they are very interesting, as in one case the female was mounted by the *second* most dominant male in the group and in the other case she was mounted by a *peripheral* male, that is, one only loosely attached to the group. In both cases the dominant male was present and observed with little or no involvement.

Fascinating as primatological data are, we cannot review that picture for its own sake but are concerned only for the light it may throw on the evolution of political society in man. So far we have illustrated the generalization accepted by all primatologists: Primate behavior is quite variable and presents nothing like a unified model from which human behavior may be considered to have emerged.

As previously remarked, the principle of phylogenetic closeness is not useful in this context. That is to say, primate species standing closest to man in the sense of physical evolution do not necessarily show the closest resemblance to human sociality. The reason is simple. Much of behavior derives from specific functions that must be carried out in certain kinds of environment. The fact that an animal is primarily an eater of fruit and insects carries with it behavioral and social implications quite different from those implied by a taste for meat.

Accepting this *mise en scène* of limitations and caveats, let us inquire into the social behavior of the primates, seeking information about whatever might be called political activity.

Role Differentiation

Primatologists divide the life spans of the animals they observe into a number of stages. There is no uniformity either with regard to the number of stages discriminated or their duration. Phyllis Jay describes five stages for langurs: infant-one, infant-two, juvenile, subadult, and adult (Jay, 1965, pp. 223–43). Vernon and Frances Reynolds distinguish eight stages in the life history of the chimpanzee: infant-one, infant-two, juvenile-one, juvenile-two, adolescent, subadult, adult-one, adult-two (Reynolds & Reynolds, 1965, p. 390). The criteria for these stages are mixtures of physical and behavioral traits and reflect some of the simplicities of role differentiation in primate society. For example, play is usually confined to the period that spans late infancy and the juvenile stage. The final role structure of a primate group varies with species, and there is a latitude of expression permitting a certain individuality. The observers, after a period of familiarization, could recognize many animals by their distinctive deportment and could predict what they would do in certain situations.

A few samplings of adult role structure in primate society from a growing literature will have to suffice. About the langurs Jay says:

> Adult males are leaders and coordinators of group activity. Their roles are extremely important in the maintenance of group unity and stability as well as in determining the group's use of its range and its relationships to other langur groups (Jay, 1965, p. 242).

She goes on to enumerate some functions from which certain roles may be extrapolated: Males are conductors in the sense of initiating and conducting group movements. They are "pillars of society" (my phrase, perhaps an unfortunate, overly anthropomorphic one) in that the dominance hierarchy of the males supplies most of the group structure. This is done in a number of ways. Dominant males are surrounded by empty space to an extent proportionate with their level of dominance (number one, number two, and so on) and temper. Dominant males also "take positions, food, and estrous females from other males" (Jay, 1965, p. 243). Finally, langur males act to reduce group tensions in two ways. Conflicts between two langurs are sometimes broken up by threat or movement of a more dominant animal, although the top dominant is said rarely to perform this function. Dominant males also start a kind of furious display that quickly spreads through the group. After a period of great activity and noise, a period that is not fully understood, the langurs relax, and the band returns to normal peacefulness.

The role prescription of· a dominant male baboon is more clearly discerned. K. R. L. Hall and Irven DeVore isolate five "key functions or behavior patterns," of which three have obvious role significance (Hall & DeVore, 1965, p. 56). The most dominant male is also the most aggressive as indicated by his participation in the largest number of agonistic episodes. When the band encounters a new or strange situation, the most dominant male goes forward to investigate and might threaten or attack. Mothers carrying newly born clustered in the vicinity of the dominant male.

Dominance

It might be thought from the foregoing discussion that one universal feature of primate society is the dominance hierarchy. Such, indeed, was the conclusion of C. R. Carpenter in the early days of scientific primate studies. His remarks are of interest and marked relevance:

> Extensive studies both in the field and in laboratories have emphasized that competition and associated dominance behavior are conspicuous characteristics of the behavioral interactions of monkeys and ape societies. *An individual is said to be dominant over another when it has priority in feeding, sexual and locomotor behavior and when it is superior in aggressiveness and in group control to another or other individuals.* The dominance of an individual is closely related to its *social status* and *prestige* in the group (Carpenter, 1942, pp. 191–2, emphasis his).

Carpenter's use of "prestige" is explained in these terms:

> By the term prestige I mean the perseveration of the effects of previous conditioning of an individual and of the reactions of other individuals to him without his showing behavior which would secure his dominance status (Carpenter, 1942, p. 192, *n.*9).

This usage departs from that suggested earlier and is closer to the meaning suggested for "authority." We prefer to associate prestige with symbolic expression for reasons previously given.

Since Carpenter's pioneering statement much more data have accumulated, and the dominance picture is less uniform than indicated. Dominance is clearest and apparently most significant among rhesus; it is least clear and apparently least significant as an organizing principle among the animals closest to man in the scale of phylogenetic evolution, the gorillas and chimpanzees.

The situation with regard to the chimpanzee is summed up by the Reynolds:

> Although there was some evidence of differences in status between individuals, dominance interactions formed a minute fraction of the observed chimpanzee behavior. There was no evidence of a linear hierarchy of dominance among males or females; there were no observations of exclusive rights to receptive females; and there were no permanent leaders of groups (Reynolds & Reynolds, 1965, p. 415).

The general tenor of these remarks is supported by Jane Goodall (1965, p. 453).

Dominance is more clearly discerned among gorillas, and its display fits some of the situations specified by Carpenter. There is also similarity to the langur in the frequent absence of actions assertive of dominance on the part of the highest male. Nonetheless, George B. Schaller (1963, pp. 240–4; 1965, pp. 346–8) has no difficulty placing his animals in a linear order roughly corresponding to age and size.

Leadership

Goodall's definition of leadership among chimpanzees seems to apply to the concept as used by other primatologists: "the leader . . . initiates group movement and regulates its speed and direction" (Goodall, 1965, p. 454). It scarcely needs pointing out that so limited a definition of leadership is almost meaningless when applied to human society. What is lacking, of course, is the most essential ingredient of leadership in human society: its application to the division of labor.

Division of Labor

As far as I know, Sahlins has not been challenged on his statement that, "In subhuman primates there is no sexual division of economic labor" (Sahlins, 1959, p. 193). Of course, females have the babies and nurse them. Beyond this point there is scarcely anything done by one sex that is not done by the other; this generalization is true of all the tasks involved in what might be identified as the economy of primate groups. As may be imagined, the category of objects called "possessions" is so limited as to be almost nonexistent. Compared to the state of any primate society, the most rudimentary material culture is in a qualitatively distinct class. (For an interesting discussion of tool use in primates see A. Kortlandt and M. Kooij. Their relevant conclusion is summed up: "Technological use of tools occurs extremely rarely in wild Primates" [Kortlandt & Kooij, 1963, p. 87].)

The basic point about all primate societies is that, with the exception of the smallest infants, all animals are essentially on their own in the food quest. Even isolated instances of food sharing are rare. Schaller observed not a single instance among gorillas. Chimpanzees also seem to lack sharing patterns, but the Reynolds, Goodall, and Kortlandt independently report observing juveniles "begging" and being given morsels by mothers. As we show further on, it is difficult to overstate the significance of the gulf between this kind of behavior and the widespread sharing known in simple ethnographic societies. Elman Service has summarized this situation most efficiently, and his remarks need no qualification because of the additional data that have been collected:

> There is one sense in which primate food-getting may favor group life and another in which it does not. *Within* a primate group, sociability is not favored in the foraging enterprises because food is never shared. That food-getting is competitive and that dominant animals (male *and* female) take it away from the subordinate animals must be a socially divisive trait, if anything. This is one of the most obvious points at which noncultural "apeness" is different from cultural humanness which so strikingly features collaboration and sharing. But group life *is* favored, with respect to an individual's food-getting, when competition among groups occurs. In competitive circumstances primate groups defend a group territory and in the course of defending themselves they also defend their food supplies. Thus even the most subordinated ape in the group has opportunities to get food in the group's territory that he could not get if he were not a group member (Service, 1962, p. 38, emphasis his).

Territoriality

Service's remarks lead us into a final but highly important topic. Let us approach the matter from the wrong direction, so to speak, by raising an old but persistent debate about the evolution of human society. The theorists of sociocultural evolution who were active from fifty to one hundred years ago made the point that the evolution of society was a development from kinship to territoriality as the basis of association. Robert Lowie (1927, pp. 51–73, *et passim*) made this thesis one of the butts of his own theory. For Lowie, territoriality was at least as old as consanguinity as an organizing principle. There is much to recommend Lowie's conclusion or, at least, in certain aspects of that conclusion. What we cannot accept is the implication that the territoriality that underlies state formation has any but superficial resemblance to the kind of territoriality that seems quite definitely to be much more ancient than the cultural recognition of kinship. We return to this part of the argument elsewhere; at this point let us consider territorial manifestations among nonhumans.

The phenomenon of territoriality[3] is known and reported in some detail among species of fish (Ratner & Denny, 1964, p. 310), mice (Anderson & Hill, 1965, pp. 1753–5), deer (Vos, 1965, pp. 1752–3), birds (Scott, 1958, p. 135), and various other animals.

A survey of data on territorial phenomena observed on wild or "provisionated" primates yields the results in Table 1.

With the exception of the chimpanzee, all primates studied in the wild seem to have more or less distinct areas within which their movements are concentrated for long periods of time. Chimpanzees move so freely from group to group that the only limits on their movements seem to be geographical, in terms of natural boundaries (Goodall, 1965, p. 456). If the ranges traversed by most primates are fairly wide and therefore tend to overlap with the ranges of other similar groups of the same species, this overlapping is less usual in what some observers call the "core areas," portions of the range most frequently inhabited. Overlapping of cores does occur but is less frequent and generally occurs to lesser depths of penetration.

Only the howler, of the six primates surveyed, seems almost incapable of being in a group which experiences peaceful meetings with other like groups. Actually, even in this case fighting is rare, but threats and display are the

---

[3] "Territoriality . . . is any behavioral phenomenon which effects the exclusion of some category of conspecific organisms from space inhabited by the territorial individual or group" (Anderson *et al.*, 1965, p. 1755).

TABLE 1.

Territoriality Among Selected Primates

	BABOON	CHIMP	GORILLA	HOWLER	LANGUR	RHESUS
Restricted area	+	0	+	+/−*	+	+
Overlapping ranges	+	+	+	+	+	+
Overlapping cores	+	+	−	−	0	−
Peaceful meetings	+	+	+	0	+†	0§
Active fights seen	0	0	0	+	0	+
Avoidance tendency	L/M	0	0	0	+	0/+**
Permeability	+	E	M/H	L	0‡	0

Symbols: + clearly reported present; 0 clearly reported absent; − concept not employed by reporting scientists; E extreme; H high; M medium; L low.

* "Howlers do not defend *boundaries* or whole territories; *they defend the place where they are* . . ." (Carpenter, 1965, p. 273; his emphasis).

† Langur groups depend greatly on avoidance and rarely come closely enough together to interact.

§ Rhesus were observed in "brief periods when all normal aggressive tendencies had disappeared" (Southwick, *et al.*, 1965, p. 144). The authors were unable to explain such periods.

** Imanishi reports that Japanese rhesus "oikia" or discrete social groups manage most interactions by avoidance based on shared perception of a dominance series (Imanishi, 1963, p. 72). Possibly because the area studied was much smaller and complete avoidance impossible, much more interaction was reported in the North Indian case (Southwick, *et al.*, 1965, pp. 143–44).

‡ Jay (1965, p. 206) says, "A langur group appears to be a closed social system and monkeys rarely change groups." The fiercest fighting she saw was associated with the repulse of a nongroup male attempting to follow a group (Jay, 1965, p. 207). Yet two adult rhesus, one a male, were observed to be apparently permanent members of a langur group (Jay, 1965, p. 211, fig. 7–8, and p. 212).

rule (Carpenter, 1965, pp. 273–5). The rhesus, too, usually finds himself in a fight if his group encounters another, but there are peaceful episodes. For the others, peaceful meetings are much more frequent than hostile encounters.

Perhaps the most amazing thing, considering the mythology about animal society and the strength of Hobbesian images of uncivilized society, is the discovery that a number of primates—gorillas and chimpanzees in particular—live in relatively open social groups. Not only is it possible for animals to shift groups, but the ones who do so most frequently, as far as we know, are adult males. The process occurs without fighting.

We can now sum up this brief overview of primate social life before venturing to review some materials about the simplest human societies known to ethnography. Primate societies lack at least three things that by their absence help account for the qualitative gap between fully cultural societies and all others. One of these things is the division of labor, another is sharing, and the third is a means of specifying different types and degrees of relationship. It is interesting that the absence of these things has a result which parallels the result of the absence of symbolic learning: the development of social structure tends to be noncumulative. The outcome is simplicity of patterning. There is nothing conceptually difficult about any primate society; problems in studying primate society stem from arduous physical difficulties, from the physical mobility of the animals, and from the trouble of telling many of the animals apart. Of course, the single greatest problem is created by inability to talk with them and find out what they think about it all.[4]

With regard to functions that may be loosely described as political, some primate phenomena are interesting. Though simple pecking orders never provide the basis of organization of a human society, all human societies include various forms of dominance hierarchy. Perhaps more suggestive are the clear indications in such primates as the baboon of dominance based upon combinations, an alliance serving to offset individual dominance (Hall & DeVore,

---

[4] My colleague, Marvin Harris, thinks that this would only introduce a further source of error probably greater than all the others and points to the heavy freight of misconceptions already carried in anthropology because analysis has been geared to the informant's mental ordering of his universe (cf. Harris, 1963, pp. 165–6).

1965, pp. 60–5). The forms of cooperation described remain insignificant, taking the form of mutual but uncoordinated harassment.

Leadership, too, is rudimentary, being confined in essence to the role of actually initiating a group movement, and setting its speed and direction. For most primates the evidence does not seem to support too strongly the view that leadership also involves disciplinary dispute adjudication. Most activity of this kind that has been described shows a more dominant animal making its presence felt by two less dominant animals who are fighting or quarreling and who break off what they are doing and scamper away. Although it is easy to find human behavior that seems to amount to the same thing, what cannot be found is the counterpart in primate society to settling disputes in human society, which serves to redress social balance. With these remarks it is necessary to turn from the fascinating world of our nonhuman relatives and to the world of our own species, divided among myriad patterns by their cultural affiliations but linked by the overwhelming commonality of their physical bodies and mental equipment.

CHAPTER 3

Simple Egalitarian Societies

"While Hobbes' state of nature was intolerable and Locke's was inconvenient, Rousseau's was idyllic" (Sait, 1938, p. 103). However appropriate their existential judgments, the social orders described by these and many other political philosophers of great eminence simply never existed. What then was the nature of the simplest cultural societies?

Matters of method compel postponing consideration of the structure of societies transitional from those of the primates discussed in the last chapter to the simplest ones known to ethnography. At the conclusion of this chapter there is a brief discussion of possibilities. Before it can be rendered meaningful, however, a review of what is actually known about simple human societies is required.

Egalitarian societies can be defined in positive terms, as in Chapter 2. The essential criterion seized upon was the social recognition of as many positions of valued status as there were individuals capable of filling them. One can also define egalitarian society in negative terms, identifying absent features or institutions that play crucial roles in other forms of society. The combination of features present and features absent should make for greater clarity.

Though there are a host of subsidiary specific details that vary in precise combination from one society to another, there are only two key institutions which must be introduced at this point. One of these is *ranking*, the other *stratification*.

Ranking exists when there are fewer positions of valued status than persons capable of filling them. A rank society has means of limiting the access of its members to status positions that they would otherwise hold on the basis of sex, age, or personal attributes. Rank has no *necessary* connection with economic status in any of its forms, though it frequently does acquire economic significance. The point is that rank can and in some instances does exist totally independent of the economic order.

Stratification, by contrast, is a term that is preferably limited to status differences based on economic differences. Stratification in this sense is a system by which the adult members of a society enjoy differential rights of access to basic resources. These resources are the physical things needed to sustain life, either directly (air, water, and food) or indirectly (things that cannot themselves be consumed but are required to obtain other things that are). Outstanding examples of the latter are land, raw materials for tools, water for irrigation, and materials to build a shelter. Though a few things would appear on the list of strategic resources of all societies, there is such evolution of cultural ecology that new strategic resources are created that are totally unknown in simple cultures. Thoreau is dead, and Walden pond, though in a state-protected reservation, has been swallowed between a suburb of Boston and superhighway 128.

Simple human societies are egalitarian and lack both ranking and stratification. How, then, do they run?

THE GENERAL NATURE
OF EGALITARIAN SOCIETIES

Volumes can and have been written on specific egalitarian societies and on comparisons at this cultural level. The present treatment must be brief and will concentrate on general features of such societies that have been described in ethnographic literature. Emphasis is placed on features relevant to political functions.

Physical Settings

One of the major differences between most ethnographically known simple societies and those that must have flourished in the Pleistocene period and persisted well into recent historical times is the nature of the habitat. Until perhaps 5,000 to 8,000 years ago competition for areas must have been relatively slight, and I presume that there was not very much large-scale displacement of societies in the inhabited regions of the earth. Without pursuing this point, I simply register the opinion that in the not so remote past, perhaps 1,000 years ago or less, many quite simple human societies were settled in well-watered areas with rich vegetation, abundant animal life, and moderate climate. At the present time there seem to be no independent cultures of preneolithic productive economy in any area of the world even remotely fitting this description. Some neolithic-like agricultural societies are still found relatively untouched in fine environments in New Guinea, but the last hunters and fishers who occupied prime territories were probably the Indians living along the Pacific in northern United States and Canada. That was in the last century; by the time they were studied their economies and political structures were already seriously changed by contact.

Societies dependent upon natural, undomesticated food

supplies are particularly vulnerable to environmental limitations. Limited technology plus limited natural food resources can only sustain small and scattered populations. But the demographic capacity of the same limited technology in a rich food area will obviously sustain a larger and potentially more concentrated population, and this will have demonstrable consequences on the development of social and political institutions.

Keeping this in mind, let us look at the environments of the ethnographically known simple societies. Physically diverse, they share what has been regularly called marginality. The word is usually employed in two senses by ethnographers, and usually both meanings apply. First, an environment is considered marginal if its return of calories for work-energy expended is minimal. Second, it is on or beyond the margins of more developed cultures; more significantly, such an environment is not desired by a developed culture for economic reasons, although in some instances the discovery of subsurface minerals or similar scarce civilized values creates a demand for portions of the area. More usually, the area's main value for more complex societies has to do with concerns of military strategy or the maintenance of trade routes.

The best known marginal societies of the past century or so have included dwellers in the icy tundra, various kinds of deserts, and relatively inaccessible jungles. Our examples shall come, therefore, from the Eskimo, African Bushman, Australian Bushman, Pygmy, and Negrito cultures and from some equally simple cultures that were found in the New World. Occasionally, when the ethnographic record permits it, we shall submit data from cultures located in more productive settings.

Demography

According to Ferdinand Okada, who made a comparative study of published ethnographies about marginal societies, the highest density reported for any such society was about three persons per square mile, a figure offered by A. R. Radcliffe-Brown for the aboriginal population of the Andaman Islands (Okada, 1954, p. 30; *cf.* Radcliffe-Brown, 1933, p. 28). The lowest density found by Okada was one person per 300 square miles reported by William Duncan Strong for the Barren Ground and Davis Inlet bands of the Naskapi (Okada, 1954, p. 31; *cf.* Strong, 1929, p. 278). These figures supply much wider limits than those offered by Julian Steward in his well-known article on band social organization. Steward set the limits in terms of his sample, which did not include the Andaman Islanders or the Naskapi, and found that "the population is sparse, ranging from a maximum which seldom exceeds one person per 5 square miles to one person per 50 or more square miles" (Steward, 1955, p. 125).

Acceptance of these figures, and let us assume that Okada's are more appropriate simply because their range is greater, is like acceptance of the Chinese census of 1954; few if any demographers believe that the census was accurate, but there is little else to go on, particularly because the 1954 census seems, to some extent, to be a projection of previous Chinese census data. In precontact and early postcontact aboriginal demography, most of the significant statements are based on fairly crude estimates. Today we have apparently reliable figures for many aboriginal populations; at least the methods used to collect the data are those associated with modern census taking. Then too, most of the populations in question are small, and the discrete populations are few in number. Access to these groups has been facilitated by modern means of communication, and contact with them tends to be much more regular than ever in the past because, through acculturation, the members of simple societies have come to value products and services that bring them to trading or administrative centers. As a result, we know, *inter alia,* that "According to the 1944 census of aborigines, carried out in all the states of the Commonwealth [of Australia] except New South Wales, the aboriginal population amounted to 71,895 persons, of whom 47,014 were 'full-blood' and 24,881 'half-caste'" (I.L.O., 1953, p. 84). It is interesting to compare this with an estimate of the number of aborigines in Australia at the time of European settlement, 211,000, according to Radcliffe-Brown, not including the 40,000 estimated for New South Wales (1930, p. 696; cited in I.L.O., 1953, p. 85). The shrinking of the population to a third or a quarter of previous size is a usual characteristic of the century or two after initial intensive contact with more highly organized societies, but thereafter it is not unusual for population to rise again. Nevertheless, some groups will have long since expired as discrete populations, although some of their genetic and cultural capital will have flowed into the dominant population and culture.

Apart from the process of depopulation itself, which is an interesting, if grim, phenomenon, the social consequences are of first importance. Population reductions stem from many causes, which often work together: New diseases, dislocated food supplies, forced movement into arid or other near-lethal environments, "anomie," and the hunting of aborigines for sport are some of the things that have produced decimation in some areas. The results have triggered further social processes, two of which are of particular interest to our present discussion. One of them is warfare and its frequency; it is discussed later in the chapter. The other involves a fascinating argument about the nature of primitive society, the character of the marginal band.

The standard position is that put forward by Steward in 1936 and somewhat enlarged by him in 1955. The leading counter has been offered by Elman Service (Service, 1960). Steward offers an ecological-demographic explanation for the organization of the band, itemizing four causal factors: low population density, dependence on the hunting of game, transport limited to shanks' mare and human back, postulated acceptance of the extension of incest taboos to all coresident members of an extended family (Steward, 1955,

p. 135). The outcome is what Steward calls a "patrilineal band," the most widespread form of social aggregation among marginal societies and the second most simple. Service takes issue with Steward on three counts: He cannot accept the family as an isolated social unit;[1] he discounts the composite band as other than a phenomenon of contact dislocation; and he feels that the narrowing of causes to ecological factors alone[2] is merely partial or actually incorrect, depending on the specific case. The stimulus for Service's criticism was the discovery "that the band societies in their *aboriginal* form do not in fact correspond to the social organizations they are supposed to have by the ecological explanation" (Service, 1962, p. 73, emphasis in original). Service also defends a point of view that overlaps with the one we stressed in earlier pages: ". . . there is more to social organization than demography. *Human* social organization is cultural and a form of explanation which is adequate for societies of wild animals is not sufficient for human societies, even those at the lowest levels of complexity" (Service, 1962, p. 73, emphasis in original). Crucial to Service's argument is the analysis of the structure and functions of sodalities, forms of social groupings that crosscut localities and, depending as they do on symbols for their very existence, cannot appear in precultural society.

Though the issue is not directly related to the central problem of this book, I cannot refrain from stating that in

---

[1] Steward says that the most simple is the "family level" in which the main social tasks are regularly carried out by family units dwelling in relative isolation. Steward's examples are Eskimo, Basin Shoshone, Nambicuara, Guató, Mura, "and perhaps other groups" (Steward, 1955, p. 119). Service argues convincingly that the pattern of isolated families acting as the sole aggregate for extensive periods of time seems to be a consequence of European contact, disruption, and depopulation—a view supported by the work of others (Service, 1962, pp. 94–107; *cf.* Wagley, 1940, pp. 12–6; Murphy, *et al.*, 1956, pp. 335–55; and so on).

[2] Service admits that Steward has avoided simple monolithic statements of the ecological position, but he points to the work of others who, in cited passages, do make such statements (Service, 1962, p. 73).

my judgment Service is correct in his criticism of Steward's family level. The cases Steward cites and the Shoshone he analyzes in detail may be considered under the composite band. Service's argument, in placing all examples of the composite band in relation to breakdown following contact or its effects, is not altogether convincing. One of the salient differences between Service and myself on this issue is the matter of primitive warfare, to which I return at the end of this chapter. Regarding one more aspect of Service's thesis, it seems to me that, in criticizing the demographic-ecological explanation of simple human social organization, Service essentially succeeds in revising and strengthening it. I believe that is the significance of his argument that sodalities are a function of dispersed settlement. Here, too, he refers to primitive warfare, and further discussion is deferred to the end of this chapter.

Economy: Means of Production

All simple societies depend on wild sources of food, which, with a few obscure and not altogether certain exceptions, are not increased by the members of those societies. Most of the work of obtaining food and preparing it for consumption according to local cultural standards is accomplished with very few tools and weapons but with natural objects like leaves and sticks. In no simple society known to ethnography is there any restriction on access to the raw materials necessary to make tools and weapons. This statement can be made flatly about resources in the habitation area of a given unit, and with moderate reservations it may be extended to resources located in alien areas. For example, a description of Eskimos west of Hudson Bay warns:

> At the outset it should be stressed that the very notion of *exclusive rights* in land or hunting and fishing territory—whether private, familial or communal—is nonexistent and outside the conception of these Eskimos. It is true that each band has a more or less traditional,

yet vaguely definable, hunting and fishing area where its hunters feel most "at home," but these grounds are open to everybody, also non-Eskimos, and any game or fish is *res nullius*, all and no one's property, as long as it has not been touched. The same view is taken of other resources like soapstone, wood, etc. (Steenhoven, 1962, p. 57).

The Eskimos are famed for presenting so clear a case (*cf.* Birket-Smith, 1929, pp. 261–2; Rasmussen, 1931, p. 173; Balikci, 1962, pp. 60 ff.). The Eskimos may be taken as almost a limiting case, but they differ from other simple societies in degree rather than kind. For example, among !Kung Bushmen each band occupies a traditional territory the boundaries of which are known to all who are likely to come into the area (Marshall, 1960, p. 331). The boundaries seem vague to the outlander, possibly because they are often set in virtually trackless country in what the Bushmen themselves treat as marginal areas. Furthermore, "!Kung hunting customs do not require that hunters confine themselves strictly to their own territory, and the ownership of the animals which are hunted is not based on territories. The animals belong to no one until shot" (Marshall, 1960, p. 331). The situation is not quite as obvious with respect to another crucial resource, drinking water. Rain water accumulated on the surface, which occurs for more than three months each year, is free to all. But Lorna Marshall tells us that permanent or semipermanent water holes are owned by the bands. What the ownership amounts to is not altogether clear. To begin with, the most significant water resources seem to be "owned" by two or more bands; furthermore, in drought years some bands split up into smaller components, which then distribute themselves about the territory, attaching themselves to other bands and thus to other water holes (Marshall, 1960, pp. 336–7). Perhaps the most serious question of limited ownership of productive resources among the Bushmen involves veldkos, the eighty or more varieties of plants that have edible parts and that, in Marshall's phrase, are what "the !Kung depend on . . . for their daily living." Although meat is much desired, it is eaten only "intermittently," whereas Marshall estimates that the veldkos account for some 80 per cent of !Kung food (Marshall, 1960, p. 335).

Lorna Marshall maintains that the fertile areas in which veldkos grow most abundantly are all thoroughly known to the Bushmen and "are owned by the bands with strict definition and jealous concern" (Marshall, 1960, p. 335). This statement is based, at least in part, upon an incident in which, despite the Marshalls' urgings, the Bushmen would not extend their area of harvest of a certain wild nut beyond what seemed to the observers to be a definite, though presumably quite invisible, line (Marshall, 1960, p. 335). Furthermore, veldkos are not shared, at least not as game is shared. We shall shortly discuss sharing patterns, including those of the Bushmen, but here I wish to say only that in the case of the Bushmen's veldkos the absence of organized sharing does not seem truly aberrant. To begin with, veldkos apparently are neither stored nor preserved but are gathered each day for that day's consumption. As the whole group is together at the veldkos patch, I cannot imagine why veldkos should be shared beyond the *de facto* sharing reported by Marshall herself: "Each gatherer owns what he has gathered and may give it to and share it with whomever he pleases. Visitors are given veldkos by the persons they are visiting or may join a gathering party as a courtesy" (Marshall, 1960, p. 336). As far as we can see, therefore, the Bushman case may join that of the Eskimos as an illustration of the absence of restrictions upon access to basic resources.

To avoid prolonging this section with further examples from a copious record, let us turn to one area in which there was a lengthy debate regarding sharing and ownership. In 1915 Frank Speck described the family hunting band as the basis of Algonkian social organization, and he attributed to it exclusive ownership of land with summary punishment for trespass (Speck, 1915; Speck, 1926). We need not review the history of the refinement of Speck's position as he and others added to the picture. In 1950 and 1951 Eleanor Leacock carried out ethnographic research among the Montagnais-Naskapi of Labrador and took as her dissertation topic rebuttal of the thesis that there is strict family ownership of basic hunting resources among the Algonkians. In brief, Leacock demolishes the case built by Speck and others. Using historical sources as well as her own field data she shows that the "family hunting territory" as an exclusive possession represents an adjustment to European-introduced fur trade. Among the interesting pieces of evidence is a French source of the middle of the eighteenth century that remarks that the Indians of the region could take beaver out of another man's trap, if hungry, provided only that after consuming the meat they would replace the fur (La-Potherie, 1753, p. 132; cited by Leacock, 1954, p. 16). Indeed, Leacock found that the Indians she studied resisted the development of family and individual hunting territories and preserved important aspects of older communal hunting and sharing patterns (Leacock, 1954, p. 9).

The evidence for significantly undifferentiated communal access to resources and the relatively permissive attitude toward "trespass" in simple societies is abundant. In addition to the cases mentioned there are many others, including the Semang (Schebesta, 1929, p. 83), Apayao (Vanoverbergh, 1925, p. 430), Shoshone (Steward, 1938, p. 254; Cappannari, 1960), Yaruro (Petrullo, 1939, p. 199), and so on.

We have alluded only by implication to the actual processes of production in these simple societies. Generalizations are made difficult by the variety of specific environments, hence of the tasks confronted. The various animals hunted have diverse life patterns of their own to which the hunt must be adapted, and similar conditions exist with regard to collectable foods. Beyond ecologically derived differences, however, loom broad areas of similarity.

All simple societies maintain fairly distinct divisions of labor between the sexes. Within these divisions, however, all adults are expected to fulfill almost all roles, particularly in subsistence-oriented activities. Nobody can exist in such a society on the basis of professional performance of a limited specialization. If there is any exception to this rule it lies not in the field of religion, for all available evidence indicates that the specialized religious practitioner in simple societies carries out a rather normal role in food production. The exception is the lazy person. Considerable pressure is directed against laziness, but, if the person can stand being the butt of jokes or if he is perhaps a little hungrier than his energetic neighbor[3] or does not care what others think of him, he may survive as a drone.

Cooperative teams are frequently required in the productive process, but the circumstances of their assembly vary widely. The mere fact of assembly does not necessarily mean that labor is concerted; a number of berry pickers may work in close proximity without any significant cooperation. It is true, however, that work of this kind is usually preferred in company that converts a simple repetitive task into a pleasurable social gathering. The obvious gain from such *esprit* may be at least partially reduced by loss of work efficiency due to diversion. Needless to say, such a way of looking at the situation would be most curious in precontact simple societies. One further comment prior to our discussion of related matters: Cooperative labor parties, whether for hunting or for gathering, take place with very little apparent leadership except for certain interesting situations like the Shoshone rabbit drive. As shown further on,

---

[3] It is by no means certain that the laggard will fare poorly in this regard (*cf.* Fortune, 1932, pp. 55–6, for the case of Negwadi, who lived a life of ease and eating among her diligent fellow Dobuans). As will be seen in the discussion of sharing and reciprocity, hunters often give out much more than they keep and beggars willing to ask are difficult to turn down (*cf.* Sahlins, 1965, pp. 186–200, for excellent bibliographic commentary on this).

whatever leadership is generated for such events is not applied to other aspects of the group life.

Economics: Distribution

Liebig's "law of the minimum" is a statement about biological evolution which calls attention to the fact that selection and adaptation respond to minimum rather than maximum features of the environment. If there is adequate water most of the year but a regular period of drought, the animals that show the best maintenance rates are likely to be those able to withstand the shortage. Such reasoning is helpful in understanding the absence of narrow rights of access to strategic resources in simple societies. It is equally useful in understanding the prevalence of sharing and the patterns of reciprocity that are also usual in these societies.

There can be no question that all ethnographically known societies have institutionalized individual ("private") property in nonstrategic objects. I agree with both L. T. Hobhouse (1922, p. 7) and Stephen Cappannari (1960, p. 136) in not applying the term "property" to things that "all the world can use." There are in all known societies things that are property on two accounts: First, while they are being used they may not be removed from the user without social disruption. Second, the user can give such a thing to someone else thereby accomplishing the creation of some kind of obligation for some kind of return and the enhancement of his own prestige. Leaving the matter of prestige for subsequent discussion, we find that the obligation for return lies at the heart of the most widespread mechanism of economic distribution, namely reciprocity.

As Sahlins has shown and so well documented:

> Reciprocity is a whole class of exchanges, a continuum of forms. This is especially true in the narrow context of material transactions. . . . At one end of the spectrum stands the assistance freely given . . . the "pure gift" Malinowski called it, regarding which an open

stipulation of return would be unthinkable and unsociable. At the other pole, self-interested seizure, appropriation by chicanery or force requited only by an equal and opposite effort on the principle of *lex talionis*, "negative reciprocity" as Gouldner phrases it (Sahlins, 1965, p. 144).

In addition to distinguishing and identifying three points along this continuum as generalized, balanced, and negative reciprocity, Sahlins notes that any particular transaction is likely to be affected by a number of additional factors, suggesting four: kinship distance, kinship rank, relative wealth and need, and the type of goods involved (Sahlins, 1965, p. 158).

The next thing to note about this mode of distribution is that it exists, as we have already indicated, in all societies from the simplest to the most complex; in the simplest societies, however, it is *the* mode of distribution. One must also realize that participation in reciprocal transactions usually occurs as a matter of course in which the donor has minimal possibilities of free decision. The chain of reciprocities to which his act is a contribution started long before and will continue into the remote future; the donor acquires this role largely by the action of other sociocultural subsystems. He is son, son-in-law, husband, father, brother-in-law, and so on. He is friend, partner, neighbor, camp mate, and so forth. He is generous, kind, a good hunter, and so on. Through the interaction of such established categories the individual finds himself with limited alternatives. Not that members of primitive societies are intellectually or emotionally incapable of defying custom. The "savage automaton" concept of primitive society, if it ever carried intellectual weight, is long dead, but this does not mean that we are incapable of recognizing the structural limits to the possibilities of individual decision making in simple society.

A general principle of reciprocal economic exchanges, particularly those in the area Sahlins calls "generalized reciprocity," is that the mechanism for balancing exchanges is vested in set formulas for distribution. Once again the Eskimos offer a clear illustration, as in this observation by Kaj Birket-Smith:

> The most important rules [according to which the kill is divided] are:
>
> If two men go hunting together and one kills an animal, he takes the fore-part and the other gets the hind part. Others say that the fore-part goes to the one who first reaches the caribou. If there are three hunters together, each of the helpers receives a hind-quarter; but if there are still more company, there is no sharing. In return the hunter is obliged to provide the inhabitants of the camp with meat in the evening.
>
> For walrus and bearded seal the rules are the same (Birket-Smith, 1929, p. 262).

In many societies the disposition of particular sections of game is not according to the rules of the hunt, but follows strict kinship protocol and specifies that certain choice portions of the carcass go to parents, to wife's parents, and so on. While pertaining to a rather more complexly organized culture than those to which we have addressed ourselves until now, H. N. C. Stevenson's discussion of the distribution of slaughtered domestic cattle includes a diagram that has always struck me as the equivalent of our own "cuts of beef" butcher chart among people living in a fundamentally reciprocal economy. Stevenson's chart doesn't show where the tenderloin or sirloin is, it shows which part must be given to which relative or affine (H. N. C. Stevenson, 1943; *cf*. Firth, 1956, p. 86, for the diagram and discussion).

Actually, even before customary procedures for distribution are brought into action, many cultures are already at work, so to speak, separating specific individuals from monopolistic possession. This method of designation is shown beautifully, though by no means uniquely, among the !Kung Bushmen, who regard as the "owner" of game not the hunter who killed it but the man who made the projectile that brought it down. The arrowmaker might not even be on the hunt; arrows are freely given as gifts or loaned (though how one tells the difference between "gift" and "loan" in such a context I cannot guess). The results are such that the ethnographer is led to remark that, "The society seems to want to extinguish in every way possible the concept of meat belonging to the hunter" (Marshall, 1961, p. 238). Other societies award "ownership" to the spotter, to the first one to strike, or sometimes to the last to strike before the animal dies. Perhaps more significantly, "ownership" does not really mean the ability to do with the game exactly what one wishes. There is no reason to believe that most hunters have strong desires other than to fulfill the role for which they have been educated, so that "ownership" really means that the man who fulfills the social requirements of "owner" is the one to whom prestige will accrue as the distribution proceeds.

In most societies this prestige is viewed as cumulative. Consistent successful return from the hunt will build a man's reputation. He is a good hunter, then a very good one, great, truly the greatest! Considering social techniques of randomizing success and the empirical difficulties of the hunt it is no wonder that the truly great hunters are sometimes held in awe and assumed to benefit from supernatural assistance. On the other hand, the prestige which even the mightiest hunter enjoys is not transferable to other areas and does not constitute a firm basis for political power.

General Social Structure

The simple societies with political forms identified as egalitarian tend to display two kinds of grouping. The smaller group is a form of family, generally nuclear as children old enough to marry usually set up their own households. The larger group is the band. Since the family is usually found in the context of a band, it is not treated as an autonomous unit. The question, however, is not entirely settled; as we have seen, Steward analyzes Shoshone society as an example of the "family level," whereas Service disagrees (Service, 1962, pp. 64–6). We need not be drawn into this dispute except insofar as an absence of warfare is implied by the individual family existing independently. It is more than probable that the harsh environment found in conjunction with a settlement pattern based on autonomous families would also ensure such general poverty and isolation as to make unlikely any need for defense.

It is improbable that human families existed as isolated, autonomous units until the bands of which they were part were forced into areas of low natural food potential or—what amounts to the same thing—were not able to leave areas that, through dessication or other geoclimatological processes, were becoming low in natural food potential. But, placing the question of the independent family to one side, there can be no disputing the significance of the nuclear family as the main component of the band. Bands like the ones now being discussed are reviewed in some ethnographic detail in another volume in this series (Service, 1962, pp. 59–109), and need not occupy us long. We make only those points relevant to our problem.

The band is a local group composed of a small number of families. The Marshall party conducted precise enumeration of thirteen !Kung bands out of an estimated twenty-seven bands that occupied the region of Nyae Nyae in South West Africa in 1952–1953; four other bands were counted approximately. Of the thirteen whose exact composition is known, the smallest included eight families, the largest fifty-seven; the average was a fraction over twenty-four. The four bands known approximately were larger on the whole, ranging from twenty-three to forty-seven, averaging 32.5 (Marshall, 1960, p. 328).

Most of the data on band size is approximate; the original sources rarely tell exactly how the figures were obtained. A sampling of the figures gathered from other ethnographies by Steward (1955, pp. 122–42) and Okada

(1954, pp. 29–45, 84–90) brackets the averages obtained by Lorna Marshall but tends to be higher. Here are some characteristic figures: The Yahgan show especially brittle band composition, and families tend to live by themselves, coming together for *ad hoc* assemblies with other families with which they may or may not cohere again. They are rarely reported to aggregate in bands of more than fifteen individuals or so at a time. The Guayaki, rare because of their matrilocality-matrilineality, run about twenty individuals per local group, the Semang up to fifty, the Waicura fifty to sixty. Most of the African Pygmies are said to run in the sixty-to-sixty-five range, but Patrick Putnam (1948, p. 335) places the average at 150, which probably reflects the aggregation of groups in the vicinity of what was then Camp Putnam, a source of goods and medical care. The Botocudo bands are said to range from fifty to 200, with perhaps the largest bands those of the Patagonian Tehuelche, running 400 and 500. These last can easily be discounted, however, as occurring in response to European influence, which included, among other tangibles, the Tehuelche acquisition of domesticated horses. Prior to this acquisition Tehuelche band size seems to have been comparable to that of the Ona, said to have ranged from forty to 120 with larger aggregates forming briefly to devour beached whales.

On the basis of the foregoing and additional similar evidence it seems reasonable to conclude that social units on this level are fairly small, particularly with regard to the interacting persons of the same sex and age status. Given such groups it is likely that all parties to social intercourse generally have intimate knowledge of the others and can reasonably expect and predict behavioral reactions. Finally, the component units of higher level (band) organization are not compelled to remain together but can and do separate and form new alignments. The apparent contradiction between this point and the one that preceded it can be easily explained. People are familiar with those in adjacent bands; very likely they are related and probably by marriage. In addition, the possible role sets in primitive society are relatively few and variation out of the expectable is unlikely although possible.

The terminology used by anthropologists in designating different types of bands—"matrilineal," "patrilineal," "composite"—reveals the frequent assumption that the charter of a band lies in kinship. Though the social organizations concerned are simple, the problem of distinguishing kinship from other bases of affiliation is not. It is complicated by the fact that the farther one travels from the immediate territory of his band the more remote genealogically and socially will be the inhabitants or relatives one encounters. Indeed, this point is one that Sahlins makes in his analysis of reciprocity, showing that there is an intimate relationship among kinship distance, residential sectors, and the quality of reciprocal exchanges (Sahlins, 1965, p. 152, fig. 1; 151 ff.; 186–200).

One of the major consistencies found from one band-organized society to another is the institution of exogamy. Steward cites this institution, phrased in terms of an extension of incest taboos to the extended family, as a causal factor in the genesis of the patrilineal band (Steward, 1955, p. 135), and Service comes to the same conclusion, although using different phrasing (Service, 1962, pp. 66–7). A much underscored remark by Edward B. Tylor, not only introduced the notion but also served to explain it in evolutionary terms, the "simple practical alternative between marrying-out and being killed-out" (Tylor, 1888, p. 267). I prefer to say today that the alternative is "dying out," to suggest that exogamy, which forces alliances, has great economic potential for expanding the area of resource exploitation. To the extent, and it is empirically known to be very considerable, that reciprocal exchanges are deeply involved with affinal ties, Tylor's dictum stands amendment.

Maintenance of band society requires that certain minimum conditions be met. The strategic condition, of course, is that the members of the band be able to live and reproduce. This minimum requires, in turn, a division of labor permitting the accumulation of foods from afar as well as from near the campsite, while taking care of the young. Exogamic prescriptions that extend the exchange and sanctuary range of the immediate group also help to ensure its perpetuation under difficult conditions. There are many other things the band requires, like a communication system and a program for enculturating the next generation; it also requires means of maintaining internal and external order. It is to these things that we shall now turn.

INTRABAND SOURCES OF CONFLICT

It has been a long time since any serious support could be mustered for Thomas Hobbes' view of primitive society: "during the time that men live without a common Power to keep them in awe, they are in that condition which is called Warre; and such a warre, as is of every man against every man" (Hobbes, 1929, p. 96). William Seagle (1941, p. 378, n.7) cites an article of Sir Henry Maine published in 1888 that referred to war being older than peace and also spoke of "the universal belligerency of primitive mankind."

The polar alternative to the war of all against all is the theory of the submissive savage. It is difficult to find important figures who have offered unqualified statements supporting this position. Rather, it is easier to find extreme statements of this theory in the work of opponents who denounce it. (The history of the concept of "unilineal evolution" shows a remarkable parallel, being more distinct and elaborated in the works of its critics than its advocates.) Bronislaw Malinowski and his pupils have said:

> The savage—so runs to-day's verdict of competent anthropologists—has a deep reverence for tradition and custom, an automatic submission to their biddings. He obeys them "slavishly," "unwittingly," "spontaneously," through "mental inertia," combined with the fear of

public opinion or of supernatural punishment; or again through a "pervading group-sentiment if not group instinct" (Malinowski, 1926, p. 10).

Both in the famous work published in 1926 and in his lengthy introduction to a later book by H. Ian Hogbin (1934), Malinowski comes no closer to specifying who the "competent anthropologists" were than offering words from E. Sidney Hartland and W. H. R. Rivers that are considerably less decisive than his own statement. I am very close to concluding that "the figment of an automatically lawabiding native" (Malinowski, 1934, p. xxvii) is really the unintended result of critical exaggeration.

During the more than seventeen months that Lorna Marshall observed Bushman bands in Nyae Nyae, South West Africa, she saw four incidents of interpersonal conflict and was told about three other incidents that occurred during that period but which she did not observe as they took place in neighboring bands (Marshall, 1961, p. 246). If the point has to be established that members of primitive societies know both deviation from established norms and conflict, there is ample evidence of both. But I believe that some earlier anthropologists were quite right to state or imply that the possibilities of both were considerably reduced by the structural absence of alternatives. There was also comparatively little incentive to violate norms.

Property and Conflict

As has long been understood despite occasional statements of denial or ridicule, there is a definite relationship between the concept of individual property and crime. Recalling our picture of access to basic resources in egalitarian societies, we can see that a major source of social unrest in more complexly organized societies is obviously lacking. The significant sources of food available to simple societies are not foreclosed to any member of the group and, as shown, usually are available to outsiders as well. Whatever men and women may fight about in egalitarian societies, it cannot be land.

It is somewhat more likely that conflict may be engendered by food. No effective means exist in simple societies to restrict access of individuals to land. But with food, different amounts are found in different hands—based on differential skill, diligence, perseverance, luck, what have you. The positive actión of society is needed to overcome the unequal distributions of nature. As we have seen, however, systems to accomplish this end are deeply embedded in all ethnographically known simple societies. It may seem one of those typical nineteenth-century overestimations of human rationality to assume that young and vigorous hunters think of the time they will be old and feeble or of what may befall their families if they are killed or injured. But the actual data of recorded mythology and the stories that are told around campfires inform us that such anxieties are indeed common, though they are not necessarily harnessed consciously to social patterns of reciprocity.

Indeed, it is possible that the patterns of reciprocity may trigger conflict precisely through the raising of unrequited expectations. What happens when people don't share as they are supposed to according to normal practice? In brief, one of four things usually results; unfortunately, considering the nature of the subject, it would be ridiculous to attempt to rank them in order of statistical occurrence. First of all, cases when nothing happens are probably quite frequent. The person who does not receive does not complain or press a case; there is no social disturbance, no breach has been acknowledged.

Second and at least equally probable, for this is amply documented in ethnographic cases, is individual retaliation by threat or actual suspension of reciprocity. A lovely illustrative case is given by Allan R. Holmberg (1950, pp. 59–60) in his description of a furious Siriono "chief" who demands a share of the game taken by a successful hunter. Refused, the man has a tantrum which ends with a vow that when he, the "chief," gets something he will certainly refuse to give any of it to the withholder. Holmberg does not tell us whether the threat is realized, but the account gives no indication of any further social dislocation stemming from this act.

Third, threat of withdrawal from reciprocity is often made into a more broadly social action by a calculated attempt to humiliate and demean the offender. In a society in which generosity and the ability to be generous are almost the sole means of achieving prestige, it is no little thing to be identified as stingy. We have no way of knowing whether identification as a niggardly person tends to develop wider social consequences. Possibly other people react to the label by avoiding transactions with the person; close relatives might align themselves accordingly, though this is not likely in bands of small size. In any case, some social disruption is likely to follow accusations of this kind. Among the results of such events is the achievement of "prepolarization," or the division of the band into latent factions to provide the basis of a later split when conditions demand it.

Fourth, beyond labeling an individual as stingy because of real or fancied slights in the process of reciprocal exchanges, there is a continuum of disapprobation, a kind of escalation of revenge. This may involve lengthy harangues in prose or poetry before the entire camp or may include more violent outbursts. Surprising to members of our own force-loving society, intraband violence seems to occur very infrequently in these simple societies. The Eskimos and some other peoples of the far north, like the Chukchee, may be an exception. They seem to esteem violence, but the frequency of their homicides does not seem so great, although more violence is reported for them than for most simple societies. Furthermore, Marshall's notation that none of the conflicts she saw or heard about were over food while four of seven "were flare-ups of sexual jealousy" (Marshall, 1961, p. 246), finds an echo in a modern ethnography of the North Alaskan Eskimo in which Robert Spencer (1959, p. 99) remarks that "killings arose less because of anti-social behavior relating to food and personal property than because of sexual involvements."

Trouble can arise if someone refuses to accept a gift. Marshall was told by one Bushman that he accepted gifts even when the last thing he wanted was to be obligated to the donor. If he failed to accept the gift "the giver would be terribly angry" (Marshall, 1961, p. 244). Again, the comparison with Eskimos is instructive:

> Mine and thine are distinguished among these Eskimos and ownership is conceptualized, though it lacks the connotation of absolute rights to which *we* are accustomed. . . . A man who has made something is owner of it as long as he needs and uses it. But at a given moment someone else will need it and the owner will lend it to the former. . . . To these nomads who in principle have no use for more property than one can load on a sled, nothing that is not really needed for daily use is regarded as property in any strict sense (Steenhoven, 1962, pp. 47–8).

And once again, the Bushmen:

> In their nomadic hunting-gathering life, travelling from one source of food to another through the seasons . . . they carry their young children and their belongings. With plenty of most materials at hand to replace artifacts as required, the !Kung have not developed means of permanent storage and have not needed or wanted to encumber themselves with surpluses or duplicates. They do not even want to carry one of everything. They borrow what they do not own . . . and the accumulation of objects has not become associated with status (Marshall, 1961, pp. 243–4).

The illustrations could be multiplied, but our purpose is served by the very clear examples already given. Conflict over things, whether land, food, water, tools, weapons, ornaments, anything, is most unlikely in simple societies because the things are either immediately open to all or so mobile as to obviate problems of possession. Equally clear is the obviation of theft, for in a sense Proudhon was right. Actually in a simple egalitarian society the taking of something before it is offered is more akin to rudeness than stealing. Once more the Eskimos are instructive as Birket-Smith reported: "Theft can never be a matter of grave importance, and a thief is regarded as something the same as a liar, i.e., an unpleasant person, and if the victim has enough moral courage and authority over the thief, he will probably demand the return of the stolen articles (Birket-Smith, 1929, p. 265).

Sex and Conflict

Statements cited above from the work of Marshall and Spencer indicate that sexual tensions are the cause of much of the conflict they saw or heard about in Bushman and Eskimo society. Our knowledge of the sexual life of people in most societies, simple and complex, is generally inadequate for the weight of generalizations it has been made to bear. As we know from the researches begun by the late Alfred Kinsey, detailed statistical data can overturn or necessitate the revision of the prevailing view of the sexual behaviour of an entire population. Kinsey reports have their limitations, procedural biases, and sources of error as a number of critics have made clear. When all is said and done, however, such information is more reliable and certainly more comprehensive than the anecdotal material usually supplied. And it is precisely the latter material that dominates anthropological study of sex in most alien societies.

What is on record indicates surprising range of variation of sexual practices in simple societies, although there is a fairly regular core built about concepts of incest, exogamy, and adultery. Unfortunately for my own argument, what little evidence exists does not seem to show a correlation between permissiveness to sexual behavior and low incidence of conflict due to sexual rivalry. The Eskimos are among the more permissive peoples with regard to sexual relations; their attitudes toward homosexuality are not altogether clear, but bestiality, although regarded as somewhat unusual, was not treated with contempt but in a matter of fact way (R. Spencer, 1959, p. 246). Sexual intercourse holds few if any secrets for Eskimo children who regularly observe copulation in their own homes. Masturbation is not taboo, and Spencer reports observation of mothers masturbating infants as a pacifier (R. Spencer, 1959, p. 245). Sexual experimentation is common around the age of puberty. Girls are advised that promiscuous relations "might complicate the system of mutual obligations between families which could arise from sexual ties" (R. Spencer, 1959, p. 245). He does not elaborate this remark, but it is evident from other statements he makes, as well as from the works of others, that sexual relations among Eskimos usually presuppose special economic relations—a more intimate and intense reciprocity than would otherwise be the case. Maintenance of too many such relationships would be very difficult and somewhat dangerous, not to say expensive.

Eskimo marriage is noted for its brittleness, if that is the proper word. The reluctance to engage in fully promiscuous relations leads to something that is structurally like the vogue for "going steady" in contemporary American adolescent society but is actually developed further into trial marriage. Two or more of these affairs might precede the first relatively durable marriage. This marriage is contracted in one of several ways, by long-standing agreement between families, by independent decision of the man and woman, or by abduction, sometimes with the connivance of the woman, sometimes not, sometimes with the aid of one's relatives, sometimes purely solo. Rape is commonplace, almost all women being considered fair game. There is also the famous Eskimo institution of wife exchange, not a casual matter but tending to establish or reinforce ties of reciprocity between the males. While most adult Eskimos for whom any details are reported are said to marry at least twice and many are said to marry six times or more, the rate of shifts of partners seems to decline as full adulthood is assumed. This does not mean, however, that sexual relations are equally circumscribed.

If the situation among the Eskimos be compared with that reported for the Bushmen wide differences are seen. According to Marshall (1959, pp. 335–65) the Bushmen are rather prudish and push sex into the background of their lives. Sexual intercourse is engaged in discreetly, but in proximity to children. We are not explicitly told about observation by others but, although it might take place, it would tend to be covert. Unlike the Eskimos, the Bushmen do not talk much about sex. Marshall attributes this to the tightness of the camp which necessarily brings close relatives of both sexes together. Avoidance taboos of various kinds operating in such close quarters, she thinks, tended to produce a general reluctance to engage in sexy repartee or joking (Marshall, 1959, p. 339), although joking relationships exist. To the polygyny of the Bushmen Marshall attributes the premium placed on marriageable women and much of the restraint which is shown toward them.[4] "Rape did not appear in stories or gossip" (Marshall, 1959, p. 360). Premarital sexual experimentation is ruled out by Marshall on the grounds that most people marry very young. (Apparently she is unaware, for example, that very

---

[4] This is difficult to comprehend by the figures Marshall gives. In the sample of 353 persons of fourteen bands, 136 were unmarried adolescents or younger children. Of the remaining 217 the greater portion, 125, was women, ninety-seven of these being married at the time of study (1952–3); the remainder comprised two young widows and two young divorcees, and twenty-four old widows. Of ninety-two adult men, eighty-eight were married (nine had two wives each, accounting for the ninety-seven married women), three were widowers and there was one eccentric old bachelor. Though the future seems dark for males wanting their own wives because among youngsters there are seventy-eight boys and only fifty-eight girls, the reverse seems true for the current crop of adults who know a surplus of females.

small Eskimo children play the "copulation game"; at any rate her view is consistent with her picture of Bushmen sexual repression.) Adultery is also said to be rare, hemmed in by incest taboos or their extensions, or by the lack of privacy. There is, however, one institution that is very much like the Eskimo—/*kamheri*, temporary wife exchange arranged by men with consent of the women.

It would seem from the evidence, of which I have given a small but representative sample, that the Eskimos are far less constrained about sexual matters than the Bushmen. If sexual access were a factor in establishing conflict, conflicts over women should be more frequent in Bushman society than in Eskimo. Hard statistical data are, of course, absent, but what we have show the reverse. I think, but cannot prove, that the vital element is not sexual access per se, although it certainly plays a role in any particular transaction. A more decisive factor seems to be the role of the women in the division of labor. Again I take recourse to a kind of social Liebig's Law according to which the minimal adaptive unit requires the combined labor of a man and woman. It is more than this: Against the infrequent situations of dire sexual need there is the constant requirement of marriage to play a full adult role in the society. While the latter probably derives from the former and in simple societies continues to rest directly upon it, the effective cause of conflict is the threat that the female's normal roles in the division of labor will be upset by attentions paid to her lover or lovers. This is exacerbated by the fact that adultery falls outside the established patterns of reciprocity. We have already seen that husbands are perfectly willing to offer their wives to other men, provided that they receive something in return and provided that they have an important role in making the transaction.

Sources of conflict in primitive society may be found in a few other institutional areas, but none are of very great significance. Apart from things directly concerned with subsistence which, as we have seen, do not usually spark contests leading to conflict, there are things which are not directly needed in ordinary life and may therefore be called luxuries. Those produced locally are no problem so long as the elements from which they are made are not of restricted access, which is indeed the usual case. There are differences of skill in making some things, but here the normal patterns of obtaining prestige through giving come into play to establish a high degree of circulation for such things. Up to a point trade goods fall under the same kind of treatment. Where they are likely to diverge from this treatment is where massive dependence on a more complex culture is involved. Frequently this dependence occurs when money and subsistence goods from the outside subvert the old economy and the society begins, often without much consciousness of the change among its members, to play by new rules.

Another potential source of conflict reminds us of dominance hierarchies in other animals. Do conflicts break out in simple societies as a manifestation of a competitive drive for power? The evidence is largely negative and confirms in a gross way the theoretical stipulation contained in our definition of egalitarian society. Rather than being structured hierarchically, such societies have as many people of paramount prestige as can display the qualities necessary. There is, however, one source of conflict in the way this kind of situation usually develops. While men in these societies do not seem to display any drive for universal dominance within their groups, they do display a considerable drive to achieve parity, or at least to establish a status that announces "don't fool with me." Among other things, this attitude helps make understandable the violence that can develop over such adulterous situations as those discussed above. As for the general structure of interpersonal relations with regard to power, we take this up further in this chapter when we discuss leadership.

Abnormal Psychic States

What we have said so far fits generally under the rubric of frustration and aggression, about which there is a fairly large and growing literature in various fields (*cf.* Scott, 1958, pp. 135–41). We are aware of John Paul Scott's warning that "frustration leads to aggression only in a situation where the individual has a habit of being aggressive" (Scott, 1958, p. 35) and recognize the special meaning of that remark for the influence of culture on expressions of hostility. Avoiding the interesting and important work that seeks to understand aggression by reducing it to chemical, physiological, or psychological constituents, I have tried here only to show that in simple egalitarian societies the structural sources of frustration-induced aggression are relatively few. But to say that there are few is to admit that there are some; also, some sources of frustration lie outside the sociocultural order, or their etiology is uncertain with present knowledge. Here must be included some of the forms of behavioral deviation that outside observers call "mental illness" and all those that threaten the ordinary continuance of social order.

There are a number of words, like "latah," "amok," and "windigo," taken from diverse aboriginal languages to express a variety of abnormal psychological states, which, if not properly handled, are potentially disruptive of normal social patterns. Though not universal, they occur in cultures of varying degrees of complexity, including some simple egalitarian societies. The Montagnais-Naskapi of whom we spoke earlier, for example, are among cultures displaying what is known as "windigo psychosis." "The outstanding symptom of the aberration . . . is the intense, compulsive desire to eat human flesh" (Teicher, 1960, p. 5). At times the windigo (that is, the person with windigo) succeeds in killing and eating others, often members of his own most intimate kin group; at other times the windigo is killed or "cured" before he can achieve his goal.

Windigo terrifies people, and they are much given to talk about real or imagined instances of the unsettling behavior. In addition to verified and possible but unverified cases the theme is built deeply into mythology, and the boundary is lost between persons who have gone windigo and evil spirits themselves. Morton Teicher, who has searched both published and unpublished literature and field materials, summarizes the results. For a period of about 300 years, for a population which even today totals about 50,000, the total number of recorded cases of actual windigo is seventy (Teicher, 1960, p. 107). Teicher admits that recording depended on the event reaching the ear of a literate person, probably a European trader or missionary, but concludes that "windigo psychosis is a relatively rare phenomenon." There seems to have been a concentration of cases during the period of most intense European contact, when aboriginal society was undoubtably undergoing its greatest stress.

One of the more fascinating aspects of windigo is the apparent frequency with which the windigo himself counsels and urges that he be killed to prevent or stop his activity. Incidentally, a surprisingly high proportion of windigos have been women, their ratio to male windigos being about 3:4 in the sixty-nine cases in which sex is specified (Teicher, 1960, p. 108). Many of Teicher's cases are so sketchy as to be of little value, but one of his generalizations fits very well the evidence he presents: The usual means of disposing of windigos is to kill them, and those who do not request death are dispatched, not as a penalty for what they have done, but to prevent them from doing it again. The second most common way of dealing with windigos would seem to confirm this emphasis on protection of others as it consists of making certain that they go far away where, if they do revert to cannibalism, believed by the Indians to be inevitable, it will be among strangers.

Windigo is of special interest because the aggressive forces it represents are usually turned inward within the band, camp, or even the family. Most of the simple egalitarian societies also know sorcery in various forms, but for the most part the action of evil magicians is turned outward. This seems particularly true of cultures in which almost all deaths are attributed to the activity of a sorcerer. We have a number of accounts of different Australian aboriginal societies in which this is true (*cf.* Berndt & Berndt, 1951, pp. 76–8 for sketch and bibliography; Meggitt, 1962a, pp. 324 *et passim*) and return to the matter when we consider political relations between groups, especially "warfare."

The special character of windigo, which is very much like amok in more complex societies, is also manifest in the fact that violence frequently receives direct, unambiguous expression. There are many forms of what is usually identified as psychotic behavior in simple egalitarian societies, but these display inversions of hostility or keep intragroup violence to a minimum. This is the way, for example, that David Aberle treats "Arctic hysteria" (Aberle, 1952, pp. 291–7), and the cases he cites show this strange condition as a kind of withdrawal, rather than as a violent onslaught. The fact is that in most cases the victim is either in the unhappy situation of making a fool of himself, or actually runs off. The Australian *bengwar*, "silly persons," although capable of "using physical violence without 'reason'" (Berndt & Berndt, 1951, p. 79) usually are protected to some extent by those about them, but we are told that they tend to die young with the implication that they cannot fend for themselves. The descriptions of the bengwars are reminiscent of Ralph Linton's description of Comanche "contraries," who usually meet the same fate although by other means (Kardiner, 1945, pp. 62–3).

LEADERSHIP

No ethnographically known human society has completely lacked leadership, the setting of a course of action followed by others. Leadership in simple egalitarian societies can be described in terms of a small number of very general patterns: First, it rests upon authority and lacks connotations of power except as shall be noted below. Second, it tends to be displayed in transient fashion, moving from one competent person to another. Third, the shifts in the locus of leadership are less associated with persons than with situations. Fourth, the limited presence of power is associated with exceptionally small groups like families and vanishes as the scope of the group widens. Fifth, authority has a much wider range than power but also declines sharply with expansion of the scope of the group considered. Finally, variations in the effectiveness of the preceding five principles are related to variations in ecology and demography. Denser populations associated with more productive subsistence regimes have more extensive leadership areas and, to a lesser extent, more power underlying leadership.

It is difficult, in ethnographies of simple egalitarian societies, to find cases in which one individual tells one or more others, "Do this!" or some command equivalent. The literature is replete with examples of individuals saying the equivalent of "If this is done, it will be good," possibly or possibly not followed by somebody else doing it. More usually the person who initiates the idea also performs the activity. Since the leader is unable to compel any of the others to carry out his wish, we speak of his role in terms of authority rather than power (see p. 12).

Though others have probably come upon the idea themselves, the notion that the state is the political order of the family unit writ large is usually attributed to Aristotle as conveyed in his *Politics* (1:2). A series of distinguished scholars have followed in this train, Sir Henry Maine and Woodrow Wilson among them (*cf.* Sait, 1938, p. 106 ff.). Despite this eminent group of spokesmen, the thesis is based upon a culture-bound view of the family, especially in those versions which assume some form of *patria potestas*, the theoretically uncurbed power of the father. It has long been clear that in many societies the kinship status of father is devoid of any of the role content usually associated with *pater;* to the extent that some portions of this role are carried out they may be assigned to mother's brother or some other person. More significantly, however, there is no abstract structural necessity for the family to be structured hierarchically with a fixed locus of power.

As already indicated, there is a range of conditions even within the restricted arc of empirically noted situations among simple egalitarian societies. Perhaps the limiting case in the direction of an absence of power is that of the Eskimo. R. Spencer (1959, p. 249) says that "the house or tent owner generally made family decisions." But he immediately qualifies this, indicating that the decisions were invariably informal and nonbinding on other members of the household. Others might cause the decision to be reversed or altered or they might simply ignore it and do what they choose as individuals. In an ultimate case in which a wife kept running away the husband might hamstring her, but this is one of those reported actions in which no examples were observed and there is only the statement of informants who themselves know no actual cases but have heard that in the old days that was the way it was done. Obviously, in such instances it is exceptionally difficult to pinpoint exactly what the old situation was, since the present account is embedded in idealization and mythology.

I must digress briefly, as the point is of utmost importance to our interpretation of ethnographic data extracted from accounts obtained by our contemporaries. Few will deny that informant accounts are a necessary source of ethnographic data, that they are extremely valuable in discovering covert as well as overt ideals. They can also throw what may be the only light on what went on in the scientifically unobserved past. It is absolutely essential, however, that the ethnographer make crystal clear what he observed and what he was told so that the different kinds of evidence can be properly evaluated. Unfortunately, the effects of this requirement upon the writing style are completely negative; perhaps that is why so few ethnographers are scrupulous in adhering to this stricture.

A good example may be taken from the work of a highly respected professional whose reputation can easily withstand such criticism. W. Lloyd Warner's work on the Murngin includes some information of use to the present analysis, including fulsome detail about sorcery, warfare, and other politically relevant activities. Unfortunately, his only remarks that throw any light on the conduct of the fieldwork are casual asides made in pursuit of some other points; even these are uninstructive: for example, "I was in very intimate contact with the Murngin natives." Most of the data presented seem to be based upon informant statements, but if Warner says anything about the language in which they were taken I missed it. Apart from what I presume were problems of translation, there is this overriding question of social fact and social fiction. Warner talks about some six kinds of warfare practiced by the Murngin and says that some are associated with fairly heavy casualties, including many dead. Perhaps it is so, but no authentication is given. In the one instance where Warner did witness a conflict the result was interesting. It was an example of what Warner calls intracamp hostilities, although one of the parties to the dyadic contest came to the camp of the other from elsewhere (Warner, 1958, pp. 166–7). We are told that, in such *nirimaoi yolno* encounters, talk is more prevalent than violent physical action and damages are more frequent among those who would restrain the parties than among the "fighters" themselves. In the case observed, no one restrained the participants, who consequently exchanged no blows. It is precisely the point of my repeating this incident to note that Warner assumes that what he saw is unusual, deviant, not the real way to handle such a situation. I should say, rather, that it *is* the usual, and I venture that, if he had returned some time later to take the story of that encounter from one of the participants, he would have found it much more violent than his notes show and it would have continued to grow more violent in the retelling until interest was lost.

While we are at it we may as well note that few things are more conducive to unsupported conclusions than the perception of political organization in simple societies by observers from more complex cultures. Burt Aginsky (1949, pp. 28–30) gives a fine example in the perception of Pomo political organization by Sir Francis Drake.

> Three days after June 26 [1579], the News [of the coming of the Europeans] having spread itself farther into the Country, another great Number of People were assembled, and among them their KING himself, a Man of comely Presence and Stature, attended with a Guard of an hundred tall stout Men, having sent two Ambassadors before, to tell the General their Hioh, or King, was coming . . . A while after, their King with all his Train appeared in as much pomp as he could . . . In the Front before him marched a tall Man of good Countenance, carrying the Sceptre, or Mace Royal . . . upon which hung two Crowns . . . Next the Sceptre bearer came the King himself, with his Guard about him . . . (Aginsky, 1949, p. 28).

I am fond of an instance drawn from the correspondence of Captain Archibald Blair, who explored the Andaman Islands about 200 years ago. While regarding the people of those islands as "probably in the rudest state of any Rational animals which are to be found," he noted that the "only Appearance of civilization was their being formed into tribes and some attention which they paid to their Chiefs which were generally painted red" (Blair, 1789, pp. 112–3). For the uninitiated it should be added that subsequent ethnographic study of Pomo and Andaman has revealed no trace of formal chieftainship, much less monarchy.

Returning to the phenomenon of leadership per se, we pick up the Eskimos once again as the leading illustration of a society with minimal regular leadership. Steenhoven and Asen Balikci are the latest in a remarkably consistent group of observers and commentators on Eskimo society. Steenhoven says that, in the large European-influenced summer camp at Eskimo Point, there was absolutely no trace of leadership in the conduct of hunting or movements away from camp. Inland, away from alien influence, a partial and intermittent leadership was found with regard to hunting. Kannajok, an informant, said to Steenhoven:

> In course of time it becomes clear who is having much success in finding the right spots. *He* will be followed by the others, but only in respect of finding the best hunting grounds. If he loses his luck and another has more success, we follow that other hunter (Steenhoven, 1962, p. 60, emphasis in original).

Earlier, among the Caribou Eskimos, Steenhoven observed the institution of *ihumakortujok,* people of wisdom of non-shamanistic kind whose advice is sought but not binding (Steenhoven, 1956, p. 30; cited in his 1962, p. 67, *n.*15). We can only agree with his remark that, "Though 'chief' is a rather loose term, it certainly does not denote an individual whose advice is taken voluntarily" (Steenhoven, 1962, p. 66, *n.*8).

Moving to the !Kung Bushman, we find a slightly more regular institution of leadership. Isaac Schapera sums up the situation: "The Bushman . . . chief . . . has no judicial functions or organized penal powers; his main duties are to direct the migrations and subsistence activities of his people and to perform certain ceremonies for their welfare" (Schapera, 1956, p. 41; the same remark is cited and glossed by M. Gluckman, 1965, pp. 86–7).

More information comes from Marshall who distinguishes between the functions of headman and leader in Bushman bands, although noting that the functions might reside in a single individual. Inasmuch as I have laid great stress on defining egalitarian society in terms of an unspecified and varying number of valued statuses, Marshall's application of a concept of "headmanship" to the !Kung seems a serious challenge. The word is necessarily freighted with connotations of hierarchy and paramountcy. I think it is the wrong word.

"The authority of a band's headman is limited almost entirely to control of the veldkos and water" (Marshall, 1960, p. 351). She says that the headman "owns" the veldkos and water (Marshall, 1960, p. 346). It is a curious kind of ownership, for those who use these resources "do not feel that they receive a gift from the bounty of the headman." This is *not* strange, because the headman "does not have the right to withhold them from rightful members" (Marshall, 1960, p. 346). It seems clear that "rightful members" comprise all persons in proximity to the resources.[5]

The headman has no authority; Marshall rules out supervision of tasks and adjudication (Marshall, 1960, p. 352). He has two or three prerogatives: to take the head of the line when the band moves, to choose the campsite, and to select his own lean-to and hearth site first. Very interesting is the indication that the headman is expected to be particularly generous, a statement that seems idealizing and exaggerating because it is difficult to imagine more sharing than has already been described. However, the position seems to have no special leadership weight, since we are told that most moves made by the band "follow long established customs and usually cause little if any controversy." If there is any discussion, "the actual plan adopted is more likely to be a consensus than the decision

---

[5] "The headman's permission should be asked by travellers or visitors before taking water, 'because he knows how much he has and knows what can be done,' someone said. But one of the listeners laughed at this and said, 'If you are very thirsty, you have no time to ask permission'" (Marshall, 1960, p. 337). We are not surprised to discover in the same context that water *is* taken without permission, which is said to show that people no longer behave properly as they did in the past. Unquestionably many Bushmen believe this, but that does not establish its verity.

of the headman alone" (Marshall, 1960, p. 351, also cites Brownlee, 1943, p. 125, for parallel observation).

Another curious thing about the position is that it is not particularly desired. Since it descends by essentially primogenitural inheritance, the desire would be fruitless for all but the next in line. To abridge an already overlong discussion, there are at least two specific indications of what this office truly represents. One clue is the absence of any necessary relationship between headmanship and leadership. We are particularly interested in observed examples of the position being filled by a juvenile who went several years before he managed to kill a buck, pass through the "ceremony of the First Killing," and get married. So much for being more generous than others! It should also be said that the person or persons other than the headman manifesting leadership did not do so in the form of a regency, but simply as themselves. The position of leader is also devoid of power, honors, or rewards (Marshall, 1960, p. 352).

The other clue is the already mentioned emphasis on genealogical inheritance of the position of headman. It seems somewhat inappropriate in this social milieu. It may be that light is thrown on this !Kung situation by what Warner has to say about a facet of Murngin culture in North Eastern Australia. I refer to concepts of the inalienable association of territories with social groups, so that even long after the extinction of a particular group, its former territory will be thought of as still pertaining to that group (Warner, 1958, pp. 18–9). I suspect that it is a kind of charter, this headmanship, that it represents the corporate access of the entire group to an entire area. Marshall comes close to stating just this (Marshall, 1960, p. 344) but veers off into what her own evidence seems to undermine—concepts of ownership and control.

LAW?

Does law exist on the social level so far described? Obviously the reply to this query hinges on the definition of law. E. Adamson Hoebel thinks that the term "law" can be extended to the Eskimos because in his usage the decisive criteria are two: some kind of court, no matter how descriptively remote from our own formal law courts, and the "really *sine qua non* of law in any society . . . the legitimate use of physical coercion" (Hoebel, 1958, p. 470). He then rests his judgment on cases such as describe the reaction of a community to recidivist homicide, which he asserts is the community imposition of a privileged sentence of death. My reading of the same data leads me to an opposite conclusion. There is no legitimacy here, for those that carry out the killing of an offender cannot know that they themselves will not suffer the same fate for their act unless they liquidate all of the offender's relatives who might try to avenge him. It does not seem useful to me to identify such action as law though it does clearly pertain to social control.

Leopold Pospisil joins Hoebel in recognizing the importance of the "court" situation but, where Hoebel subordinates that principle to legitimate coercion, Pospisil finds "the casuistic approach" the best touchstone of law. This is a logical product of his view that a crucial aspect of the "process of law" is that it must have the form of a decision. (This statement represents my fusion of his ideas as he sets them forth in Pospisil, 1958, p. 258, and in an unpublished paper, 1965.) Apart from the question of the form of a legal decision, he offers four attributes of law: "authority, true *obligatio*, intention of universal application, and sanction" (Pospisil, 1958, p. 258). I think this is an outstanding characterization of law but it seems to me that Pospisil does not apply it consistently, being inclined to value the criterion of "having the form of a decision" above the others.

If we apply Pospisil's formula to the Eskimos, it is my opinion that we have only the "form of a decision" and none of the other criteria. There is no authority for it is not recognized by the malefactor or those who would avenge him. For that matter, the recognition that he might be avenged indicates that even those who carry out the action have no faith in its legitimacy. To talk of *obligatio* under such circumstances is ridiculous: Nothing that happens is binding upon any of the parties except as they are members of a society carrying out the patterns of their culture. This statement also would seem sufficient to take care of any intention of universal application. All Eskimo cases are notable for the fact that they seem to exist by themselves; the only precedents that may be formed are those advanced by outside observers.

As for sanction, the last criterion offered by Pospisil, it obviously exists to the extent that at some point violence is directed against an offender. But, while law without sanction is chimerical, sanction itself cannot define law. In this case we move full circle, back to the criticism of Hoebel, noting again that there is nothing in the case record of aboriginal Eskimo situations that establishes anything like an effective concept of legitimate employment of sanctions.

It seems unnecessary to repeat what I have said about the Eskimo for the African Bushman. It appears, however, that my argument regarding the absence of law in simple egalitarian societies is most likely to be challenged from a curious direction—the Australian aborigine. This arises, at least in part, from the the fact that many distinguished writers have applied the term "law" to customary actions or idealized versions of situations described by informants. Hoebel, for example, speaks of the law of Australian aborigines (Hoebel, 1954, pp. 301–9), although he concludes that on "the particular level of social development" found among Australians, Andamanese, and "for the most part among the Shoshones" law is weak because "the responsibility for adhering to established procedure still rests for the most part with the two contending parties" (Hoebel, 1954, p. 310).

Actually, it is not so much that commentators and analysts like Hoebel apply the word "law," it is that the primary documents produced by ethnographers in the area utilize the word. Warner, to give one instance, speaks in various contexts of "law" or "customary law" or "tribal law," all apparently meaning the same thing and that thing being rather vague (Warner, 1958, p. 605, index item, "law, tribal").

A more recent example is afforded by an excellent ethnography of the Walbiri of North Central Australia. Its author, Mervyn Meggitt, identifies the Walbiri word *djugaruru* with the English word "law," noting that it may also be translated as "the way." If I understand it correctly, the word has a sense closely parallel to the concept expressed in the phrase "the Hopi way" or the Chinese concept of *tao*. The parallels, if correct, are very instructive. To my knowledge no one has confused either the Hopi way or *tao* with law, recognizing both of these as important parts of the idealized-ideological self-image of the culture in question. Violations of such standards are more likely to be regarded as normal than would be adherence.

Meggitt goes on to find the equivalent of the traditional distinction between law and custom in Walbiri (Meggitt, 1962a, p. 252) on the basis of the presence or absence of physical sanctions. Meggitt's argument distinguishes between the illicit use of ceremonially acquired meat, which is met with ridicule or humor, and the failure to share a kill, which is said to be reprobated by physical attack. No cases are given as far as I could discover, and I must note that the job was made difficult by an index which managed four references to penis holding and not one to "sharing," "reciprocity," or even "economic activities."

Meggitt leads directly to theoretical conflict by admitting the "absence of individuals or groups in Walbiri society with permanent and clearly defined legislative and judicial functions" (Meggitt, 1962a, p. 251; 1962b) and then, a few pages later, discussing the legal use of personages who decide whether a breach has occurred, what the punishment should be, and who is to administer the punishment and prevent retaliation by the relatives of the person disciplined. If the latter statements were validated I, for one, would have to accept the existence of law in aboriginal Australian society, at least in Walbiri. But what is offered falls far short of this desideratum. Supernatural sanctions and mythology are what we are actually given (Meggitt, 1962a, p. 260 ff.). Unfortunately this is precisely what we have had up to now.

As an instance I would like to cite the famous emphasis upon kinship that is attributed to the Australians. A key aspect of this concern is the assertion of abhorrence for incest. A. P. Elkin (1964, p. 144) tells us that, "a couple caught committing an act of serious incest would be speared on sight." Hoebel says that "Incest . . . results in the spearing to death of both offenders after judgement by the elders" (Hoebel, 1954, p. 303). Meggitt collected no cases of incest, but Ronald and Catherine Berndt discovered one actual case, the parties to which lived in a community they studied. A man took his own daughter (not a classificatory daughter) as his second wife, the girl's mother remaining as first wife. The daughter had a child by her father. Of this situation the Berndts tell us simply that, "There appears to have been no fight or severe quarrel resulting from this union; there was some talk at the time, but it soon died down" (Berndt & Berndt, 1951, p. 59).

I should like to emphasize that I do not believe that isolated cases of lack of enforcement obviate law; if that were the case law would not exist in any society yet known, including our own. On the other hand, I do wish to question the assertion of law when the record of observed cases does not accord at all with idealized normative statements about hypothetical cases or with legendary or mythical case accounts. I think it is a grave error in such instances to assume the validity of the informant's story and rationalize the discrepancy with observed behavior on the grounds of dislocation produced by European contact. The latter, of course, is usually taken to have upset the old social structure. It is at least equally possible that European contact, usually associated with imposed legal standards and equally imposed ethical standards, creates a demand for a new mythology that bridges the gap between the acculturating native society and its new master.

The question is not solved but remains moot. It is made especially difficult by unavoidable semantic disputation. Beyond this difficulty lies a diminishing supply of pristine cases, perhaps already shrunken to zero. It seems to me, however, that when an assertion of the existence of law in a simple egalitarian society is encountered, one may expect that the burden of proof will lie with the author of the assertion.

EXTERNAL RELATIONS
IN BAND EGALITARIAN SOCIETY

Maintaining the internal character of the group is only one aspect of the political life of any society; there is also the problem of holding itself as a unit in a world of other integral units of equal or larger scale. The topic is a large one; the present treatment will be relatively brief, compressed, and highly selective. Only a few topics will be discussed: the bounding of the group's territory and membership, some of the main means of conducting peaceful intergroup activities, and a consideration of the extent and character of hostile interactions between units.

Territoriality

Elsewhere in this chapter (pp. 71–72) we reviewed some aspects of the relationship between individuals or small units and basic productive resources, especially land. Little remains to be added, although an extensive catalogue of details might be supplied. Such simple egalitarian societies as most Eskimo groups are broadly permissive with regard to the territories they inhabit. While there may be a strong attachment to certain areas, which they know best, there is no concept of trespass. We have already discussed the status of resource ownership among the !Kung Bushmen, noting that nominal rights to water and veldkos are said to be vested in a headman who cannot, in effect, deny permission for their use.

With regard to Australian aborigines, Meggitt's information on the relations between local groups and territories conforms with the work of earlier ethnographers and has the advantage of being a conscious attempt to clarify aspects of aboriginal social and economic organization which had been more or less neglected by generations of scholars interested in other kinds of problems. It is interesting, therefore, to see that the Australians deal with territoriality much like the African Bushmen, except that the Australians seem to place much more emphasis on ritual connections with certain sites and, a matter we must shortly investigate, are represented as much more warlike than most other simple egalitarian societies. For all of this, however, Australian band territories are not closed, however well described their boundaries.

I cannot refrain from noting here that there seems to be a sharp qualitative difference between all noncultural societies and those of human beings with regard to the concept of territorial boundedness. There is nothing short of a fully symbolic medium of communication, other than an extrasensory transmission of whole cognitive patterns, that can convey concepts of boundary such as Meggitt describes:

> The older Walbiri men . . . have no difficulty in defining the limits of their own countries fairly precisely . . . The positions of the boundaries are fixed, validated and remembered through the agency of religious myths. These stories not only plot the totemic tracks and centres but also specify the points at which the

custody of the songs, rituals and decorations associated with them should change hands as the tracks pass from one country to another. An investigator able to spend long enough in the field could produce from such data a detailed map of the borders of the four countries [of which they believe their territory to be comprised] (Meggitt, 1962a, pp. 48–9).

Having cited this passage at length, I should like to demur at the use of the term "country," which seems inappropriate because of its usual political charge. Also, let us note that the implication of the passage is that the Walbiri do not ordinarily think in terms of continuously bounded territory, but are capable for special purposes of saying that this area stops and that area begins at a fixed set of points, or the border is conceived as marked by a line. C. W. M. Hart and Arnold R. Pilling, for example, explicitly deny that the Tiwi, Australians who live in the Melville and Bathurst Islands, twenty-five miles north of the continent, thought of boundaries as sharp lines. Thus, for the Tiwi

the boundary was not a sharp line but a transitional zone—perhaps of several miles—where the change from trees to open savannah became noticeable, with the band territories thus fusing into one another . . . The Tiwi, so to speak, thought of the landscape as a sort of a spectrum where a man moved gradually out of one district into another as he passed from one type of horizon to the next (Hart & Pilling, 1960, p. 12).

Because the Tiwi have one of the highest population densities for Australian aborigines it might be expected that their boundaries would be even more sharply conceived than those whose sparse numbers inhabit vast desert stretches. On the other hand, it is true that these islands inhabited by the Tiwi have sharper landscape contrasts, possibly offering more raw material for boundary marking. In either case, the model seems to be one of core area with relatively vague surroundings, not unlike the territoriality displayed by a number of other primates.

Ethnographies differ on the degree to which local groups could move into the lands usually associated with neighboring groups. Spencer and Gillen (1912, p. 232–3; 1904, p. 31) and Warner say that adjacent groups usually had friendly relations. The latter in particular has remarked: "The ownership of the land includes the use of it, but there would be no thought of excluding the members of other clans from using it; rather, mutual use would be encouraged if the two groups were friendly" (Warner, 1958, p. 147). The Berndts have recently offered a summary statement:

> Sometimes, however, it is difficult to know to which tribe a certain territory belongs; or members of one tribe may have hunting rights over country held by another . . . Contrary to popular belief tribal territories and boundaries are, or were, relatively flexible. Also, people are not invariably afraid to move across the territory of an adjacent tribe. As a rule they have grounds for fear only if they deliberately or inadvertently interfere with a sacred site (Berndt & Berndt, 1964, p. 34).

Meggitt, however, carried out a careful survey of relations between neighboring aboriginal communities and discovered great variation in their quality, ranging from open friendship to naked hostility. Proximity by itself does not seem to Meggitt to be a decisive variable in deciding rational quality; factors ranging from "cultural similarity to temperamental characteristics" seem to him more reliable determiners. I can see some connection between cultural similarity and proximity, and, although I do not quite understand "temperamental characteristics," I accept variability in the quality of relations among adjacent peoples, satisfied that they may vary according to historical circumstances involving what can be defined in this situation as chance factors. An accident precipitates a hostile reaction between two groups, and this newly exposed hostility may require that older breaches with others be at least temporarily neglected. Thus over time several adjacent cultures may change their attitudes toward one another without affecting physical distance.

Meggitt acknowledges that aborigines' territories are not always sacrosanct but may be entered and used by aliens upon occasion. Here we encounter something quite reminiscent of both Eskimos and African Bushmen: Sharing seems to *increase* with scarcity. Says Meggitt, "Outsiders may enter the territory uninvited only in an emergency, such as when they face the threat of starvation in their own country . . ." (Meggitt, 1962a, p. 44). This hospitality should be compensated. Presumably, the reciprocation thus reinforced remains a characteristic of the interaction unless disturbed by other forces or events.

Membership

To some extent, albeit usually a limited one, all human societies are open systems with regard to membership. Individuals can enter alien groups at almost any point in their life cycles, but formal procedures must be followed. In most cases it seems that the membership thus acquired results in few, if any, immediate disqualifications, but the entrant usually has a special and somewhat equivocal status, particularly with regard to the ceremonial aspects of life. Apart from this reservation, members acquired other than by birth can be significant to the group. Being at least theoretically open as membership aggregates enables these societies to extend their gene pools beyond limits set by marital restrictions in force. More important, however, is the increase in potential for cultural development as carriers of new elements can be incorporated. Obviously, from the point of view of this book, another matter of significance is the implicit limitation of hostilities in the acceptance of members from outside. Finally, to the degree that adopted members stand outside the regular kinship system they complicate the political relationships within the group.

Actually, the reasons for shift of permanent group affiliation seem variable in aboriginal society. Among the Australians it appears to have been a rare phenomenon, made especially difficult by the elaborateness of ritual and the closeness of the association between ceremonial life and territorial features. But, of almost equal significance for our argument, the Australians seem to have been frequent visitors to other camps, often drawn by invitations to particular ceremonials.

One of the important consequences of the mechanisms which permitted people to enter alien bands was the growth of composite social structures in the decades following the original post contact breakdown of aboriginal societies. Thus in many parts of the world came to pass what Stefansson has described for the Cape Smyth Eskimo. Visited twice, thirty years apart, the population was found to total roughly the same number, about 400. But on the second visit only four of the inhabitants were found to be survivors or descendants of the original company (Stefansson, 1919, p. 104; passage cited with comment in Service, 1962, p. 104). I agree with Service that heterogeneous camp membership, at least in larger-scale manifestations, is likely to be a consequence of population loss and dislocation following contact. The "composite band" structure that results usually requires more complex political arrangements since there is no unified framework of kinship upon which most if not all relationships can be articulated.

War and Peace

The problems that arise in defining war are much like those encountered in defining law and social control. There are some scholars who see war as a universal cultural phenomenon while others would define it by such criteria as to have it appear only in fairly complex societies. Harry Holbert Turney-High, for example, identifies a number of features as characterizing "true war": tactical operations, definite command and control, capacity for sustained attack should the first assault fail, clear motivation phrased as a group end, and adequate supply (Turney-High, 1949,

p. 30). Contrast this with the definition used by Maurice R. Davie: the competition between groups struggling for existence, particularly as manifested in contests by force (Davie, 1929, p. 12). Stripped of social Darwinist implications, Davie's formulation is much like John R. Swanton's: "War is . . . the most violent relation that may exist between groups of people" (Swanton, 1943, p. 1). For my own purposes I favor a slightly amended version of a definition proposed by Quincy Wright: "the . . . condition which . . . permits two or more *hostile groups* to carry on a conflict by armed force" (Wright, 1942, p. 8, emphasis his).

Even using such a definition the problem of the universality of war is vexing. Davie asserts at the outset of his study that, "War, then, is universal" (Davie, 1929, p. 8). Hobhouse has opined that warfare was not the perpetual state of primitive society but he was equally certain that it was not one of perfect peace (Hobhouse, 1956, p. 112). His review of a number of primary reports indicates that of a sample of fourteen simple societies seven had prolonged feuds and four others indulged in hit-and-run ambushes and attacks. A few had such low incidence of intergroup violence as to seem institutionally peaceful, but these are among the most sketchily known societies in ethnography, such as the Kubu and aboriginal Vedda.

Primary data relating to warfare in simple societies can lead the analyst to despair of generalization. He may read that, "Warfare is one of the most important social activities of the Murngin and surrounding tribes. Without it, Murngin society as it is now constituted could not exist" (Warner, 1958, p. 155). Compare this with Steward's remark, "Except for temporary conflict with the white man, warfare was an unimportant factor in amalgamating the native population . . . Paiute bands did not fight with one another or with the Shoshoni. Conflicts over pine-nut areas were brief and never involved weapons more dangerous than the sling, which did little damage" (Steward, 1938, p. 55).

To some extent the differences in these remarks may be attributed to genuine cultural differences. I wonder, though, if time and the character and results of contact with more complex societies might not have produced some of the seemingly aberrant features. Thus, as previously indicated, the passage of time and the presence of an impressionable audience in the form of a notetaking ethnographer may act as an inflationary factor with regard to conflicts in the past. This is one way of explaining why there is so much less fighting in the actually observed present than in the recollected past. Of course, to be fair, it should be noted that the expansion of "civilization" usually is the extension of the monopoly on killing by a state, so that reduction of hostilities may well reflect the presence of armed police.

Unfortunately, it is not possible to make a flat generalization at this time characterizing egalitarian band societies as either peaceful or warlike. However, on the basis of fairly extensive but not always reliable evidence a few highly provisional generalizations may be offered about intergroup fighting in a simple society.

Frequency

Even among peoples on this level who have been described as warlike, the time applied to actual hostilities, including preparations and postbattle ceremonials, seems little. The time devoted to hostilities can only be figured as extensive on this level if the latency periods in the course of feuds are considered. In that case some societies can be treated as if never at peace. This is an ethnocentric application of the highly formalized treatment accorded war in complex societies to simpler societies in which such institutions as peace treaties have no place. Conversely, ceremonies which may have as their point the purification of warriors after contact with ritual defilement of blood and death are often taken as celebration of the closing of hostilities. Finally, there is no time devoted to material preparations for conflict on this level. None of the societies described in the literature build fortifications. None have been reported to stockpile food and supplies for military purposes. None engage in special training activities for warriors. None possess a special military technology but use ordinary tools and the weapons of the hunt when they fight men. Discounting latency periods when frictions lie dormant, and apart from the few hours or few days that are actually consumed in a clash or raid, it may be said that a state of peace prevails.

Intensity

What has already been said explains the low intensity of combat in simple societies. Protracted attacks and sieges do not occur. The typical action is a raid involving few attackers; the appropriate word for what takes place seems to be clash—there is a sudden violent set-to and most of the participants return hoarse from screaming threats and insults but are otherwise unscathed. Again it is tempting to compare this behavior with that of the other primates who, we are told, expend most of their energies in combat situations carrying out threatening behavior rather than actual onslaughts. This is not to say that warfare on the egalitarian-band level is devoid of casualties. Warner, for one, estimates that in the general region he studied there were perhaps 200 deaths from warfare in twenty years.[6] Possibly closer to the norm for societies of this level are the Siriono who were reported to be warlike by Nordenskiöld. On the basis of his own observation of the Siriono, what the Siriono told him, and study of their history and present distribution, Allan Holmberg concludes:

---

[6] Warner's "statistics" are pathetic, but he cannot be blamed for the vagueness of his informants and the absence of independent documentation. He can be faulted, however, for not making absolutely clear exactly what he himself observed as opposed to what he was told. In view of the likelihood that his totals represent, at best, the multiple inclusion of the same event, I think his estimates grossly exaggerated (*cf.* Warner, 1958, p. 158 *et passim;* also Schneider, 1950, pp. 772–7).

Warfare between bands simply does not exist, and where the Siriono have come in contact with other peoples, Indian or white, it is they who have been raided and rarely they who have done the raiding. In fact, the entire history of the Siriono, from what little we know about it, seems to reflect a strategy of retreat rather than one of attack. Whenever they have come in contact with other groups, they have been forced to retire deeper and deeper into the impenetrable jungle in order to escape defeat, and in retiring from previously occupied lands they seem to have made few firm stands in defense of their territory (Holmberg, 1950, pp. 62–3).

This comes close to what Steward says about the Shoshone:

In aboriginal times most of the Shoshonean people had no national or tribal warfare. There were no territorial rights to be defended, no military honors to be gained, and no means of organizing groups of individuals for concerted action. When war parties of neighboring peoples invaded their country, the Shoshoneans ran away more often than they fought (Steward, 1955, p. 112).

Service has recently argued that "the fact that bands are not warlike in modern times does not mean that they never were" (Service, 1962, p. 49). He attributes this relative peaceableness to being "enclaved among more powerful neighbors." While he admits that warfare must have been on a small scale and sporadic, he argues that its psychological effect would have been a factor in producing virilocality, hence the patrifocal band. Basing his case in part upon very early accounts of contacts with these simple societies, Service seems partially to refute his own position when, some pages later, he remarks that "fighting often greatly increased when the first contacts with the Europeans produced dislocations and migrations, and greatly diminished in later times when control had been established" (Service, 1962, p. 49).

Admittedly, the problem is a tough one. There are indications, for example, that the Vikings feared people whom they knew as "Skraelings," who seem to have been Eskimos, for these people paddled right out to the Viking ships and attacked the Norsemen fiercely. This also reminds us of the awesome reputation of some of the Andamanese who are reported to have destroyed many crews of wrecked vessels over the centuries.

The problem is worthy of much more serious attention than it has been given because the nature of warfare throws much light upon many problems of comparative sociology. The final revelations may be surprising. Some simple societies of the ethnographic present may be discovered through combined archaeological and ethnohistorical techniques to have previously been more complex, with the more complex structures having been among the casualties of massive contact.

Military Organization

It does not take great imagination to picture the reaction of people living in ghost- or demon-ridden cultures to a small number of howling savages, stark naked or dressed in furs from top to toe, brandishing obviously lethal spears or bows or clubs. Knowing the terrain, as the aliens could not possibly know it, and accustomed to hitting by raid, a tiny party of such warriors could strike terror in a more civilized crew and do quite a bit of damage, too. By the time the survivors returned to their native shores it would not be unlikely their attackers had grown in number and their grasp of military organization and tactics would become commensurate with the invaders'.

Speculation? Almost entirely, yet without some sort of explanation like this it is very difficult to understand even the few military successes that have been recorded for the impacted simple societies. What we do know about military organization in such societies indicates a complete absence of command or coordination; every man stands and fights or runs away by himself. Radcliffe-Brown's description of Andamanese warfare could apply, with little or no alteration, to most intergroup combats in simple society. He tells us that stand-up fights are rare, most encounters being surprise raids. Since most raids are for revenge, the person seeking it gets some relatives and friends to come along, but there is no leadership. If the attackers "met with any serious resistance or lost one of their own number they would immediately retire" (Radcliffe-Brown, 1948, p. 85).

The absence of any leadership in military affairs in simple societies is of exceptional significance. There have been many influential social analysts who have rested considerable weight in their schemes of the evolution of political society upon the role of war leaders, for what could be more logical than to assume a war chief would refuse to relinquish his powers in peacetime and thus become a permanent monarch? Herbert Spencer, to give but one illustration, put it in this way: "how command of a wider kind follows military command, we cannot readily see in societies which have no records: we can but infer that along with increased power of coercion which the successful head-warrior gains, naturally goes the exercise of a stronger rule in civil affairs" (H. Spencer, 1893, p. 337).

As yet in the development of my own argument I cannot apply anything that has been said to the emergence of the state, because that event lies still far ahead, after ranking and stratification have come upon the social scene and been matured. What has been said, however, does apply to the evolution of ranking and stratification from an undifferentiated egalitarian base. Whatever emerges when we attempt to show how this occurred, it seems evident that it will not be related to any prior evolution of military organization or command. On the other side, I think I will be able to show that the evolution of warfare and military statuses, at least during the earliest breakthroughs to more complex forms of society, followed and was dependent upon developments in technology, economic organization, and nonmilitary aspects of social organization.

THE TRANSITION TO BAND EGALITARIAN SOCIETY

I have deferred my comment on the relation between band egalitarian society and nonhuman primate society until now when a sufficient picture has been drawn of the former. Despite recognizing the validity of a few objections made to his presentation, I believe that Sahlins' essay (1959, pp. 186–99) is still the best overview of an admittedly difficult subject. My treatment takes off from his, but has the advantage of the publications of several extraordinarily productive years in primatology since his article was written.

The paramount invention that led to human society was *sharing* because it underlay the division of labor that probably increased early human productivity above the level of competitive species in the same ecological niches. Sharing and the division of labor are also eminently suited to the solution of maintenance problems as the human species radiated over much of the globe, encountering most of the possible types of environment. At times the question was obviously of simple survival and to this the sharing pattern was particularly adaptive. We have reviewed enough evidence to be able to agree with Service that, "The more primitive the society and the more straitened the circumstances, the greater the emphasis on sharing, and the more scarce or needed the items the greater the sociability engendered" (Service, 1962, pp. 42, 38–9).

Of almost equal importance was the concomitant reduction in the significance of individual dominance in a hierarchical arrangement within the community. In part the structural possibility for such a hierarchy was undermined by the demands of sharing; at least such demands altered the form of dominance by introducing the factor of symbolically expressed prestige which could substitute for physical dominance. Another restraint on simple dominance was afforded by the invention of a symbolic environment, especially by the differentiation of the social world into symbolic categories: females I can copulate with, females I must not copulate with, and so on.

These basic inventions, plus a few others of very great significance in such areas as tool and fire use and symbolic communication per se, must have placed our early man ancestors at an enormous advantage because their success dominates the history of the past two million years. Though the bands probably very rarely exceeded fifty individuals until Upper Pleistocene times, they obviously kept splitting, sending off shoots until, as remarked above, most regions of the earth had some people as inhabitants.

The threat to this very successful level of sociocultural development was less a hostile, untamed environment, niggardly resources, or fierce predators, than the emergence of new forms of society. Even at that, many of the simplest societies persisted, some of them in excellent environments, until the primitive world model was genuinely shattered by completely new inventions in technology and innovations in economic and political organization. This is the subject of our remaining chapters.

CHAPTER 4

Rank Societies

A rank society is one in which positions of valued status are somehow limited so that not all those of sufficient talent to occupy such statuses actually achieve them. Such a society may or may not be stratified. That is, a society may sharply limit its positions of prestige without affecting the access of its entire membership to the basic resources upon which life depends. It is usually unwise to treat as wealth such sumptuary marks of prestige as bird plumages, dentalium shells, or other paraphernalia of rank, because that term conjures up a vision of universal exchangeability. In our society, of course, wealth is comprised of a variety of holdings all having monetary values. All items can circulate freely, being exchanged through the explicit or implicit use of monetary equivalencies. Such is not usually the case in a rank society. The phrase "spheres of exchange" has been suggested by Paul Bohannan (1963, pp. 248–53) to express a vital character of this kind of system, although recognition of the division of an economy into more or less exclusive sectors, such as subsistence versus prestige, has been extant for decades. In any case, there is usually little or no infiltration of objects of value from one sphere into the other. The marks of prestige cannot be used to acquire food or productive resources. The significance of this point to my argument is probably apparent: Accumulation of signs of prestige does not convey any privileged claim to the strategic resources on which a society is based. Ranking can and does exist in the absence of stratification.

THE GENERAL NATURE OF RANK SOCIETIES

The spectrum of rank societies is much greater than that in egalitarian societies. While part of this impression may be illusory, based upon the relatively recent eliminaton of many egalitarian societies as a direct or indirect consequence of the expansion of the modern states, there can be little doubt that the greater spread of rank society has a firm demographic base. Before we look into that aspect of the problem, a brief overview of environmental factors is called for.

Environments

Most of the egalitarian societies known to ethnography have been located in areas remote from the centers of complex cultural development over the past 5,000 or 6,000 years or more. Particularly as we approach our own time, we find egalitarian societies in relatively impoverished habitats, frequently extreme in climatic conditions and poor in natural food resources. On the other hand, rank societies have managed to come down into our own historical period still in occupation, if not control, of some of the most desirable stretches of the earth's surface. Indeed, some of the areas occupied by such societies have been so bountiful that population size and density have seemed to be out of proportion to the development of their technologies, as in the Pacific Northwest until the last century. Fortunately, environmental determinism as a single-cause interpretation of cultural development has been dead for some time, and I have no intention of trying to revive it. Environment plays an important and active role in ecological formulas, however, although always in combination with a number of other variables. It is not accurate, therefore, to treat the habitat simply as a permissive factor. This is particularly the case with reference to what may be called the pristine development of ranking.

As my argument unfolds, I will make use of a distinction between pristine and secondary situations, applying this distinction also to the development of stratification and the state. A pristine situation is one in which development occurs exclusively on the basis of indigenous factors. In such a situation there is no external model of more complex design to help shape the new society. Neither is there the presence of a more complexly organized society to stimulate the process of development. Any stimuli that motivate change in the pristine situation are internal to the developing society. One further observation must be added to ensure clarity: To the extent that no society exists in a superorganic vacuum, but is necessarily surrounded by other sociocultural entities, part of its developmental process will result from and be influenced by interaction with those external entities. However, there are situations in which none of the external cultures are any more complex than the one being considered, and these situations can be regarded as pristine.

The pristine emergence of ranking is significantly dependent on the availability of food. So far as is known, only a few societies in the long course of history have been fortunate enough to occupy areas sufficiently rich in natural food resources to permit the growth of population beyond the low levels characteristic of technologically unsophisticated band egalitarian society. The foremost means of breaking this barrier, of course, was the complex of inventions that we know as the "neolithic revolution." Before that "event" took place, however, probably a few societies did enjoy exceptionally favorable habitats as far as food resources were concerned. Possibly the horse hunters of Western Europe during the Solutrean period of the late Paleolithic were so favored, and it may be that their social organization was of the rank type. This possibility may ultimately be confirmed by archaeological discoveries of socially differentiated burials, but ranking societies do not always dispose of their dead in ways that confirm to later generations the existence of differential status. There was one culture area where ranking societies flourished that did not have neolithic control of their food supplies. The North Pacific Coast lacked plant and animal domestication but had a fairly complex ranking system, although the full development of that system seems to have awaited contact and commercial relations with European-derived culture.

Demography

There is a dramatic demographic difference between ranking and band egalitarian society. This difference is poorly expressed in ratios of population per square mile, although the minimal figures for this ratio in ranking society far exceed those of the bands. What makes these ratios misleading is the fact that the bands, invariably gatherers and hunters, use most or all of their territories in the food quest, while ranking societies, usually agricultural, use only a portion of it during any particular time period. Thus, the actual social density of population tends to be several times the figure obtained by dividing the total units of area by the total population. This is the case even after adjustments are made for the fact that hunters and gatherers also tend to cluster at any given time within a portion of their range, and for the fact that agriculturalists, particularly those with primitive farming techniques, are likely to continue to ex-

ploit larger ranges for wild foods as well as for new or re-
vitalized crop land in the cycle of land occupation required
by swiddenage.

Differences in population between egalitarian and rank
society are manifested not only in density figures, but also in
the size of the total residential community. Though few
egalitarian bands manage to surpass fifty individuals living
together with any degree of stability, few rank communities
would fall below this figure, and most would have populations in the hundreds. Reliable statistical data are absent,
but it is likely that the age and sex distributions vary significantly between egalitarian and rank society. It may be
guessed that infant mortality is reduced with growing control over the food supply. Simultaneously, warfare appears
to be much increased, which might account for a significantly lower proportion of males in the adult population.
Actually, the composition of the population seems to be a
result rather than a cause of the distinctive features of rank
society.

One other hypothesis about population in rank society
can be offered. Population growth in this type far exceeds
anything known in band egalitarian society. Fairly constant
population increase coupled with limitations of subsistence
technology and immediately exploitable land resources tend
to produce, in turn, a pattern of physical expansion,
frequently in the development of satellite communities.
Actually, the term "satellite" is less than .appropriate. In
some instances relations are maintained between the original
and the new settlement and in part of these cases the relations have elements of subordination, particularly in matters of ritual. In other instances, connections may be weak
and almost devoid of content, forgotten with the passing
of the pioneer generation which could actually look to a
parental group in the old village. Where relations are maintained, the ranking system of the offshoot village usually
articulates with that of the parent village, a situation reinforced by using kinship categories and terminology.

Subsistence Economy

Ranking may develop, as previously indicated, in the absence of domesticated sources of food, but such situations have probably been very rare. Expectably less rare are situations of secondary ranking, that is, ranking that has grown not out of indigenous factors but through the imposition of a model of organization developed outside the society in question. I shall not belabor the point here, but one of the best described instances of this process is given by Julian Steward (1938, pp. 149–50), describing the rise of Tümuko, a Shoshone, to a chief's position in the middle of the nineteenth century.[1]

A distinctive feature of the ranking society is the employment of all individuals in labor tasks typical of their age and sex. Rank does not bring assignments that take its possessor out of the regular labor force, nor does the manipulation of rank suffice to excuse the manipulator from regular tasks. Indeed, if anything, the holder of rank in such a society is compelled to work more arduously than any-

---

[1] Steward argues that "Basic patterns of organization and chieftainship obviously could not be borrowed unless conditions to support them were present. If such conditions were present they would automatically develop without the necessity of borrowing" (Steward, 1938, p. 246). There is considerable reason to support an amended version of the first statement: Borrowed patterns of organization and chieftainship will collapse and disappear unless conditions capable of supporting them are also borrowed or developed. On a very similar theme related to Steward's work but using data from a much more complex sociocultural system, see Fried (1964, pp. 47–62). But there is nothing that will prevent abortive attempts, and it may take some time before the experiment is realized to be abortive. As for the "automatic development," I agree with regard to long-run phenomena, but think that the lag in time prior to the autochthonous development of the institutions in question gives ample room for diffusion. Actually, the type case I have in mind is one in which the model of organization is imposed *in toto* by an external, ruling power. For purposes of its own rule, such a power may treat a politically inferior society as if it were more complexly organized, going so far as to recognize chieftains not in the native system. The Reindeer Tungus have been treated in this way (Shirokogoroff, 1929, p. 192).

body else, because he is expected to be more generous in his distributions.

There is no indication that ranking develops out of any managerial necessity occurring in hunting and gathering society. Such vectors of supervision that develop on that level, such as might be associated with leaders of rabbit drives or whale hunts, are dispelled with the end of the activity, and no halo effect is discerned. The genesis of the ranking society, in terms of individual psychology, may well lie in the demand for affect, so that some individuals seek reinforcement by giving more and more frequently than they should, thereby creating obligations among those that have received goods. It is thoroughly consistent with such a model that the "high-ranking" individual at times might appear to an observer as not particularly a wealthy person in the society (*cf.* Smith, 1940, p. 125; McIlwraith, 1948, pp. 179–80).

In rank society the division of labor is much the same as in egalitarian society, being determined primarily by age and sex. No conspicuous specialization of craftsmanship develops, except as natural divisions of interest occur. These bestow no particular benefit on their possessor except for a transitory prestige (*cf.* Leacock, 1955, pp. 31–47). In any case, no political power derives from such specialization.

The major subsistence event underlying rank society is the transition to domesticated food supply, although, as indicated, it is possible that temporary shifts to this more complex societal level occurred much earlier in windfall environments. If such developments have occurred in fact, there has also been a subsequent local devolution back to the simpler level of integration. This is not surprising for there is nothing impossible about reversibility in an evolutionary process, and relatively short-run reversals may be fairly probable. What most concerns us, however, is not the abstract dynamics of cultural evolution, but the connections between a domesticated food supply and ranking. The relation seems to be centered in the demographic effects of the more certain and more concentrated food supply: Communities become larger on the average and much more permanent. Though they are larger population aggregates, rank villages are still built on the framework of kinship with the kin network becoming more formalized than in simpler band egalitarian society. One of the major developments is the emergence of a clearly distinguished descent principle requiring demonstration of relationship. The basic technique of accomplishing this is the specific genealogy which, at least in theory, specifies all consanguineal ties and many affinal ones, and thus stands distinctly apart from the vague, mythological "genealogies" that, in equalitarian society, act as the charters for band membership. Incidentally, it should be remarked in this context that the descent lines and genealogies are not necessarily unilineal as was assumed to be the case some years ago. Various forms of postmarital residence option can be integrated with demonstrated genealogy, so that corporate kindreds as well as lineages become a typical form of grouping at this level. Literature on this point has accumulated rapidly in recent years. One of the most comprehensive statements occurring in the context of an extensive ethnography is to be found in Harold W. Scheffler (1965, p. 47 et passim). Given such forms of grouping and the device of the genealogy, it is possible to develop a hierarchical arrangement of kin such that, for example, proximity or distance to a particular ancestor becomes significant (Kirchhoff, 1959, pp. 260–70; Fried, 1957, pp. 1–29). This factor does not succeed in explaining why ranking comes about, but it does suggest one means by which it can be realized. We shall return to the larger problem at the end of this chapter; at this juncture there are still other characteristics of ranking to consider.

Redistribution

To the extent that things circulate through an egalitarian society, instead of being consumed on the spot by a producer, the form of circulation is the reciprocal exchange previously discussed. Reciprocal forms continue to be significant in all subsequently developed types of economic integration, but they may be replaced as the paramount form. In rank society the major process of economic integration is redistribution, in which there is a characteristic flow of goods into and out from a finite center. Invariably that center is the pinnacle of the rank hierarchy or, as complexity mounts, the pinnacle of a smaller component network within a larger structure.

A classic example of a redistributive economy is that of the cultures of the North Pacific Coast:

> Among the Indians of the North Pacific Coast the social units—localized kin groups—were the owners of wealth, not individuals. . . . major riches such as the lands, houses, and important wealth tokens were group property. Even the objects possessed by the individual were made available to the group in case of necessity. Though the highest-ranking member of each group spoke of himself, or was spoken of by others, as the "owner" of his group's house or houses, its real estate, and most if its treasures, he was the administrator of his group's possessions, not an individual owner (Drucker, 1965, p. 50).

It is significant that the core of redistribution (or pooling) lies less in the spectacular exchange displays, such as the frequently misrepresented potlatch, than in the basic daily relationship between a community and its productive capital and the consumable yield of that capital. Of great importance is the fact that redistribution has its locus on the level of the village or even larger organizational unit. This becomes clear in an example drawn from Fiji:

> The village is and has been an economic entity as well as a political one. It is a proprietary unit, with titular ownership of all land and the lagoon offshore vested in the paramount [chief]. . . . Yet insofar as a village traditionally achieved a collective economic existence, this was organized and directed by the old-time chief.

The paramount could summon the community's labor on his own behalf, or on behalf of someone else who requested it, or for general purposes. . . . Besides his right to summon labor he accumulated the greater proportion of the first fruits of the yam crop . . . and he benefited from other forms of food presentation, or by the acquisition of special shares in ordinary village redistribution . . . Thus, the paramount would collect a significant part of the surplus production of the community and redistribute it in the general welfare (Sahlins, 1962, pp. 293–4).

Unlike even the strongest economic roles in societies based exclusively upon reciprocity, the regularity of the role of village redistributor conveys prestige and bolsters political status. This is not altered by the fact that in some societies the acquisition of the role of paramount redistributor depends in some measure upon personal achievement often measured in cumulative instances of unbalanced reciprocity. It is the carrying out of large-scale distributions on the way to achieving the status of redistributor that accounts for the often puzzling observation in the past of the impoverished chief. Now we know that such persons were rich for what they dispensed and not for what they hoarded.

Settlement Patterns

The characteristic mode of settlement is the village. Population size is quite variable, but the range presented in the galaxy of ethnographic reports may not be reliable as a guide to pre-European situations. This is one way of interpreting the existence in contemporary times of very tiny villages comprising only a single household. Considering that in the past warfare was both serious and endemic in these societies, one may question the viability of such tiny settlements. At the large end of the scale the limits on village size are primarily set by the predominant mode of obtaining subsistence. Curiously, among the largest villages reported for this level are those of the North Pacific Coast.

Though they grew from the exploitation of marine resources, their greatest size was probably reached as the result of trade with Europeans. Actually, these peoples show a movement from summer to winter quarters or, more accurately, a movement from the main winter village to a less permanent summer habitation site or sites, the number being an outgrowth of the diversification of natural food resources.

Warfare has a major effect on village size and organization. As noted, it tends to set lower limits on population size since a minimum force is necessary to forestall raids, even though size alone does not eliminate the possibility of attack. Upper population limits probably reflect circumstances of warfare. Given existing levels of swidden agricultural productivity, a fair amount of land must be kept out of operation for every unit cultivated. It might be thought that a further limitation is the increasing element of danger as distance from the center of population is increased. Although logically evident, this proposition is difficult to document.

In rank society villages tend to exist as largely independent, autonomous social systems, although most have some point or points at which they are articulated with a larger and usually cooperative network. For one thing, most such villages, even if not ritually exogamous, see a significant portion of marriages occurring outside the village. The affinal ties thus established may have considerable significance for the ranking system as a whole. A well-known instance is offered by the so-called *mayu-dama* system of the Chingpaw (Kachin) of northern Burma as described by E. R. Leach (1954, p. 78 ff.). Apart from kinship alliances, the hierarchical rank structure of a village tends to be specific to it although two major exceptions may be mentioned. In one, an over-all ranking system may crosscut the rankings associated with particular villages, so that a kind of moiety arrangement is superimposed on all interacting villages. The Toda organization described by W.

H. R. Rivers (1906) may be an example. Also of this type is the organization of the Lolo, although this society is more accurately classified as stratified (see p. 186; this position is based on Lin, 1961, pp. 97–106). The other exception is a relatively unformalized version of the first and refers to the formation of special marriage alliances between high-ranking families, an institution that is functionally equivalent to the development in some societies of special endogamy to preserve rank privileges; this often leads to marriages among high-status families that may be considered incestuous in other sectors of the society.

Important as the village pattern of settlement is in rank society, it is obviously not specific to this form of social organization. Unfortunately, what I surmise to be the most significant aspect of settlement pattern is not ususally given with clarity and accuracy in the ethnographic accounts. I refer to the density of village settlement—the number of villages to be found in delimited and measured districts and their component populations. Some work has been done on reconstructing general population densities, and in Chapter 5 we briefly review the problem.

Kinship

The articulation of most interpersonal relationships in rank society is an aspect of the kinship system. "It would scarcely be possible to overemphasize the importance of kinship in the social structure," says Philip Drucker (1951, p. 274), speaking about the Nootka. "As it is said," Raymond Firth (1957, p. 234) reports for Tikopia, "'the whole land is a single body of kinfolk.'" There are exceptions, such as the Australians with their remarkably widespread network of kin relations, but in general the significance of the web of kinship is greater in rank society than in band egalitarian society and in stratified and certainly in state society. In band society there may be de facto descent groups, but these tend to be precipitated out of ecologicallý favored residential rules. Unlike rank society, which is dominated by the ideology of kinship, band society seems to be dominated by the ideology of coresidence. (As previously mentioned, this type of territoriality is only superficially like that which is associated with the nation-state.) Stratified society shows growing concern for a class-and-territory focus. It should be mentioned, if only because misinterpretations have been common in this field, that just as kinship plays an important role in band society, despite emphasis on coresidence, so kinship continues to play a major role in stratified and state society. In rank society, however, the role of kinship seems to occupy the greatest relative proportion of the total social field.

Despite the great importance of kinship as *the* principle of association, there is little uniformity about the precise character of the kinship system. In brief, examples may be found which are either unilineal or bilateral, matri- or patrilateral, multilateral, or given to one or another kind of option. In conformity with this variable situation we find variability of kin terminology. The previously mentioned Nootka, for example, have a variant of Eskimo terminology, while that of Tikopia is bifurcate merging with Iroquois cousin terms. It is patent that kinship terminology has little or no diagnostic value as a criterion of egalitarian, rank, or stratified organization.

There is no particular uniformity in postmarital residence choices, but at least one important generalization may be essayed. Though there are some societies on this level which maintain fairly rigid postmarital residence rules (and these are the societies with the firmest unilinealities, as might be expected), most of these societies place *ad hoc* benefits before other considerations in the determination of any specific case of residence. This applies not only to persons of low rank, who look for easily available, high-yielding resources and compatible neighbors, but also to those of high rank, who can shop about to achieve optimum rank possibilities. In all cases, of course, the persons in question live with some relatives; the question is which ones and how to trace the relationship.

The Nootka, to continue with the examples already introduced, stated a verbal preference for viripatrilocality but actually moved about so freely that most abstract possibilities actually occurred ethnographically: "Chiefs tended to stay most of the time with the group in which they owned property . . . , whether this came from the paternal or maternal line. But even they moved about, and might spend a fishing season, a year or even 2 years, with another group to whom they were related" (Drucker, 1951, p. 278). As for common folk, they moved even more frequently, unless they were seduced into staying more permanently in a particular house because of special privileges offered by the chief. This feature of Nootka society was but a somewhat extreme version of something that is rather commonplace: the qualification, in the sense of modification, of the residence rule. Sometimes it is institutionalized as a pattern of visiting, thus disturbing the basic residence procedure very little, as in Tikopia. In Moala, Fiji, there are significant deviations from normal patrilocal residence. Of the variant modes ambipatrilocality is the most common. Marshall Sahlins (1962, p. 103) is careful to establish these patterns as aboriginal features of social organization and not the result of contact derived from disruption of aboriginal patterns. Indeed, one of the outstanding examples of the social use of diverse residence preferences in association with extensive use of the principle of ranking is to be found in the Trobriands. The most common type of postmarital residence is viri-avunculocal, and it is associated with land rights. But higher ranking subclans have taken advantage of rank and a secondary preference for viripatrilocality to acquire agricultural lands superior in quality to those with which they were mythologically associated (*cf.* Fathauer, 1961, p. 244).

What seems to be general about residential preferences in ranking society can be summarized: First, from the point of view of those of low rank, the process is often dominated by *ad hoc* opportunism and a search for advantages; Second, from the point of view of those of high rank, the problem is to attract and keep a suitable number of lesser families in the community. Third, in spite of possibly improving rank through moving, it is common for a group of closely related persons, usually males, to constitute the nucleus of a group; thus, even a nonunilineal society may have a tight kin core. Consider, for example, the Choiseulese, among whom "Anyone is said to be always welcome in any descent group of any *sinangge* with which he can trace a consanguineal connection, and many persons are in fact living with groups into which they were not born as a consequence of parental residence" (Scheffler, 1965, p. 47). Despite this: "through patri-virilocal residence the men of a cognatic descent category come to form the 'core' (*kapakapa*) of a residential segment" (Scheffler, 1965, p. 46).

The character of this core group seems to me to be of the greatest importance for it not only lies at the heart of the concept of the rank society but contains the seed of the next stage of development, stratification. This is the way it looks in Choiseul, where, despite the general significance of cognatic ties, the core group that forms may begin to resemble a patrilineage:

> Those who trace their descent from the apical ancestor of the descent group solely through males are said to be *popodo valeke,* "born of men," of agnatic status. These men are said to have primary rights and interests in the property and affairs of the group; they are "strong" within it. Primogeniture is said to determine precedence in the agnatic line and thereby who will be *batu,* or manager, of the people and their estate (Scheffler, 1965, p. 46).

Even when brothers do not live together as a core unit of a community, they may function as a specially united group; again the Nootka are illustrative (Drucker, 1951, p. 274). Emphasis on closer rather than more distant kin is not an invention of rank society in one sense, but in another it is. Band egalitarian society, as we have seen, and as Sahlins (1965, p. 186 ff.) has neatly begun to document, knows the distinction as is conveyed, for example, by M. J. Meggitt's (1962a, p. 120) description of a Walbiri, Australian aboriginal man, asked to part with a very scarce object: "If he is asked, the man usually gives the single article to an actual or close father or son, but he refuses distant 'fathers' and 'sons.'" On this social level, however, there is a very strong relationship between kinship distance and physical distance, a relationship which in good part flows from the previously discussed emphasis on coresidence. The basic formula for the band egalitarian society, then, is "we are probably close relatives because we live together." In rank society the formula is, "because we are close relatives, we probably live together." As we have seen, this is particularly the case as the ranking system matures and tends toward stratification. One visible indicator of the difference is the presence of specific kinds of unilineal descent groups. Elman Service has stressed the character of "clans" as sodalities linking distinct residential groups; for him the clan is not a local group (Service, 1962, p. 126). This usage is diametrically opposed to that suggested by George P. Murdock (1949, p. 68), stressing "residential unity" as one of three criteria of clanship. My own preference in defining the essential aspects of clanship is for criteria that leave the question of localization for empirical testing. The most important criteria are unilineality, corporation, and the means of establishing membership. The last is usually accomplished by birth, as far as any individual is concerned, but with regard to the membership of the whole and the connections among these members the linkage at crucial junctures is by agreement or what I have called elsewhere "stipulated descent." By this is meant that ultimately membership is based on an unestablished, unestablishable descent from a common ancestor. In the absence of any means of demonstrating genealogically exactly how all the different members of the clan are related it is simply assumed that because they are members they must be related. The problem in a clan is then to clarify the relative kinship statuses of the members so that they may act properly toward each other. What has to be done is to identify the generational standing of the members, for frequently within generations members are equal. Note that, for purposes of the central argument of this book, the clan by its structure defined here is an inclusive unit, tending to include all possible members even though that means offering shares in the clan's corporate resources. In some societies clans contain members or groups of members of obviously alien origin now assimilated under the ethic of kinship. (Under certain circumstances therefore even birth can be dispensed with as a means of entrance.)

In contrast to the clan is the lineage, similar in structural detail except for the means of establishing membership. In the lineage this requires demonstration of relationship to all the other members of the lineage. Since all existing members already know their precise ties, the newly arrived can easily locate himself vis-à-vis all others. The fact is that this is done, though there are alternative means by which it is accomplished. The lineage differs from the clan in tending to be exclusive, refusing entrance to some and generally paring membership to the minimum. Lineages differ also in offering members partial or restricted access to corporate resources. While this exists in potential in all lineages, it does not always appear as a major operating principle. When fully active, however, it usually signifies the presence of full stratification, as is discussed in the next chapter. Apart from its use in narrowing access to productive resources, lineage functions to narrow access to status, in particular to the scarce and valued statuses that comprise the basis of rank society.

Before moving more deeply into the implications of the last remarks, let it be made clear that clans and lineages can and frequently do coexist in a single society. For example, in contemporary Taiwan there are thriving clans and not quite so vigorous lineages, both serving different social ends. Some of the clans include numbers of lineages although the clan is not simply or even in any sense the expansion of the lineage network. Conversely, that a whole lineage may constitute a corporate segment of a clan does not affect its autonomy and separate origin. The fact that clans and lineages serve different purposes and sometimes contradictory purposes may be one good reason for their coexistence, as societies are rarely harmoniously integrated systems but more usually display some measure of conflict and disequilibrium. In the case of clans and lineages, the latter may serve as instruments of ranking and stratification, tending to produce a society of potentially hostile socioeconomic class segments. At the same time the clan may operate to crosscut these class lines thus discouraging incipient class conflict.

This takes us to the heart of the distinction between lineages and clans. What matters in the lineage is precisely what Paul Kirchhoff (1959, pp. 260–70) pointed to when describing the structure and significance of what he calls the "conical clan." The crucial thing was to establish for every member of the society his closeness of relationship with the founding ancestor. Actually, this is not the clearest way to phrase it, despite the ease with which the point is understood by people who have grown up in a ranking (and stratified) culture. It would be better to say that what must be known is the distance of relationship between any member and the highest-ranking person of his generation. This is frequently interpreted in the folk ideology as distance from the founding ancestor. The concept is made possible by adding a simple principle of seniority to that of descent, so that even in the case of multiple births, siblings can be sorted out on the basis of different moments of birth and given different privileges on this basis. In such a society the first born of a first born is considered closer to the ancestor than the first born of a second born, and so on. The line of descent is not simply the transgenerational tie that recedes toward the first-known ancestor (for example, the sun!), but the string of first born through time. This may be further delimited by specifying that only one of the sexes can be recognized as an authentic link.

Kirchhoff recognizes that such concern for descent had several concomitants. Genealogies, unnecessary in a clan, become charters of preferred status in a lineage. The keeping of genealogy becomes a serious matter, a preoccupation of what Kirchhoff calls the "aristoi," although at times the actual work of remembering (later of recording, or tracing) went to nonaristocratic specialists and scribes. Marriage, always problematical and usually beset with traditional taboos and exhortations, becomes even more constrained as ranking systems become more sophisticated. The marriage arrangements of the Australian aborigines are perhaps more impressive for their systematization of a society, but are nothing as confining as the self-imposed limitations developed in a rank society. Often in such a society the end result is a revolutionary violation of previously held norms of exogamy as a highly ranked innovator marries a woman from a previously tabooed kin group. Kirchhoff also suggests that emphasis on nearness of relationship rather than type of descent might lead to bilateralism as a consequence of the attempt to manufacture suitable family trees (Kirchhoff, 1959, pp. 266–7). If such factors have indeed produced bilateralism, it has been the history of our own society that offers one of the best examples. In other traditions the growth of ranking and stratification can be contained within strongly unilineal systems. It is understood now, for example, that even the strongest unilineal systems provide significant roles for what may be called "the other side" of the descent picture. This may include transmissions of certain kinds of scarce value, while withholding others as inalterably associated with the uniline. The latter situation is exemplified in a number of Indonesian societies, such as the Minanangkabau, which differentiate between "earnings" and "heirloom property" (Josselin de Jong, 1951, pp. 56–7; cf. Gough, 1962, pp. 588–90).

INTERNAL POLITICAL FEATURES
OF RANK SOCIETY

A member of an egalitarian society put down by a set of curious chances in the midst of a rank society would probably experience relatively little dislocation. He might marvel at the opulence of life, the stability of settlement, and the size of habitations, but in his social life little would strike him as really strange. The institutions which flowed from and supported the social ranking system would pervade his life but in a gentle and subtle fashion, unlikely to rouse his anxiety. As we shall see, this is a far cry from what might be expected to occur when a member of an egalitarian society is introduced into a stratified society. In such a case the very basis of livelihood is threatened and almost every aspect of life is changed with the almost total reversal of the expectations of economic behavior. In rank society the changes in economic behavioral expectations are relatively mild, but there are some important shifts in political behavior.

As in egalitarian society, most of the institutions that apply to what was earlier defined as the political areas are embedded in other institutional activities. What this means is that in rank society, as in egalitarian society, few if any activities are carried out as explicitly political. Actually, this may be somewhat misleading, as even in stratified and state societies political activities are frequently carried out in the context or guise of other activities. In rank society, as in egalitarian society, the analyst has difficulties in discriminating the political action, whereas in stratified and state societies there is little question except for certain borderline phenomena. Accordingly, in the following analysis, as in our discussion of egalitarian society, the political nature of the activity or institution in question is often secondary or even more remotely tied to some other functional goal.

Division of Labor

The age and sex bases for the division of labor noted in egalitarian society continue but with differences. Where the universally valued role of the male as a hunter in many egalitarian societies contributes to his ritual and political superiority, there is often an increase in the direct participation of women in decision making, apparently correlated with the importance of the female role in agricultural productivity. There is, of course, no direct relationship between significance in the labor process and political importance: Slavery should establish that fact. Furthermore, the range of participation of women in the political activities of rank society vary widely with the society. Perhaps the optimum role played by women is that described among the Iroquois, where they had a right similar to recall that could control the way in which certain sachems used their positions (Morgan, 1922, p. 84). A contrary example is offered by the Kapauku of New Guinea. Women are considered important economic assets because of their gardening and pig raising (Pospisil, 1958, p. 57; 1963, pp. 63–4), but they are supposed to be docile and obedient and leave decisions to men (Pospisil, 1958, p. 57). Yet Kapauku knows Xantippe and because the society has no institutionalized role for assertive females, such a woman enjoys "an uncontrollable status" (Pospisil, 1958, p. 58) but does not seem to have much influence beyond her own henpecked household.

Apart from age and sex, there is little significant division of labor. For the most part everybody does the same tasks. There is the barest beginning of professional specialization, as some people can do certain tasks better than the average, and there is a small but visible tendency to relieve persons of high rank of some or all participation in some phases of work.

In Tikopia, for example, degrees of skill are not recognized in basic agricultural production, although degrees of industriousness are recognized. In deep-sea fishing, however, a distinction is made between those who are proficient and all others. Despite this distinction, Firth tells us that "Skill as such does not entitle a person exclusively to his individual product, any more than industrious labor" (Firth, 1965, p. 63). The ultimate device by which this is achieved is what he calls "forced exchange" (Firth, 1965, pp. 316–8), which we have already seen operating on the egalitarian level. In Tikopia it is usually accomplished by coupling a request with an unsolicited gift, but in other societies the request might be made without such an accompaniment. Sahlins describes *kerekere* as "the prevailing form of economic transaction among kinsmen as individuals." "More goods change hands through *kerekere* than through any other form of distribution, excepting familial pooling" (Sahlins, 1962, p. 203). He vigorously denies that *kerekere* is either "borrowing" or "begging"; it is a request or solicitation for some good or service and "often a request cannot be directly refused" (Sahlins, 1962, p. 205). Interestingly enough, there is a form of *kerekere* in which the request is prefixed by a gift, called "a more unsociable form" by Sahlins (1962, p. 207).

A particularly clear example is recorded by Philip L. Newman on the basis of his work among the Gururumba of West New Guinea. He was impressed with the incessant banter among people of all ages and statuses, banter which was largely compounded of pestering demands for all sorts of things. If I may take a little liberty with his account (Newman, 1965, p. 52), the form of the request may be seen as equivalent to standard American "Gimme!" and the reply to "Take, dammit!"

Yet in all of this there is a strong current of rank, such

as not detected in egalitarian societies. This is perhaps most conspicuously manifested in the growing tendency for exchanges of this kind not to be strictly reciprocal, with an inhibition becoming manifest on the likelihood that the person of superior status will make such demands of his rank inferiors. To do so is to risk a loss of prestige.

A logical expectation of increasing significance and formalization of rank differences is that they should be accompanied by decreasing participation of high-ranking individuals in the primary productive labor of the society or, as put by Sahlins (1958, p. 7), "the segregation of chiefs from subsistence activities and their dependence upon the produce of other members of the society." Conversely, there is an expectation that this withdrawal from the crude labor process is related to a development of managerial responsibility for larger-scale productive enterprises and for management of important parts of the distributional system. One curious wrinkle may develop in the unfolding of this generalization. In societies which blend emergent ranking systems with substantial egalitarianism the persons holding the rank positions may be the hardest working people in the system. This is a foreseeable concomitant of the fact that their positions rest upon generosity, with the bulk of things that must be given away being their own in the sense of resulting from their own labor and that of their households.

This is the case in Siuai society in the Solomon Islands as described by Douglas Oliver (1955, p. 338): "Some recognition is also accorded men on the road to becoming wealthy—in other words, men who are *effectively* industrious . . . the man who toils abnormally long hours producing taro or pots, etc., for sale is regarded with respect and wonderment, even though he may not be considered a potential leader." The qualification about potential leadership fits quite well into the previous argument. Wealth alone does not a *mumi* (big man) make; he has to give much of it away—in the approved fashion, by throwing well-attended feasts (Oliver, 1955, pp. 360–1). Compare this with what is said about the Mandari of the South Sudan:

Of equal importance with the power of giving judgments is the obligation of the *Mar* to feed his people . . . The *Mar* is expected to give assistance to those in need as well as providing food entertainment for the elders . . . and visitors. In theory, a *Mar* should never refuse a request for shelter, food, implements or weapons for hunting, and because chiefs are anxious to keep their dependents, and in the past, to attract new clients, they give economic assistance where they are able (Buxton, 1958, pp. 81–2).

The anxiety of the Mandari chieftain to please and retain his followers reminds us of Drucker's remarks about the Nootka, each of whose chiefs

was in every way dependent upon his tenants. Every chief recognized this; it was taught him from childhood. His problem was, therefore, to attract lower-rank people to his house, and to bind them to him as much as possible. This he did by good treatment, generosity (giving many feasts and potlatches), naming their children, etc. (Drucker, 1951, p. 280).

Whereas in most rank societies the chiefs worked as hard and often harder than the rest, things were otherwise in Nootka, where chiefs are said to work not at all. Actually, this is not completely true. A chief does little or no menial labor, but he does participate in some of the important productive activities. For example, he might initiate and take part in the first fishing expedition of the season; indeed, it is only after he or a formally chosen surrogate ritually opens such a significant activity that the generality of folk can participate in it (Drucker, 1951, pp. 244, 251–7). This was not the case in Moala, where the prerogatives of chieftainship

did not exempt the chief and his household from manual labor. Moreover, the traditional economic obligations of the chief to dispense goods must have matched his ability to amass them. The chief would be required to subsidize the labor he called and to distribute food and goods in great quantity at life crisis rites. His gardens were open for appropriation by his people, and his house for hospitality (Sahlins, 1962, pp. 293–4).

Similar observations are made by Firth about Tikopia. Chiefs work. "Most of their food comes from their own exertions" (Firth, 1965, p. 191). By initiative and example a chief inspires and directs community production (Firth, 1965, p. 231). He gives elaborate feasts, and this generosity "sets the seal upon his status" (Firth, 1965, pp. 222–31, 230). There is perhaps no other area of social theory where the variables cohere so neatly.

Leadership

In rank society leaders can lead, but followers may not follow. Commands are given, but sometimes they may not be obeyed. Does this mean that they are not commands? Perhaps, but then there is no society in which all commands are obeyed. In rank society, however, there are few if any effective sanctions that can be used to compel compliance. What there is tends to be similar to what was seen operating on the egalitarian level, although there are some new elements. Certainly there is a different feeling and intensity about the situation of leadership, and this is often best conveyed by religious and ritual phenomena. Before analyzing a few examples of the conjunction of religious and political elements, a closer look at the role of rank in the economy will be of advantage.

In egalitarian society the size of cooperative work parties is usually very small; when large parties are assembled they are for periods of short duration and subsequent reassembly is not likely to duplicate previous membership. Furthermore, no trace of authority displayed at the collective activity is transferred to any other aspect of social life. In rank society there is clear departure from these generalizations: Authority is regular and repetitive and extends into various aspects of social life.

It is through his role as feast giver and host in intergroup celebrations that the person of rank most commonly shows greatest influence on the productivity of his society. By his actions in initiating such activity he encourages maximum output by a number of his followers, though often it would seem that he does not succeed in galvanizing all of his potential followers. He also succeeds in scheduling the productive activities. Again, a qualification must be added: Though some headmen or big men in some situations do manage to set a kind of calendar for some productive tasks, it would seem that in many cases the scheduling is imposed on the community by ecological factors substantially beyond its control. Thus, reaching a cyclical peak of the pig population, which varies with other food availabilities, might be the incentive to a big man's invitation to attend a great feast (cf. Vayda et al., 1961, pp. 69–71).

Desire to have someone undertake leadership may itself lead to a productive outburst, although the level may not be thereafter sustained beyond what is considered normal. H. Ian Hogbin (1951, p. 134) tells of such a case among the Busama of New Guinea. As usual with the Busama, leadership was being declined by a preferred candidate and "to prevent him from withdrawing at the last moment his fellow clubmen rallied round and put a huge garden into cultivation."

The Camayura of the northern Mato Grosso in Brazil show, among other things, the haplessness of classification. In terms of their social organization and its operation they are egalitarian. But the effective unit of social organization is the village of about 100 people which has a chief whose descent line may go back to the sun and who receives a special burial (Oberg, 1953, pp. 50, 68). Nevertheless, "When an Indian is asked who is the chief of the village he will mention the chief's name but will immediately name one or two other men who are considered chiefs as well" (Oberg, 1953, p. 46). The main function of the Camayura chief seems to be economic. Though the Camayura chief is not mentioned for generosity, his role in distribution as well as in production is clear, as this description of a fishing expedition shows:

> Early one morning while it was still dark, Tamapu, the chief, could be heard walking up and down in the plaza in the village, giving instructions to his people . . . He detailed certain men to go and prepare their weirs and hand traps . . . Tamapu, himself, made a new conical hand trap in order to show the details of its manufacture.
>
> [During that day the preparatory tasks were carried out.]
>
> The next morning all the able-bodied men, boys, and little girls set off for the stream [where final preparations were being made].
>
> Tamapu now gave instructions to the timbo beaters. [Afterward the beating went on for about two hours.] . . . While the beaters were thus occupied, the older men, Tamapu among them, went up and down along the shallow weed-filled margins of the stream with their conical basketry hand traps . . . [Poison was put in the water and bowmen began to shoot the fish that surfaced for air.] . . .
>
> After the shooting began, Tamapu and the men too old to shoot, sat on the shore giving instructions and advice to the bowmen . . .
>
> Tamapu kept watching the [bow]men . . . and was evidently dissatisfied with their performance. Eventually he called out that they were missing too many fish because they had had sexual intercourse the night before [a violation of ritual propriety—M.H.F.] and

that they had better let the boys do the shooting. This obviously was not meant as a joke, for the men obeyed and were replaced by the boys. . . .

The next day . . . the chief saw to it [first] that every house group had its fair share of the several hundred fish caught (Oberg, 1953, pp. 27–8).

Firth's detailed analysis of the productive role of the Tikopian chief (Firth, 1965, pp. 190–212) need not be repeated here. Examples of most of the functions have already been given. In one particular function, however, there is something additional and important. This is the use of the sacred powers of the chief to declare taboo some activity, food, or location. Firth concludes that:

Some of the taboos . . . merely limit immediate production and consumption in specific places while allowing similar effort elsewhere; others divert productive energies partially or entirely from one field to another. Most marked here is the effort of a chief . . . to take charge of the economic forces of his clan or district in the interests of the community, and limit present application of labour in order to get an increased product later (Firth, 1965, p. 212).

Again we see a calendric function in the work of the chief. Actually, Firth would take us even further. In keeping with his conviction that "an analysis of a primitive economic system . . . can be made without sacrifice of the basic approach of modern economics (Firth, 1965, p. 13),[2] Firth views the chief as "to some extent" a rational manager of a multifaceted economic enterprise, although not as "an exploiting capitalist, taking in return for productive risks the profit of the enterprise" (First, 1965, pp. 232, 231). A scrupulous ethnographer, Firth offers evidence of the limitations under which such a generalization would operate. It would be infernally difficult to tell exactly how much economic

---

[2] In Firth's own qualification this applies to formal and not to substantive analysis.

value lay in the chief's decisions to taboo something, and the chief himself usually applies the taboo for some ritual purpose. Perhaps more significant is the absence of power by which the chief can force compliance. The case record shows workers coming late or not at all, or otherwise defying the chief's wishes. This makes the chief unpleasant and he grumbles (Firth, 1965, p. 232).

Ritual Leadership

The individual of high rank is frequently also of comparable religious standing. This is almost automatically the case in societies dominated by lineage organization. Given the value of nearness of relationship, recognizing the overlap between the ancestors and the significant gods, acknowledging the close tie between religious ritual and episodes of feasting, it is understandable that rank and religious status would be vested in the same individuals.

In Tikopia, for example, there is an extensive pantheon in addition to venerated ancestors, but worship and ritual tend to be associated with the clan or *kainanga*, whose *ariki*, or chief, is simultaneously high priest. While some of the rituals, particularly certain dances, attract almost universal participation, much of the activity is carried out by the ariki alone or with the assistance of his immediate family (Firth, 1940, pp. 10–1). In a very real sense, however, all of the religious activities carried out in Tikopia (which had a population of about 1,200 in 1928, when Firth's original studies began) are integrated and form one consistent pattern despite the autonomy of the clans which carry out portions of the ritual. The absence of political paramountcy among the chiefs, not to mention their lack of power, does not seriously hamper the course of the ceremonial cycle. The four clan chiefs are arranged hierarchically, rather than in order of the burden of ceremonial obligations. It is reported, however, that there is a Tikopian belief in one deity being supreme over the others; this is the *Atua i Kafika*.

The very best ethnographies are more than adequate condensations of the observations made on a particular society by a particular observer. A truly outstanding ethnography permits a symbolic equivalent of fieldwork to go on with the reader as fieldworker. Firth's extensive account of Tikopia, available in a number of publications, several of them revised to include new theoretical interests as well as some new data acquired on a subsequent field trip, is one such outstanding resource. While working through Firth's account of Tikopia, it became apparent that the Atua i Kafika should have been both more and less than Firth reported, if my speculations about the relationship between rank society and ancestor worship have any validity. In brief, I expected at every mention of this divinity that Firth would identify him as ancestor of the Kafika as well as its leading deity. Each time, however, he identified the figure as a god and said nothing about ancestry. The best I could discover was a mention such as this: ". . . 'The yam has only one deity, the god in this family,' said the Ariki, meaning by his last statement the Atua i Kafika" (Firth, 1940, p. 94). Finally, my study of Firth's work included his *History and Traditions of Tikopia* (1961), and patience was rewarded:

> it was through his special relation with powerful gods that he [the Ariki Kafika] was believed to exercise his superior role in the social and economic as well as in the religious spheres.

> These gods were first of all his culture-hero ancestor the Atua i Kafika . . . who was generally recognized as the supreme deity of Tikopia (Firth, 1961, p. 53).

With this statement Firth introduces a set of themes which lie at the heart of his study. The gods are ancestors, and the ancestors are gods. The keeping and telling of the tradition, its conservation or amendment, its rejection and subsequent return, all are part of the political activity most characteristic of rank society. Though most of the versions of im-

portant tales collected by Firth are similar from informant
to informant, first in the unauthorized versions obtained
from nonspecialist informants and then in the versions told
by the chiefly priests, there were significant discrepancies.
This, he decided, is because "the traditional tales may not
reflect a unitary society. They may reflect the social structure, but in its competitive, opposition aspects rather than
in its integrative ones" (Firth, 1961, p. 174). "The lack of
agreement between . . . different versions, often in conflict,
is due not so much to differential memory as to differential
interests (Firth, 1961, p. 175).

Firth comes to the conclusion, after some very interesting comparative analysis of versions of tales and degrees
of agreement on such key matters as aboriginal priority in
the land, that the tales reflect less the social *status quo*
than the dynamic situation of continual realignment. I am
not prepared fully to accept this intriguing suggestion, but
neither can I here do it justice in attempting to qualify it.
I feel, however, that both streams are of great importance
and that to neglect one is to miss the point. (This is not a
criticism of Firth, who *does* analyze both.) I really wonder
if the lack of a monopoly on the ideology is not particularly
characteristic of rank society. In the absence of a higher degree of political power there is no genuinely "official" version.

Returning to the problem of leadership in ceremonial
aspects of life, we may note an apparent discrepancy in
the religion of the cultures of the North Pacific Coast.
Drucker summarizes the situation: "Although social life
revolved about minute gradations of rank, the Indians did
not endow their deities with a divine counterpart of gradu-
ated status" (Drucker, 1965, p. 83). Actually, this is less
disturbing to the thesis alluded to above than is the seeming absence of genealogy and claims of descent from gods.
On the other hand, there is no absence of evidence of connection between chiefly rank and leadership in ceremonial
activities. For example, in Drucker's account of major Nootka

rituals chiefs frequently figure in key roles. That chiefs figure so prominently in a number of rituals is due to their close association with the economic activity involved, that is, hair seal hunting, sea otter hunting, whale hunting, herring and salmon fishing, and so on (Drucker, 1951, pp. 168–81). Though chiefs of old might have carried out shamanistic activities, or so legends credit them with doing (Drucker, 1951, p. 181), most shamans are common folk. He believes that shamanistic success was used as a pathway to prestige in a society where most prestige was already ascribed. Shamanism was not, however, a lucrative profession (Drucker, 1951, p. 183).

More like Tikopia is what we are told about the previously mentioned Mandari of the Southern Sudan. The *Mar,* chief, "is the guardian of the rain, the land and natural phenomena." He conducts major sacrifices and is considered a more potent religious practitioner than the *bunit,* who is more like a curing shaman (Buxton, 1958, p. 83). Although it is said that the *Mar*'s sacrifices are not to divinities as ancestors while those of the *bunits* are, the importance of descent is very great. No single founding ancestor of the Mandari is recognized, as the population arrived at different times from different places. However, priority of arrival is an important factor in legitimizing rightful claims to land. "The people of Bora extraction represent the largest group who claim a single ancestor, and clans of this stock are found throughout the country. They base their right to land and their religious superiority on an important myth [about their descent] known in some form to all their descent groups" (Buxton, 1958, p. 70).

Among the Tallensi there is exceptionally close interweaving of political and religious roles. Beyond his status as symbolic owner of the land of his lineage, the chief takes ritual responsibility for most things considered to have some aspect of supernatural danger about them like firing the bush, responsibility for serious accidents or for the safety of special expeditions, and so on. "His office is sacred, imposing upon him observances and taboos" (Fortes, 1940, p. 259). Chiefs not only conduct the great ceremonies but supply much of the major contributions which make them possible. Meyer Fortes makes it clear that in a very real sense the playing out of the ritual life of the Tale is a major portion of the political life of the community (Fortes, 1940, pp. 258–64).

Without further expanding this section, for which the materials are almost superabundant, due to the traditional interest anthropologists have taken in the religious aspects of the societies they have studied, it should be clear that variations in intensity and greater variations in detail cannot obscure certain conspicuous general characteristics. The charter of the ranking society tends to be its view of the supernatural world as represented in tales and sometimes in genealogies. Frequently the demand for certain kinds of ceremonies, logistically organized by lineage heads, big men, or chiefs, coordinates or provides the stimulus for the coordination of different sectors of the economy. Yet, in all of this, the chiefly figures bring little in the way of power to their priestly roles. Instead, it seems more accurate to believe that such small power as they control is likely to stem from their ritual status, although even here there is minimum possibility of transfer of power from one situation to another.

Conflict

All the sources of interpersonal conflict found in egalitarian society persist in rank society, as indeed they persist in all subsequently evolved types of society. Certain kinds of irritation not present in egalitarian society make their appearance in rank societies, although their expression may still be relatively subdued. For example, while access to basic resources within the corporate unit is not significantly altered, there tends to be much more consumer's property in rank society. Patterns of reciprocal exchange do operate to keep these things in circulation, but there is a qualitative break with egalitarian societies as accumulation of nonstrategic values is often the basis or means of validation of rank distinctions.

Even against this background, it is difficult to speak of conflict arising in these societies out of situations conveyed by words from our own culture. The word "theft," for example, seems to be simple in its connotation: Something belongs to somebody and is taken without his permission. Epistemological questions to one side, we must immediately ask what is meant by "to belong," "to take" (or "to be taken"), and "permission"? As we have seen, ownership in simple societies usually connotes the right to give something away. This expression is somewhat better than the more usual reference to the right of disposition, for the latter suggests a very wide range of possibilities where the actual situation may be quite limiting as certain relatives, in-laws, neighbors, and so on, must be taken care of in given order of priority and with respect to fixed quantities and qualities. As previously indicated, this system can engender its own conflicts, quite apart from notions of "theft" as individuals can quibble over what they receive as compared with what they think they deserve, or over the way they are treated during the transaction, or the time it takes before they receive what they think is coming to them. Such conflict, probably endemic in all societies, tends to be among the most minor irritants, usually being expressed in gossip or by deliberate snubbing. It may, however, trigger a sequence of escalated insults which, if not contained, can end in community-splitting acts of violence.

The situation is exacerbated on the level of ranking society by the tendency to convert any act of actual or potential hostility into a threat to status. The potential progression is a real one in some societies: Acts of omission, the failure to give gifts at appropriate junctures, can be interpreted as "stealing" (Scheffler, 1965, p. 86). This, in turn can be treated with great seriousness "as though the offender were saying to the offended, 'You are a man of no account, and I can do as I please with regard to your property'" (Scheffler, 1965, p. 219). Here, Scheffler is discussing stealing, especially misappropriation of garden produce, but the remark seems appropriate to the broader problem. Where the progression goes so far as to threaten to compromise the status of a high-ranking person, the next event could be violent, involving an attempt to kill the offender. As we shall see, there are numerous social baffles operating against such an event.

Especially with reference to theft, it is difficult to proceed further without raising a warning, the long familiar plaint that care be taken to differentiate between societies operating under aboriginal as opposed to postcontact conditions. The concepts of property in aboriginal society are exceptionally subject to alteration upon relatively slight degrees of contact, not to mention such massive encounters as leave in their wake wage employment, cash cropping, money, and an imposed, if only dimly comprehended and unwanted, legal system. Add to this the widespread, if not universal, experience of the encroaching aliens from more complex societies, who find the natives stealing everything they can get their hands on. From the native point of view, of course, what is usually happening is explained either in terms of anticipatory balanced reciprocity or, because the aliens are so far outside their own inner circle, negative reciprocity, which places a premium on divesting the other of what he has while giving minimum return. One result of this is the emphasis placed on theft and its punishment in colonial law codes, and the probably high rate of diffusion of such attitudes into the changing aboriginal society.

Though it has nothing to do with ranking, the fact that ranking societies tend to be more sedentary introduces another source of potential conflict, namely the area which in our own legal culture is known as personal liability. Because few anthropologists have been explicitly interested in legal aspects of the cultures they have studied, few have expressly dealt with the area. Leopold Pospisil's study of the

New Guinea Kapauku is a conspicuous example to the contrary. His treatment of the category is limited to cases of damage inflicted by hunting traps and by domesticated pigs loose in somebody else's garden. Even in Pospisil's unique account of a New Guinea society, the only one that is said to believe in and practice a capitalist economy (Pospisil, 1958, p. 15) and that has a neat little legal system to go with its cherished private property, cases of liability seem at least as likely to end in conflict as in the payment of damages (Pospisil, 1958, pp. 197–200).

Unfortunately, it is impossible, except by inference, to say anything about compliance with decisions rendered in Pospisil's Kapauku judicial system. He relates a few cases in which the defendant absolutely refused to abide by the decision, but in many of the other cases the outcome is merely a statement of the acceptance of the "verdict," with no explicit following up of subsequent events (Pospisil, 1958, p. 272). Of course, even in our own complex and discrete legal system, judgments are not always met; failure to specify actual case dispositions, however, weakens Pospisil's account. This is of considerable theoretical significance, since Pospisil may stand alone among New Guinea ethnographers in claiming that societies at this level know law in their aboriginal state.

Do Rank Societies Have Law?

Apart from Pospisil, ethnographers dealing with rank societies sometimes explicitly deny that these societies operate under an institutional system with the characteristics of law; most, however, do not address themselves directly to the problem, but are often content to describe the system of social control without characterizing it. As an example of the former, Scheffler's characterization of the Choiseulese may be cited: "The single most fundamental fact about Choiseulese society seems to have been that it was without formal juridical institutions" (Scheffler, 1965, p. 180). Yet Oliver, describing a society virtually adjacent to those on

Choiseul, and similar in many structural features, says that "in a descriptive work like this one it seems best to . . . leave it up to the reader, using his own favored terminology, to decide . . . whether a control measure is a 'custom' or a 'law' " (Oliver, 1955, p. 523, n.4).

What is permissible or even desirable for an ethnographic monograph does not necessarily convey advantage to the synthetic work of comparative analysis and generalization. What in any study of a single culture may be a semantic problem becomes the very end of the analytical process in the attempt to generalize about cross cultural and trans-societal regularities.

When we turn to the actual data on conflict resolution in ranking societies, even if Pospisil's Kapauku case record be included, I think it relatively a simple matter to establish the absence of law whether the criteria used be those suggested in Chapter 1, or even those of Pospisil himself (see Chapter 3, pp. 90–1). The most that can be seen in the available illustrations might well be called "law-like" processes of repairing social breaches. Law-like, because one or more of the criteria of law are present and active, yet at the same time one or more of the criteria of law are absent so that, like John Austin more than a century earlier, we can analytically distinguish legal institutions from those that fall short, thereby assisting in discovering what developments go with others in the evolution of general sociocultural systems.

The Siuai of Bougainville, like all other people known to ethnography, whether simple or complex, egalitarian, ranked, stratified or what have you, possess a fairly extensive catalogue of behavioral norms. The Siuai tell ethnographers, and whatever other questing souls may come their way, that this is the way they behave and possibly they do think they behave that way or attempt to behave that way. As Oliver, after often being misled, observes: "deviations from family-household norms are numerous and occur much more frequently than generalizing informants would have us believe" (Oliver, 1955, p. 442). Oliver selects the family-household level because beyond this level social norms are followed with even less regularity and are "maintained . . . with even less *organized* social control than occurs in the case of the family-household" (Oliver, 1955, p. 443, emphasis in original). With regard to all levels of this society, however, the major means of achieving conformity with norms is through indoctrination and continuing ideological reinforcement, particularly of ritual character. On the family-household level there is more power than at any other. But even here the Siuai are unaccustomed to the employment of physical sanctions. Oliver speaks of the native catechist in one village as somebody whose children fear and obey him. He beat them freely when they were small. "He learned this custom when he worked for a white family" (Oliver, 1955, p. 195). Oliver regards the Siuai as, in general, tending to the overindulgence of children; even should one parent tend toward strictness, the other parent would probably compensate by additional leniency. Most attempts at correction are verbal, so often reiterated as to lose significance and rarely if ever accompanied by action.

When all is said and done, Siuai social control rests upon the inculcation of norms which are supported by ritual and the force of public censure and ridicule. Should one faced with such pressures nonetheless breach norms he would face sorcery wielded for vengeance. Siuai *mumi* (big men) are leaders; indeed, Oliver's book is a specialized study of leadership. Leadership in Siuai, as is generally the case in rank society, is a matter of frequencies of initiating behavioral streams as opposed to carrying on a behavioral stream initiated by someone else. Oliver (1955, pp. 331–2) speaks of "orders" and "obeying" but his own examples suggest that the words are too strong for what actually occurs. At the core of a mumi is a generous and popular host whose authority rests on the threat that he will not proffer an invitation. Sahlins describes the "big-man":

the indicative quality of big-man authority is everywhere the same: it is *personal* power. Big-men do not come to office; they do not succeed to, nor are they installed in, existing positions of leadership over political groups. The attainment of big-man status is rather the outcome of a series of acts which elevate a person above the common herd and attract about him a coterie of loyal, lesser men. It is not accurate to speak of "big-man" as a political title, for it is but an acknowledged standing in interpersonal relations—a "prince among men" so to speak as opposed to "The Prince of Danes." In particular Melanesian tribes the phrase might be "man of importance" or "man of renown," "generous rich-man," or "center-man," as well as "big-man" (Sahlins, 1963, p. 289).

In the final analysis, a Siuai big-man exerts whatever authority he has to prevent a serious breach (Oliver, 1955, pp. 443–4) because once such a rupture occurs, it is beyond his power to repair. Fiji, much more structured politically than anything to be found in aboriginal Solomon Islands society, knew similar uncertainty about breach: "Given pervasive rivalry in the village, the private right to secure redress and the chief's only limited command of force, the traditional chief's peace was an uncertain business, depending largely on the willingness of contending parties to adhere to it" (Sahlins, 1962, p. 327).

Precisely the same state of affairs is described for the North Pacific Coast (Drucker, 1965, pp. 74–5). One particular case is recorded in which a chief turned bully and terrorized a village. One man, a "commoner," wanted to kill him because the bully had maliciously destroyed work on which he had lavished considerable time and energy. (The bully was reported to have already committed three murders!) The commoner was dissuaded by others "with great difficulty," but the offending chief "became frightened and moved [away]." He lived elsewhere but occasionally re-

turned to the village in which he had committed his violent
acts; nothing was ever done to him. Drucker concludes:

> there was no formal machinery to punish wrongdoers.
> People did not know quite what to do about the situ-
> ation. They talked against [the offender] and refused
> to cooperate with him, but his rank gave him a certain
> immunity from physical harm. To the advice and pleas
> of his elders he turned a deaf ear. Finally the resent-
> ment became so obvious and unpleasant that thick-
> skinned as he was he had to leave. Informants do not
> know what would have happened to a man of lesser
> rank who behaved [thus]; none ever did (Drucker,
> 1951, p. 319).

The remark about rank conferring immunity from physical
harm does not quite jibe with the rest of Drucker's account
for, as in Siuai and Fiji, the usual means of control is the
counsel and cajolery of kin. Beyond this is public ridicule.
Beyond that, the fear of vengeful sorcery or immediate re-
taliatory violence. Beyond that, nothing. Everything is done
to avert open breaches within the community, especially
between persons contained, as almost all were, within one
or another web of kinship ties—agnatic, cognatic, or affinal.
Again, Drucker has put it well, although others before him
have said the same thing in almost the same words: "In the
rare instances in which blood was shed, usually nothing was
done about it. The group would not take vengeance on itself, nor demand *wergild* of itself, and there was no higher
authority" (Drucker, 1965, p. 74). Drucker goes on to say
that "serious crimes" such as clan incest were punished by
death, but in most societies, including those of this kind,
there is a tremendous gap between the ideology, including
its own reinforcing mythology, and social reality. Drucker's
own account of the Nootka and Chickliset, for example,
states flatly that while such unions were avoided, they
"aroused no feeling of horror" and no adverse social action
seems to have followed marriages, much less temporary sexual unions between close relatives (Drucker, 1951, p. 301).

Probably the outstanding recent attempt to controvert the view so far presented is that of Pospisil. As already indicated, he has undertaken in both comparative and ethnographic study to establish the existence of law as a cultural universal, with his own research among the Kapauku of present day Irian as his primary example. Unlike some other analysts whose assertion of the universality of law is based ultimately upon a definition which makes it coterminous with custom, Pospisil offers a straightforward, clear-cut set of criteria. What is more, Pospisil willingly foregoes the device of the will of the whole community or society, agreeing that "such expressions are virtually identical with a statement of the absence of authority" (Pospisil, 1958, p. 258). If he does not take refuge in such usual qualifications, he does so in a more unusual one, in something akin to what Julian Steward has called "levels of sociocultural integration." For Pospisil there is not one legal system in a given society but a plurality of systems. Indeed, "every functioning subgroup of the society," in his view, "has its own legal system which is necessarily different in some respects from those of other subgroups" (Pospisil, 1958, p. 272).

Pospisil compounds his rejection of law defined as a special emergent system of social control that develops in response to the need to regulate behavior attendant upon the expansion of the community and the declining effectiveness of kinship. Not only does he fragment law so as to make it equivalent to a congeries of partially overlapping, partially discordant value systems, but he is led to the following declaration: "I dare to say that it is inconsistent to make a qualitative distinction between the law of the state and the 'criminal gang's ethics.' Both of these phenomena . . . belong to the same category; both should be classified as laws" (Pospisil, 1958, p. 278).

If it is true that there are as many legal systems in a society as there are subgroups, then every member of the society must be operating simultaneously under multiple conflicting directives. Now, we are fully aware of "double-bind" and similar situations in which individuals do, in fact, face contradictory norms or inducements, but few of these are associated with the terrible paraphernalia of law which ultimately intends the destruction of those who do not conform and possesses the physical means to carry it out and to prevent further vengeance. Pospisil enumerates four criteria of a legal system, but his own case record requires him to dilute each to the point of abandonment. Of 176 "cases" presented in his monograph exactly fifteen were personally observed by him. I have nothing but respect for Pospisil's ethnographic talents and readily grant that he took great pains while collecting stories about other cases to check details with as many informants as possible (Pospisil, 1959, p. 145), but this is one area in which memory may not be the best servant. This is underlined not only by such ethnographies as Oliver's on Siuai (Oliver, 1955, p. 442; see p. 145), which compares the generalizing of informants with what the ethnographer actually observes, but also by examination of the fifteen cases Pospisil recorded on the spot.

Many of the episodes observed and recorded are devoid of even law-like character. Here is one case:

> Imo, a member of the Enona sublineage of Botu, took wood from an old felled *uwaa* tree which grew on the territory of Jamaina sublineage. He was stopped by Jok [headman of Itod] and asked to lay down the wood he was carrying. Since he did not obey, the authority [Jok] knocked the whole pack of wood from his shoulder. A violent argument started which threatened to evolve into a fight. However, the culprit quieted down and left the wood in Itod (Pospisil, 1958, p. 181).

Lest it be thought that I have selected one conspicuously weak "case" upon which to base my criticism, let me present three more in succession. The first involves the same Jok, the headman who was the "authority" in the previous anecdote.

[The "plaintiff"] Mab's father loaned Jok, his daughter's husband, money for buying an additional wife. [Years later] Mab, because he wanted to get married, came to Jok's house to ask for payment. The debtor explained that he had no money on hand and promised to pay in the future. The infuriated young man . . . left with an ultimatum which gave the debtor only three days' time . . . Jok, though a brave warrior and a courageous man who had killed many enemies, strangely enough was scared by the threats of a boy who belonged to a confederacy too weak to fight the political unit of the debtor.

Outcome: Jok collected the necessary shell money and repaid in due time.

Comment: The concern of the debtor can be interpreted as fear of losing face in public because of his violation of the rule (Pospisil, 1958, p. 227).

Ipo was sick and impatient. He ordered his wife around so much that the latter was quite upset. When she was cooking, he shouted at his wife again. Annoyed, she threw a stick into the fire, thus unintentionally scattering some ashes over the meal.

Outcome: The husband beat her with a stick. She wanted to leave him and go back to her village, but later she changed her mind and stayed (Pospisil, 1958, p. 239).

Ama went to . . . visit her parents. Although her husband had reminded her to leave him enough sweet potatoes at home, she had forgotten about it in the excitement.

Outcome: After she returned, she was slapped twice by her husband (Pospisil, 1958, p. 239).

One can only imagine what a jurisprude like Austin might have done with "cases" such as these. Most generously, he would probably have rejected them for their spontaneity and formlessness, which is to say that there is no reason to believe that they would recur in anything like their reported form and Austin would probably have concluded that "the party who will enforce [the same sanction] against any future offender is never determinable and assignable" (Austin, 1954, p. 143). More seriously, such cases make a shambles of Pospisil's own criteria of law. Pospisil dissociates authority and power.[3] While I recognize that the law usually involves authority,[4] I am much more impressed with the role of power. Pospisil, on the contrary, not only strips power from the law but removes formality from authority thus making an authority comprise "one or more individuals who initiate actions in a functional group and whose decisions are followed by a majority of the group's members" (Pospisil, 1958, p. 259). In not one of Pospisil's cases, including those dredged from informants' memories, is there a possibility of showing that the decision, was followed by a majority of the members of the group. In a substantial portion of the cases, as a matter of fact, there is no final disposition beyond a notation of the promise to do something. In additional cases it seems that the disposition of the case is synonymous with its "hearing" interpreted as a scolding for the malefactor. The so-called Kapauku authority has the legal status of the child who led "Our Gang."

In the absence of a volume of genuine cases showing the repetitive application of uniform settlements and penalties, Pospisil establishes "the attribute of intention of universal application" by linguistic criteria. In essence, this attribute is said to be manifest when such usages are employed as is conveyed by the expression "it is always

[3] Once again we come upon a point which has been of much concern in the past; see Carl Friedrich, 1963, pp. 216–31.
[4] "He who believes upon authority, entertains the opinion, simply because it is entertained by a person who appears to him likely to think correctly on the subject" (Lewis, 1849, as quoted in Friedrich, 1963, p. 216).

to the definition of "tribe" offered by E. Adamson Hoebel
(1958, p. 661): "a social group speaking a distinctive language or dialect and possessing a distinctive culture that
marks it off from other tribes. It is not necessarily organized
politically." The definition, when scrutinized, proves to be
a thicket of difficulties. For example, what is meant by the
concept of a "social group"? If a tribe must be a "group,"
as that word has been used as a technical term, all its
members would have to interact or at least participate in
a theoretically interacting structure. Precisely on these
grounds Oliver refuses to classify the Siuai as a tribe. They
do possess a common language but, notes Oliver (1955, p.
103), "They do not all together cooperate . . . in any kind
of common enterprise, nor are they united in any sort of
separate hierarchy." The Siuai do not act together in land
use, are fuzzy about boundaries, intermarry with people
speaking another language, and, as a matter of fact, are
bilingual. All Siuai do not comprise a potentially exclusive
interactive network; what is more, some Siuai interact more
frequently and regularly with some adjacent non-Siuai than
they do with Siuai. Consistent with a terminology of which
he approves, Oliver prefers to consider the Siuai an aggregate rather than a group. It should be made clear, before
the point gets lost, that however a tribe be defined, it should
be in terms of an aggregate and not of a group, although
expectably rare cases may be found in which a true group
exists.

Returning to Hoebel's definition, which I am using for
sake of convenience and not because of any desire to single
him out for criticism, let us confront, albeit briefly, the question of delineating distinctive culture. Apart from considering the problem in terms of social structure, what is at
stake is a question of inventory. Three different focuses
can be induced: First, there is the inventory of trait types,
each trait type being considered a unit without regard to
frequency or functional importance. Second, given parallel
inventories of trait types, units may be differentiated on the

basis of dissimilar frequencies of specific elements. Third, rather than compute total profiles in contrasting frequencies, units may be compared with regard to one or a few traits that have extraordinary significance in one unit but are no great matter in others. In fact, all of these three inventory methods are unsatisfactory for distinguishing ethnic units and equally unsatisfactory for tribes, as Moerman and others have indicated. The problem, seemingly insurmountable when approached in terms of the ethnographic present, becomes ludicrous when treated through history. This is not to say that functions do not exist for a myth of ethnic or tribal purity through time. Like racism, which it resembles and with which it overlaps, tribalism as a mythic structure is a contemporary sociocultural response to contemporary situational stimuli, but this is a matter I discuss later in this chapter.

Another topic can be disposed of at this juncture. Informant statements of tribal self-identification provide no way out of the dilemma, although such statements comprise a valuable body of data that throw much light on other questions of social process. While I do not believe that Edmund Leach invented the point, his exposition of ambiguities of self-identification in *Political Systems of Highland Burma* (1954) has been the point of departure for many statements about alternative identities. Rather than repeat any of the better known examples, I offer one from testimony recorded in the Progress Report to the Legislature by the California Senate Interim Committee on California Indian Affairs:

> Mrs. Morris, Jr., a Hoopa resident of mixed Indian ancestry raised the question of the eligibility of her sons to fish upon their return from overseas service with the armed forces. The following exchange between Mrs. Morris and Princess Brantner, President, Yurok Tribal Organization, Inc., would indicate the complexities involved in the matter of tribal affiliations:

Brantner: "Are you enrolled at the Yurok Tribe?"

Morris: "Well, that is what I would like to know, because my mother was born in the Yurok Tribe."

Brantner: "Well, I said, did you sign up as a Yurok Indian, or did you sign as a Hoopa?"

Morris: "Well, I am just in the middle. I don't know which one to be."

Brantner: "Well, you will have to decide which one you want to be, because there are many of us that are the same. There is a lot of Indians that belong to the Yuroks, that are half Yuroks or half Hoopas, and they have decided they want to be a Yuroks Indian, and some have decided they want to be a Hoopa Indian. Some have decided they want to be from the Smith River Tribe. So right now we have a chance to eat salmon up here—if you want to eat salmon, you better say you're a Yurok and join us" (California, 1955, p. 411).

Because of such difficulties, many anthropologists have seized upon the criterion of linguistic discreteness, which also featured prominently in the sample definition of tribe that we borrowed from Hoebel. Raoul Naroll's summary discussion (Naroll, 1964, pp. 283–91, 306–12) is a useful point of departure: Some ethnic groups, differentiated by name, speak tongues that are regarded by linguists as the same or, what is probably merely another way of putting it, form part of a continuum that cannot be divided for sound linguistic reasons. Of course, such linguistic continua are often divided for other reasons, such as the already held notion that the speech communities are distinct in other aspects. This is interesting, because there are examples of the joining together of two or more different language groups under the rubric of a single tribe. Naroll ends with the warning that "the operational difficulties of applying the linguistic criterion are formidable." Actually, it seems to me that few, if any, ethnographers have systematically examined the linguistic data of their societies toward this end. In this regard some comments by H. H. Vreeland prove illuminating. His work, deeply involved with and related to the production of area handbooks, required the acceptance of sociocultural units, not necessarily tribes. For a long while, Vreeland was satisfied with essentially linguistic criteria for these units, although he was aware of their shortcomings. Now he is less certain of their empirical utility. At least, he has come against cases that do not respond to linguistic handling (Vreeland, 1958, pp. 82–4).

The retreat from overemphasis of a linguistic criterion for tribe or ethnic group is usually coupled with movement toward a common sense group of criteria so manipulated that no single criterion is absolutely essential. Under such procedures, the sets of criteria may vary from case to case, with obvious deleterious effect upon comparability. In the previously mentioned contribution of Naroll, four types of "cultunits" are differentiated at the junctions of two sets of criteria. Naroll's critics have taken issue with him for neglect of specific additional criteria; Frank Bessac wants to add the possession of a common group name; Simon Messing wants to include demographic size of the unit, and so on. Thus it goes, an interesting and useful discussion despite some total disclaimers such as that of Leach (Naroll, 1964, p. 299). Whatever its value in establishing comparable sociocultural units for structuring HRAF-type analyses, however, it tends to drift away from our central concern with the concept of tribe.

More interesting to me at this time is the last element in Hoebel's definition, a disclaimer of the necessity that a tribe be a politically organized body. By this is usually meant that the tribe as a group does not necessarily have a consistent body of sanctions applied by any individual or group to the membership at large, nor is there necessarily any gathering together of the group as a whole or even males sent from each constituent smaller grouping to comprise a military force for offense or defense. According to H. Ian Hogbin and C. H. Wedgewood, this would seem the traditional, not a modern view. They have written:

> The word "tribe" has in the past been used for any large cultural or linguistic group irrespective of whether the component members form a single political unit. Recently, however, the distinction between a large group with an organized political unity, and one whose members are associated only through the possession of a common language and generally similar culture, has been seen to be very important (Hogbin & Wedgewood, 1953, p. 251).

They then cite the definition of tribe given in the most recent edition of *Notes and Queries in Anthropology:* "A tribe may be defined as a politically or socially coherent and autonomous group occupying or claiming a particular territory" (Royal Anthropological Institute, 1951, p. 66). The statement of Hogbin and Wedgewood is not altogether justified, although it is certainly in step with the concept of, for example, *Tribes Without Rulers.* Nevertheless, further along in the same edition of *Notes and Queries* one reads that: ". . . there may be no supreme tribal authority; and the political unity of the tribe emerges only in co-ordinated or collective action, by the more or less independent subdivisions of the group each under its own elders on special ceremonial occasions or in opposition to enemies" (Royal Anthropological Institute, 1951, p. 136). This does not differ too significantly from the definition that appeared in *Notes and Queries* half a century ago: "A group of a simple kind, nomadic or settled in a more or less definite locality, speaking a common dialect, with a rude form of government, and capable of uniting for common action, as in warfare" (Freire-Marreco & Myres, 1912, p. 156). This usage differs from the one, for example, Frederic Seebohm used in his influential study, *The English*

Village Community, in which is identified the Welsh tribe, as a collection of free households united by kinship under a *brenhin,* or chief, the households seeming "to have been grouped into artificial clusters mainly . . . for purposes of tribute or legal jurisdiction" (Seebohm, 1883, pp. 190–1).

The range of this small sampling of definitions is a suitable introduction to the confusion that surrounds this term. But the word "tribe" carries confusion back to its origins. A *tribus* was one of three segments of the Roman patriciate. Each segment was thought to have been a completely autonomous political unit in the past. As far as is known, neither of these conditions applied in ancient Rome: The word "tribe" lacked sociological rigor from its inception.

It was precisely in the dual sense of common descent and autonomous political integration that the concept of tribe was applied by Lewis Henry Morgan to the Iroquois and, indeed, to "the great body of the American aborigines" (Morgan, 1878, p. 103). Rather than dwelling on the seven "functions and attributes" of tribeship described by Morgan as his preliminary to the analysis of the Iroquois examples, and which include such items as the right to invest sachems and chiefs elected by the gentes, and the right to depose them (Morgan, 1878, pp. 114–7), I offer my own list of what I take to be the essence of Morgan's view of the criteria of a tribe: first, the presence of a number of kin units (gentes in his specific view) mutually interconnected by affinal ties; second, possession of a common language.[6] Third, possession and defense of a territory; fourth possession of a name; fifth, possession of a structure of government surmounted by a supreme authority which embodied the popular will. It is, of course, to the last point that we must now direct our attention. First, let us note that Morgan is explicit in identifying the tribe as a "necessary and

----

[6] Morgan actually says: "The exclusive possession of a dialect" (Morgan, 1878, p. 103). He recognizes exceptions but believes that tribe and linguistic unit tend to be coextensive; as he says, "the tribes were as numerous as the dialects" (Morgan, 1878, p. 102).

logical" stage "in the growth of the idea of government" (Morgan, 1878, pp. 102–3).

Treating the tribe as a political structure, Morgan made a uniform analysis of examples from the American Indians, heroic Greece, and formative Rome. To these, Engels added a comparable analysis of the Germans. The crucial political point was believed to lie in the significance of democratic institutions, as in each of these cases ultimate control was believed to rest in some form of popular assembly. In the Iroquois case, it was the famed requirement of unanimous decisions at various levels, so that sachems in the highest council of the confederacy were, at least in theory, merely expressing opinions that had been iterated and approved on levels even lower than the tribal. In the Greek case, it was the *boule;* among the Romans, the *comitia curiata;* and among the Germans, the *Umstand.* Once again, I would like to take the opportunity to note that for better or worse the societies analyzed by Morgan, and. of course, by Friedrich Engels as well, were all subject in particularly strong ways to what may be called the skewing effects of secondary situations. That is, all were undergoing the shift in the complexity of their political institutions in the presence of more highly organized political societies, although in this regard some were more directly and continuously exposed than others, and to stronger or weaker emanating centers. Simply by way of illustration, let me recall for you that Morgan's account of Greek history was dependent to a considerable extent on the work of George Grote (1846–1856). Though disagreeing with Grote on various matters, such as the interpretation of the Grecian gens vis-à-vis the Grecian family, he could not but adopt Grote's view of the age of Greek civilization, to wit, that it began to enter history with the composition of the Homeric poems in the ninth century B.C. or even later, at the time of the first olympiad, in 776 B.C. Curiously silent about developments in Egypt and Mesopotamia, Morgan noted that when the Greeks entered the stage of history they "were striving to establish a state, the first in the experience of the Aryan family, and to place it upon a territorial foundation, such as the state has occupied from that time to the present" (Morgan, 1878, pp. 222–3). *Ancient Society* appeared, of course, in 1877.

Rather than develop a dialogue with the long dead, no matter how important their role in the history of anthropological theory, I prefer to move this discussion into our own century and decade. Let me turn first to the recent work of Carl J. Friedrich (1963). Friedrich specifies the tribes as the second of four levels of government, coming after the local community and preceding the national community and the imperial community. (He also has a provisional fifth, the world community.) Actually, he identifies the "tribe" with the "regional community." As Friedrich sees it, there is often an intermediate level of government between the strictly local community and "the 'all-inclusive' community of nation or empire" (Friedrich, 1963, p. 543). Indeed, he thinks that intermediary levels such as this are "bound" to exist in larger states. What makes this interesting is that he sees the level as being associated with "distinct political institutions," stating that the units on this level may have "a distinctive tribal foundation." As illustration, he gives the Bavarians, Swabians, Saxons, etc., of Germany, noting that the Weimar Constitution began with the phrase, "the German people, united in its tribes" (Friedrich, 1963, p. 543).

Friedrich associates tribalism with "marked linguistic peculiarities, the dialects," also with what he calls "distinctive . . . features of folk culture." For him, tribalism and regionalism seem much the same; this is consistent with his terminology, as previously indicated. This approach suggests certain parallels in the thought of Friedrich and J. H. Steward—parallels that are all the more provocative for being the products of discrete intellectual environments. However, Friedrich is not terribly concerned with technical problems of sociocultural evolution, and he turns instead to the second of the two questions raised at the outset of this discussion. In this regard, he makes several interesting observations, which I shall merely bring to the reader's attention. He sees considerable significance in tribal or regional phenomena in the modern political world. He notes the clashes between different language groups in India and comments that such differences are having much more impact on modern nation building than has older provincial organization. However, he warns against the assumption that a well-drawn linguistic map solves problems of political organization, "because language is only one of the factors entering into community-building" (Friedrich, 1963, p. 544). He pursues a similar point with regard to newly emergent African states, noting that "the effective and traditional African community is the tribe . . . definitely distinguished on the basis of language and other cultural traits." Finally, while Friedrich admits that "tribal units could either be destroyed or employed as the basis of political organization," he does claim for tribes a natural reality, which is to say in his terms that, given "conditions in which the people themselves have a voice in their political association" and given the probable prior dissection or agglomeration of tribal units by the previously dominant colonial power, "they naturally tend to reunite."

If Friedrich is correct, we can expect to find ongoing political activity wherever there is a discrepancy between ethnic boundaries and political boundaries. We must be sophisticated about this. We can readily recognize that ethnic groups are transitory phenomena with variable memberships oscillating about shifting mythic charters. Simultaneously we can recognize that such associations do possess at least contemporary reality and may raise demands that have to be dealt with on the political level. Indeed, reverting to Harold Lasswell's epigrammatic definition of politics —who gets what, when and how—it may be noted that ethnic groups have functioned politically with varying degrees of success and may be expected to continue to do so. What the political situation is in tribal groups will be taken up below.

"Tribe" as a Stage in Political Evolution

Unlike many others who have used the words "tribe" or "tribal," Marshall Sahlins and Elman Service have been precise, clear, and consistent in attempting to apply them to a specific level of sociopolitical development. Like Friedrich, Sahlins and Service identify tribe as a second level of general political evolution. Their first level is that of the band, an explicit community comprising a small population in constant face-to-face interaction, sharing life in a locality, although usually wandering about some restricted range, camping together. Being exogamous, each band must maintain at least some relations of affinality with one or more adjacent counterparts, but these gossamer ties do not constitute any significant alteration of the independent nature of the group. (Note that bands are groups in the narrowest sense proposed above.)

The distinctive thing about a tribe in Service's view is that it must be more than *"simply* a collection of bands" (Service, 1962, p. 111). The increment of difference is found in his analysis of tribes as a boundable system of relationships whose armatures, the devices connecting the members of the component polar bands, are sodalities, cross-cutting associations devoted to kinship affiliations, age-grades, secret societies, ritual congregations, and ceremonial parties. Like bands, Service's tribes are characterized by embedded political structuring, since the major institutions of social control are distributed throughout the sociocultural fabric and are carried out through available roles and statuses, none of which are specialized for governmental functions. Since Service's tribe, as defined, is an exceptionally fragile structure, he looks to its superorganic environment for the stimulation to its development and maintenance. The *raison d'être* of a tribe is conflict, basically for scarce resources. Tribalism extends the peace group; it also presents military possibilities that Service believes superior to those available to bands (Service, 1962, pp. 113–15). Without retracing the steps of his reasoning, we note that it is consistent with the foregoing when Service boldly identifies the emergence of tribal society with the neolithic revolution. Sahlins agrees:

> The tribal level may have emerged in a few exceptionally favorable environments in the food-collecting, Paleolithic era. However, it was the Neolithic Revolution that ushered in the *dominance* of the tribal form, that precipitated great sectors of the cultural world to a new level of general standing (Sahlins, 1961, p. 324).

Unfortunately, and I say unfortunately because the Sahlins-Service argument seems very elegant to me, the arrangement of band and tribe in a general evolutionary sequence of forms leaves much to be desired. It seems possible, for example, to place both on the same temporal level and level of complexity, with the band representing the semipermanent membership group sharing a common camp, and the tribe constituting the shifting grouping of camps (that is, bands) that comprises an area of relative peace and that would include a demonstrably high frequency of intermarriage. In other words, it seems to me that Service has not justified his statement that a tribe must be more than simply a set of bands, for if that is the case, his band societal level becomes semantic and somewhat hypothetical, like Steward's family level. As Steward puts it,

> I classify the Shoshoneans as an exemplification of a family level of sociocultural integration because in the few forms of collective activity the same group of families did not cooperate with one another or accept the same leader on successive occasions. By another definition, however, it might be entirely permissible to view this ever-changing membership and leadership as a special form of suprafamilial integration. While the Shoshoneans represent a family level of sociocultural integration in a relative sense, their suprafamilial pat-

tern involved no permanent social groups of fixed membership despite several kinds of interfamilial cooperation (Steward, 1955, p. 109).

It requires very few alterations to convert that into a parallel statement about tribes conceived in the Sahlins-Service sense. What is more, we have their repeated assurances that tribes by their structural nature involve, to paraphrase Steward, no permanent social groups of fixed membership, despite several kinds of interband cooperation. Sahlins is explicit about this: "a tribe will automatically return to the state of disunity—local autonomy—and remain there when competition is in abeyance" (Sahlins, 1961, p. 326). This suggests, of course, that tribe in this conception is one form of a series comprising a cycle, rather like the cycle of family forms that have been described in certain societies, and thus is not an aspect of any general evolutionary process as has been defined elsewhere by Sahlins and Service (Service, 1960a, pp. 747–63).

Actually, Sahlins seems to have some doubts about this very point but his resolution of the problem has been far from satisfactory:

> In comparison with groupings of intermarrying bands, pantribal social institutions are perhaps the most indicative characteristic of tribal society. Such institutions clearly demarcate the borders of a tribe, separating it as a social (and ethnic) entity. Intermarrying bands may carry a vague sense of tribalism—as in Australia—but as dialect shades off into dialect and customs change gradually from band to band, no one can say where one so-called "tribe" ends and another begins. This is a clearly less integrated condition than that of tribalism properly so-called (Sahlins, 1961, p. 343, *n*.3).

As we have already indicated, the ethnographic record does not support this view. Boundaries separating tribes are no clearer than those separating bands; indeed, they cannot be clearer, for to the extent that bounding mecha-

nisms exist, they are precisely the same for band and tribe.
Purely by way of illustration, let me cite P. Brown and
H. C. Brookfield to the effect that the Chimbu (New
Guinea) "tribes" in the pre-European period were "unstable
. . . composed of shifting alignments of clans, phratries
and parts of phratries" (Brown & Brookfield, 1959, p.
46). While otherwise according very well with Sahlins'
conception of a tribe, it is patent that tribal borders need
not be more clearly demarcated than band borders. Actually, most so-called tribes seem at close range to be curious
melanges rather than homogeneous units. Here, for illustrative purposes, a sample from the Philippines:

> The name "Kalinga" is an Ibanag word meaning
> "enemy," and was widely used in Spanish times for
> mountain peoples adjacent to the lower and middle
> Cagayan valley . . . the upper Saltan communities ad-
> jacent to Abra show strong marks of Tinguian infiltra-
> tion, and the Tinglayan communities adjoining the Bon-
> tok higher up the Chico are transitional to that ethnic
> type. Yet there is still much to be learned about the
> congeries of people classed under the Kalinga rubric.
> . . . Spanish writers . . . used a variety of district and
> ethnic names in characterizing the Kalinga groups.
> Beyer, in his 1917 survey of the Philippine population,
> was led to say, "[They consist] of several distinct peo-
> ples who are now so exceedingly mixed in physical
> type, language, and culture that it is difficult if not im-
> possible in the state of our present knowledge to sepa-
> rate the constituent groups and define their distinguish-
> ing characteristics" (Keesing, 1962, pp. 221–3).

To which Roy F. Barton added this amen: "As Professor
Beyer has said, the Kalinga tribe is an ethnological hodge-
podge" (1949, p. 13). It is precisely because tribal units are
ill defined that we have the ongoing discussion mentioned
earlier in which anthropologists seek stable and repetitively
useful criteria for ethnic groupings.

  While the remarks of Beyer, Barton, and Keesing are

still before us, so to speak, I would like to abstract three generalizations from the sector they illuminate. First, with regard to so-called "tribal" names, it is a commonplace that such names are often derived from two particularly frequent sources: from a designation applied to a population by outsiders, or from a word equivalent to the concept "person" or "human being." I would like to argue, although I cannot substantiate the point now, that such names are proteanly flexible through space and time and probably have always varied situationally as well.

Second, if residence is relatively stable, particularly among peoples with agricultural subsistence bases (although we note the significance of swiddenage as an incentive to a certain physical mobility), the agglomeration of units into what have been called "tribes" is likely to have been very variable. Given a series of settlements or camps, there has been a tendency in ethnography to assume that the synchronically observed pattern of agglomeration represents a reality transcending time, whereas diachronic observation might well have revealed shifting assortments.

Third, there seems to be a widespread tendency among anthropologists to assume prior conditions of purity and homogeneity whenever the data indicate a later situation of heterogeneity. Actually, putting it this way fails to bring out all of the gratuitous assumptions usually associated with this view. An analogy from human paleontology will be useful: Fossil populations like that found at Skhul or in the upper cave at Chouk'outien have usually been interpreted as the result of the fusion of previously discrete pure racial elements. Similarly, with regard to such societies as the Kalinga, it is often assumed that the heterogeneous condition they display could only be the product of modern conditions, and efforts are made to separate them into their pristine constituents. It seems more likely that, apart from certain conspicuous elements derived from modern societies, the heterogeneity of these societies is a relative matter that should go back into time, shifting with changes in associational alignments, microecological changes, and so on. Incidentally, this point of view is compatible with the new archaeology and its emphasis on statistical rather than archetypal site profiles; it is less inclined to view cultural changes as the result of migrations with seemingly recurrent genocide and is more inclined to accept migration as a more or less constant factor in human history, shifting the emphasis to the containment of the migrants and their novelties.

To retreat to the Sahlins-Service view of tribes once more, I should like to say a few more words about tribe as a way-station between band and state in the evolution of political organization. As we have already seen, the tribe and the band do not differ with regard to boundaries and distinctiveness of character as much as Sahlins and Service would like. But apart from this, there is, at least in Sahlins' work, the explicit recognition of what can only be called the "unprogressive nature" of the tribe as he defines it. This I take to be the significance of the finding that tribes as political structures are *ad hoc* responses to ephemeral situations of competition. It is the chiefdom, the next stage visualized by Sahlins and Service, that bears the weight of evolutionary advance, for it genuinely bridges a previous level of organization, the acephalous society, with the state. But, as Sahlins and Service imply, tribes and chiefdoms are not the same thing.

It may seem as if the tribe is a necessary construct for logical reasons, if for no other. How else can the gap be bridged that lies between the discrete autonomous settlement and the nation-state? It was reasoning such as this, for example, that led Steward to deal with "tribal society" as a level of sociocultural integration, one that he believes overlaps Robert Redfield's "folk society" construct. Yet Steward, too, recognizes that the tribal designation is unusually difficult to explicate. "It is significant," he says, "that the term 'tribal society' remains an exceedingly ill-defined catchall" (Steward, 1955, p. 53). Indeed, in the same paper

Steward was inclined to define "tribes" in terms of a group of negative traits, in terms of the lack of state organization, absence of classes, absence of literacy, and so on; he also offers the opinion that "there are *no* features shared by tribes that are common to all mankind" (Steward, 1955, p. 44), by which I assume he means that there are no specific positive features common to all tribes.

In fact, there is no absolute necessity for a tribal stage as defined by Sahlins and Service, no necessity, that is, for such a stage to appear in the transit from a single settlement with embedded political organization, to a complex state-structured polity. Such a developmental process could have gone on within a unit that we may conceptualize as a city-state, such a unit as Jericho might have become in its later stages or as villages became cities in Mesopotamia, India, China, and elsewhere.

"Tribes" as Secondary Phenomena in Political Evolution

While being bold, I shall go on to say that most tribes seem to be secondary phenomena in a very specific sense: They may well be the product of processes stimulated by the appearance of relatively highly organized societies amidst other societies which are organized much more simply. If this can be demonstrated, tribalism can be viewed as a reaction to the formation of complex political structure rather than a necessary preliminary stage in its evolution.

Whatever be the truth about this problem, it is already abundantly clear that there are important social aggregates usually called "tribes" that have nothing to do with anything I have said so far. These are the "tribes," so-called, that spring up in colonial situations. One of the most illuminating examples I have found is that presented by Elizabeth Colson in her study of the Makah Indians of the Northwest Coast.

In eighty years, the entity of the Makah Tribe has been created from the descendants of the formerly independent villages about the Cape Flattery region. . . . It was undoubtedly their common residence at Neah Bay and their status as Indians and wards of the government *vis-à-vis* the Indian agency which created the tribe from the former independent villages . . ." (Colson, 1953, p. 79).

The story is somewhat more complex than this and skillfully analyzed. What it amounts to is a tribe created by governmental action, its members showing considerable diversity in culture, language, and in physical type (Colson, 1953, p. 87).

The Makah represent a kind of limiting case, since they exhibit the scrambling of all the categories normally implied in a discussion of "tribe." The significant point, however, is not their diversity, but the means by which they became organized. Colson describes the Plateau Tonga of Northern Rhodesia in similar terms:

In a sense it is probably false to regard the Tonga as a definite group or real unit which is set off by definite criteria from other peoples . . .

Today the Tonga exist within one political unit, the Plateau Tonga Native Authority, but this is of recent origin and due to circumstances beyond their control. Government has placed them within the bounds of a single administrative district and has organized them into [seventeen] chieftaincies . . . [which] represent Government policy and convenience, and not cultural, linguistic, or political distinctions among the Tonga themselves (Colson, 1951, pp. 95–6).

Rather than press the extreme view that all contemporary tribes are the result of contemporary political and economic forces, I conclude by taking the more moderate view developed by May Edel in a posthumously published paper.

As she sees it: ". . . however much tribal affiliation and identification may enter, the issues and conflicts of today are rooted in problems and social interactions of today, and are not just atavisms rooted in some pre-existent past and continuing on a momentum of traditionalism" (Edel, 1965, pp. 358–9). She quotes the much-cited work of A. L. Epstein: "Intertribal relations on the Copperbelt . . . and the cleavages within political organizations along tribal lines, cannot be explained simply as vestiges from a tribal past which have survived into the present. On the contrary, they reflect processes at work within the urban social system" (Edel, 1965, p. 359, from Epstein, 1958, p. 239). She also summarizes her view of M. Gluckman's position which comes to much the same thing, although I would be less charitable and say that Gluckman's position strikes me as being variable (cf. Gluckman, 1960, pp. 55–70; 1965). Confusion seems to predominate in one of his most recent treatments, where he states that, "basic to a tribal society is the egalitarian economy, with relatively simple tools to produce and primary goods to consume. The powerful and wealthy use their might and goods to support dependents; for they are unable to raise their own standards of living with the materials available" (Gluckman, 1965, p. xv). Gluckman's attached list of tribes includes the Bushmen and the Eskimo as well as Nuba and Dahomey (Gluckman, 1965, pp. xv–xx). He also applies the term "tribal" to Scots, Welsh, Irish, French, Jewish, Lebanese, and African denizens of British towns on the ground that they "have their own associations, and their domestic life is ruled by their own national (sic) customs insofar as British law and conditions allow" (Gluckman, 1965, p. 292).

Like Colson viewing the Makah and the Tonga, Edel described Chiga tribalism as a condition of response to contemporary stimuli:

> For such a people as the Chiga, whatever sense of ethnic unity they possess can only be an emergent one, a response to experiences of the recent past. For the

Chiga as I knew them in the nineteen-thirties had no "tribal" unity whatsoever . . . The only sense of common Chiga identity came from a common rejection of alien overlordship (Edel, 1965, pp. 368–9).

I do not believe that there is theoretical need for a tribal stage in the evolution of political organization. Such a stage explains nothing but does divert attention from more important questions: How does ranking begin and how does it undergo adaptive radiation? How does stratification get its start, and how does it catalyze societies? How does it reinforce itself, and what are its effects on other societies? These questions, it seems to me, do not necessarily involve tribalism. Indeed, if I read the evidence correctly, tribalism is an evolutionary cul-de-sac, part of a spasmodic cycle that in and of itself lacks the institutional raw materials capable of leading to more complex forms of polity.

It seems to me that the so-called "tribal" groups to which I have so far turned my attention (and I admit the smallness and inadequacy of the "sample") are not social organizations whose integrity recedes into a remote past. Rather, there are clues indicating that the tribalism displayed is a reaction to more recent events and conditions. That such tribalism can be made to play a major political role in a real present is not a modern discovery. Long before recent European colonialism, not to say neocolonialism, the Roman, the Chinese, and other expanding state societies had grasped the essentials of divide and rule. What is more, in the relations between these states and simpler organized societies it was understood, within the complex cultures, that effective manipulation demands a certain minimum of organization within those simple societies. There have been examples in which "tribes" have been consciously synthesized to advance a scheme of external political control. It is not beyond belief that groups within former colonial powers would consciously or unconsciously do whatever they could to create and maintain factionalism.

Having completed this critical synopsis of a group of classical and current theories about probable events and transitional institutions in the evolution of political society, from acephalous conditions to chieftaincy, we turn to an alternative view and consider the emergence and evolution of the rank society from an egalitarian base. Let us first consider rank societies as units viewed, so to speak, from the outside. What, for example, is the composition of the social groups that they comprise?

Groups

While a completely definitive statement must await an exhaustive check of the entire literature, my own spotty sample reveals considerable uniformity. Most rank societies are strongly based on villages. However, the conspicuous feature is that the largest continuously functional unit and the village tend to be congruent. While there are supra-village aggregates, the village is essentially autonomous, and significant agglomeration is either rare or quite transient. The major qualifications appear to be two. Where a more complex political society has encapsulated the rank society, there is often a formal policy of enlarging villages by incorporating a number of previously discrete groups into a single administrative unit within which extensive interaction is strongly encouraged. The other qualification has to do with a certain kind of environmental situation that happens to pertain in a significant portion of all ethnographically known rank societies, that is, many of these societies tend to be on relatively small islands. Although various barriers may interfere with movement on land, distances are short and the lagoon or the sea offers a more rapid means of communication. Where this landscape occurs, there seems to be a higher degree of intervillage integration than is the case elsewhere. The title of Firth's book, *We, the Tikopia,* is instructive. The phrase translates a Tikopia saying; moreover, there is no doubt that in the sense urged by Oliver the Tikopia form a group, albeit a secondary group ultimately linked through the relations among their chiefs (Firth, 1959, p. 257). The consciousness of being Tikopia should not obscure the functionally more significant identification of villages as the largest effective social groups in that society.

Territoriality

A Siuai returned from laboring in New Guinea gold fields told Oliver that his own Siuai landscape was great and asked how anybody with sense could want to live elsewhere (Oliver, 1955, p. 104). Such feeling of identification with a whole region is rare in Siuai, as it is rare throughout rank society. As just noted, the village is usually the largest effective social group, and it is the land associated with this group that tends to be the largest expanse which people regard as theirs to have, hold, and struggle over.

Since rank society is associated with domestication or with the exploitation of rather concentrated resources, such as fish-rich streams, it is also associated, as we have seen, with greater demographic density. As a further consequence, even though productive regimes by no means simultaneously exploit the total territory in intensive fashion, the gross size of the territory tends to be very much smaller than the enormous ranges within which the simple egalitarians wander and camp. Another concomitant is the sharper bounding of the area believed to be associated with the residential group. This matter of boundaries and the identification of a specific group with a specific territory can be grossly overdone. In Tikopia, for example, there has been considerable physical mobility, many persons move from natal villages to others where they cultivate gardens on land turned to their use by cognatic or affinal relatives. This represents a departure from the normal continuity of viripatrilocality, but is too frequent to be merely a deviation. What is more, as Firth's restudy of Tikopia indicates, membership in the four locality crosscutting clans was much more widely dispersed in 1952 than in 1929. There was a process of clan dispersion under way that might ultimately turn all Tikopia into precisely the kind of group that was mentioned earlier (Firth, 1959, p. 201). This process was encouraged by the underlying egalitarianism in usufruct that enables individuals to share land access with those whose strict genealogical title should exclude them. The curious thing is that this is going on in Tikopia just as the island is experiencing what may be its most serious population crisis ever, an increase from some 1,300 to 1,750 people, a matter of 35 per cent in less than twenty-five years. Although such an increase is quite modest compared with areas experiencing rates in excess of 2.5 per cent a year, Tikopia is a tiny island that was already pushing its resources in 1929. In times past population was held in balance by various things, including infanticide and natural disaster, but some reliance seemed to be placed upon war, with the people of a defeated village not only being driven from their site but from Tikopia, perhaps to perish at sea during a journey to nowhere (Firth, 1961, pp. 129–39). With the older violent solutions being refused to the Tikopia by impinging external government and by missionaries, it would seem that much of the interstitial area is being slowly filled. Actually, part of the immediate solution is already discernible in changes in the social pattern; if they continue, Tikopia will drop from the lists of rank societies and become stratified and a more integral part of the externally supplied state organization than it is at present.

The vagueness of the association between some rank villages and their territories is reflected in ethnographies from geographically separated areas. Without going into much detail, one additional example may be given from Africa, particularly because the work done by Colson among the Tonga of Nothern Rhodesia has shown outstanding concern for this particular problem. She says, "In a sense a village does not even exist as a territorial unit, though it has a spatial distribution" (Colson, 1951, p. 119). The distinction is a nice one and very important. The fact is that in this Tonga society, as in most rank societies, the concept of title, of legally specific ownership, is absent. A population, with its ranked head, is associated with area but, "In former days a headman and his people could not prevent a strange village from coming to settle nearby unless they resorted to force" (Colson, 1951, p. 119). Newcomers might appropriate bush by what amounted to squatting or they might go through the motions of discovering the original user and ask the right to use it from him. It is worth remarking that Tonga village headmen are described by Colson as leaders whose effectiveness rests upon prestige and authority rather than force and privileged access to sanctions. Of great interest is the observation that the headman and only the headman is considered to have everybody in his village as his following. His name and the village name are the same (Colson, 1951, p. 115), indeed, "the position of the headman . . . apparently establishes the identity of the village and differentiates it from other groups of like nature" (Colson, 1951, p. 116). Despite this, "the headman cannot allot land, for he possesses none save that which he has cleared himself" (Colson, 1951, p. 119).

I stress the fact that the intensive study of ethnographies is an occupation that immediately produces staggeringly variable detail. While some societies handle land tenure matters more or less like the Tonga, others show great variation. The compendiums of principles underlying land tenure in various colonial regions testify clearly about this matter. Nonetheless, two factors can be discerned to appear in a multitude of guises. The underlying egalitarian economy in rank society drastically limits the power of those in high-ranking statuses to manage the distribution of usufructory rights to strategic property. Beyond this, however, the ranking system itself not only is one of the templates of local organization but offers a potent means of linking discrete communities. It usually does so not merely by reinforcing existing kin ties of various kinds, but by channeling these kin relations and setting them within an implicitly hierarchical structure. Viewed metaphorically in terms of process rather than as a frozen level of organization, the ranking system has great potential for the presentation of a societal skeleton upon which the musculature and specialized organic development of stratification can grow.

External Polity

At the risk of being querulous, I must again take issue with Service for his finding that the "external polity of tribes is usually military only" (Service, 1962, p. 114). To the extent that this remark covers what I designate as rank societies, it seems misleading, although I hasten to agree with Service that rank societies tend to be combative, that many of them exist in what may be seen as a chronic state of war, and that terror and psychological warfare are common means of maintaining group integrity in the face of competition for survival. I suspect, but cannot prove, although I hope others will subject this hypothesis to severe test, that this aspect of rank society has temporal and ecological dimensions. Briefly, I think that it should be possible to find a significant statistical correlation between the intensity and frequency of martial orientations in rank society and pressure of populations on resources. Apart from this, however, it is necessary to recall that most rank societies engage with equal or greater frequency in other intercommunity activities, most notably in feasts, parties, ceremonies, and other events predicated upon organized hospitality. It is in the conduct of such events that ranking reaches its apogee as the effective organizer of the population. Warfare produces nothing like it in rank societies, even when the manifest purpose of the conflict is to protect a specific ranked individual or group.

So much has already been said about the role of great feasts in rank society that I can be brief in this treatment. We begin with an example, drawn deliberately from the account of certain districts in the eastern highlands of Australian New Guinea. The source is a work of Ronald Berndt, an interesting analysis of warfare and social control. Precisely because the stress is laid on war and because of the extended discussion of torture, cannibalism, and other acts of terror, Berndt's treatment offers strong support to the Service contention mentioned above. Yet, without belittling the significance of military postures among these people, we can indicate that actual periods of hostilities are brief, "Few interdistrict fights last longer than two or three days" (Berndt, 1962, p. 235). Though "potential hostility from members of other districts is part of the normal process of living" (Berndt, 1962, p. 240), the periods between overt clashes are of much greater duration, so that it seems possible to say that this society, in a sense oriented around war, is generally in a state of actual peace.

While war is irregular in spacing and concentrates little energy, major intervillage ceremonials are comparatively regular, require long periods of elaborate preparation, and play a significant role in regulating the general economy of participating villages. In one district studied, activities that culminate in a great pig festival span a period of almost six years with the final six months being extraordinarily active ones. Not only a mountain of food must be assembled, but also sufficient quantities of firewood, water, leaves, and other essentials of the feast. Perhaps the two most important tasks are the raising of the pigs and the delivery of invitations to surrounding villages and districts. Quite apart from the feasting and distribution at the formal ceremony, the arrangements negotiated from village to village to solicit loans and contributions represent a major portion of the ties binding discrete villages into a wider-ranging, if loose, social system. While hostilities might follow such a feast, they are customarily suspended during the six months of intensive preparation (Berndt, 1962, p. 64). At the actual distribution, lineage headmen, as a group, act as hosts and call in turn the names of districts and lineages to receive food. Hearing the name, "the headman or warrior leader" comes to get his share, dancing, and returns to his group where his younger brothers take the meat back to their own village. Incidentally, from Berndt's own accounts of warfare it would seem that the term "warrior leader" is inappropriate since the leadership qualities are not pronounced. Instead, these individuals seem better indicated by such a phrase as "outstanding warriors" (*cf.* Berndt, 1962, pp. 174–5).

Perhaps the best known ceremonies of the general type described are those formerly carried out among the Indians of the North Pacific Coast. Although it is now established that the climactic, tremendously elaborated potlatch was a product of European contact and trade-borne wealth, the early potlatch, though less sumptuous performed similar functions (Codere, 1950, p. 94). The structure of the potlatch was such that it simultaneously expressed the rank structure of all relationships, both between villages and within villages, and served as a device for organizing discrete villages into overlapping economic networks (Codere, 1950, pp. 64 ff.; Drucker, 1965, pp. 56–66, 127). Describing Tsimshian mortuary potlatches, Drucker conveys all the familiar points. Preparations, primarily the stocking of foods and gift items, took a year or more and required the host village to solicit aid of various kinds from near and distant villages. Invitations were sent and required smaller ritual occasions when presented and accepted. Although the usual Northwest Coast procedure was to treat high rank first, the Tsimshian went from low to high rank in making presentations. In any case, the affair was saturated in ritual commemoration of rank differences.

Potlatching has been called "fighting with property" and could lead to out-and-out fights. Apart from the metaphor, or what might be the results of a local inability to respond to crushingly lavish hospitality, the potlatch represented a peaceful activity. It brought out the highest development of administrative abilities in the societies concerned. In this respect it differed sharply from war that was carried out in much less organized fashion.

Warfare

Although rank societies tend to be warlike for the reasons previously indicated, the degree to which intergroup relations are settled with violence varies considerably. As I put it earlier, there may be a correlation between frequency of intergroup violence and density of settlement. I think that a somewhat less direct relationship exists between the significance of ranking and the amount of warlike activity. Some information on the relationship has been presented by A. P. Vayda (1956, pp. 2, 222 ff.) in the context of Polynesian ethnology. The Maori, whom I would treat as representative of simple ranking, are characterized as having warfare small in scale, brief, with relative absence of command and discipline. The model of Maori military organization, to the extent that one can find it organized, is, like that of the equally simple Pukapuka society, based upon existing kin and village structure (*cf.* Beaglehole, 1938, pp. 373–4; Fried, 1961, pp. 141–5). On the other end of the continuum, in the more complex ranking societies and stratified societies of Polynesia, such as those of the Society Islands and Hawaii, warfare is more thoroughly organized.

A similar picture is presented by the situation in the North Pacific Coast region. The highest development of ranking occurs among the Nootka and Kwakiutl and the societies in their part of the area. Military sophistication also increases as one moves into that area. Unlike the situation, for example, in the New Guinea Highlands, observed by Berndt, where outstanding warriors are simply those who are individually strong, crafty, and fearless, but who have no visible command functions, the Nootka had some specialization of military function. There was a commander-in-chief, tactical splitting of parties for flanking or other maneuvers, and the employment of sentinels and scouts.

Despite this, discipline was poor with no provisions for replacing a fallen commander while still in combat. Drucker notes that, "the lack of succession of command . . . caused attacking forces to withdraw when on the verge of victory because of the loss of their commander" (Drucker, 1951, p. 341). This may be compared with Vayda's comment about the Maori: "Even when on the verge of victory, an attacking force might withdraw because of the loss of a leader" (Vayda, 1960, p. 26).

Perhaps the most important question for the present inquiry has to do with the relation between military prowess and political position. It has been held quite frequently and by some of the major thinkers in sociology that political status originated in either religious or military roles and of these the latter are often adjudged the more significant since they appear to convey intrinsic physical power that can be used to sanction the behavior of others. But as has already been indicated, the military organization of rank societies is but a partial utilization of the pre-existing kin and community structure. If a direction must be found in the developmental sequence, it would seem that significant military leadership status depends upon prior general status. The leading possible exception to this is in a society where war leaders are distinct from peace leaders. Yet where such a division exists it rarely develops that the war leader enlarges his sphere of influence at the expense of the peace leader (cf. Drucker, 1951, p. 343). When he does, there will usually be special circumstances, the most common being the impinging of a more complexly organized society.

FROM EGALITARIAN TO RANK SOCIETY

The question has long been a favorite one: Why have people permitted themselves to be seduced, bilked, murphied, or otherwise conned into relinquishing a condition of egalitarianism for one of inequality? The question, of course, is loaded, not only politically but culturally. Apart from being biased, however, the question is wrong in its implication that individuals faced a conscious choice and selected the alternative of rank society. I believe that the evidence is quite to the contrary and that events conceived retrospectively as cataclysmic actually passed without notice until they were fully accomplished. Rank society grew out of egalitarian society without the conscious awareness of the members of the society in which it occurred; I believe that stratified society and the state emerged in the same quiet way and were institutionally fully present before anyone fumbled for a word by which to designate them.

In the move from egalitarian to rank society, the first thing to note is the persistence of the main frame of economic relations. In terms of access to the things necessary to maintain life, equality is retained. Standards of living, even with regard to items beyond subsistence, are also generally equal. The outstanding differences are essentially based upon varying increments of prestige and upon the hierarchical ordering of status positions.

What would lead to the narrowing and institutionalization of positions of rank? Undoubtably there are many circumstances involved: problems of maintaining connections between parent settlements and those that have budded off; possibilities of diversifying the consuming sector of the economy by maintaining regular trade relations with communities exploiting somewhat different resources; the possibility of better handling of food supply by organizing special labor forces for simple irrigation tasks; rationalization of a sequence of habitation in which original settlers are joined, albeit peaceably, by subsequent settlers; the formalization, as Service has pointed out, of trans-settlement sodalities, often as a means of enlarging the area of relative peace. These are but a few of the more obvious and probably most widespread stimuli to the emergence of ranking.

If I had to select the two most significant factors, I would choose ecological demography and the emergence of redistribution. These have already been analyzed at the beginning of this chapter; a more detailed investigation is not attempted here. Neither of these factors, of course, comes out of the blue. Both stem from an underlying revolution in the relations between man and environment, expanding and stabilizing subsistence. Once accomplished, rank society is quite durable but as we already know and now must investigate, there are circumstances under which further developments occur which introduce a much more fundamental kind of inequality. This is the stratified society.

CHAPTER 5

Stratified Societies

Of the several types of societies discussed in this book, that called the "stratified" society is the most difficult to illustrate with ethnographic examples. That is to say, stratified societies lacking political institutions of state level are almost impossible to find, although the stage of stratification-without-stateship must have occurred several times in the evolution of complex political and economic organization.[1] The cause of this rarity is not difficult to isolate. Once stratification exists, the cause of stateship is implicit and the actual formation of the state is begun, its formal appearance occurring within a relatively brief time. Justification of this statement is the task of the present chapter. The main argument can be stated

---

[1] The actual road to the state is variable. All states did not have to go through a stage of stratification-without-stateship. But each pristine state certainly had to traverse this stage or level.

briefly. The maintenance of an order of stratification demands sanctions commanding power beyond the resources of a kinship system, which is adequate for the purposes of egalitarian and even rank society as the previous chapters have shown. By differentially distributing access to basic means of livelihood and by simultaneously making possible the exploitation of human labor in the conventional Marxist sense, stratified societies create pressures unknown in egalitarian and rank societies, and these pressures cannot be contained by internalized social controls or ideology alone. Furthermore, the pressures are usually exacerbated by the transformation, attenuation, or destruction of kin relationships in the stratified society, thus making it unlikely, to say the least, that kinship relations will provide a universal means of social control and adjudication within the society. But these remarks run ahead of the analysis; let me return to the definition of stratification.

A stratified society is one in which members of the same sex and equivalent age status do not have equal access to the basic resources that sustain life. It seems both convenient and tactically wise to consider the basic resources[2] of a society in an ecological context and therefore to some extent relative rather than absolute. Thus, different societies may be said to have different basic resources, the variation being due to differences in geographical environment, technological equipment, and what may be called the historically determined perception of the exploitable environment. For example, few American Indian cultures of the Plains regions drew any portion of their subsistence from the rivers that flowed through the areas in which they farmed or hunted and it would be pointless to consider riparian resources in any way basic. Conversely, other American Indian cultures, such as the Yurok of California, did derive part of their subsistence by river fishing, and access to

---

[2] I have elsewhere (Fried, 1957, p. 24) defined "strategic resources" in essentially similar terms. The present term "basic resources" seems closer to the mark.

those waters would have to be considered as access to a basic resource. Elsewhere, the raw materials for making tools and weapons may be limited to stands of wild bamboo, fortuitously distributed stones, or deposits of ore. Similarly, in the simplest situations water is a basic resource only for drinking purposes, but in more complex situations it may be basic to agricultural production, to the generation of power, or to the carrying off of wastes. Though our analysis does not carry through to highly organized political systems dependent upon the most complex technologies, it can be expanded to include them. In some instances, particularly in our discussion further on of recent types of state formation, the flexible nature of the concept of basic resources is advantageous.

It should be emphasized that our concept of basic resources refers to what might be considered capital rather than consumer goods. Central are the things to which access must exist in order for life to be maintained for the individual. Given those things, or, better, given unrestricted access to those things, anyone can manage his own support, particularly given a domestic division of labor. We are less interested in such actual consumables as food itself, or specific tools, than in the ultimate source of food and the raw materials from which tools are fashioned. Accumulations of harvested food supplies and stockpiles of tools in a primitive society confer only limited and transitory advantage. Storage and preservation facilities for the former are lacking and overaccumulation of the latter might be disadvantageous where survival depends on mobility. The most obvious and efficient means of investing supplies beyond consumption is to give them away, establishing a pattern of exchange, and this fits the model we have discussed. It is possible, however, for individual accumulation of consumables to occur. In addition to having only transitory character, such accumulation is an explicitly antisocial act, fostering hostility. It is interesting that in prestratified societies individuals or families hoarding food in famines must move away from their less fortunate neighbors to enjoy their advantage, because if they remain in association with the destitute there is no way to avoid their demands. This behavior should be compared with that displayed in stratified societies in similar circumstances. Shortages raise prices, and profiteers withhold essential commodities unless their prices are met. The actions taken by complex governments to establish war or emergency price and rationing controls confirm this distinction, as does the reality of the black market.

Dangerous deprivation of individuals in nonstratified societies usually does not occur until there is a sharp reduction in the standard of living of all. All individuals physically capable of securing food can attempt to do so for there are no barriers between them and the basic resources. Where stratification, in the sense in which the term is used in this book, does not exist, each individual, bound only by such division of labor as accords with age and sex, has unimpaired access to the raw materials of survival. In stratified societies there are impairments in the way of access; they can be exceptionally diverse but can be reduced to two very broad categories: First is total exclusion by virtue of assigning all available usufructs to specific individuals or groups, the latter being composed of members fewer than the total population of the society. This condition implies that periodic redistribution of usufructory rights either does not occur or is confined to a portion of the population and not the whole.[3] As a consequence it is apparent that some members of the society face problems of subsistence different from those who enjoy direct access to the basic resources. A second category of impairment of access arises as a consequence of societal size and complexity. In com-

---

[3] This limitation helps to locate, vis-à-vis the categories we are using, the nonstratified peasant communities that periodically avoid land concentration by redivisions taking account of waxing and waning family size. In the short run some of the families may seem to be moving ahead of others but a longer view reveals a process of leveling which obviates stratification.

plex societies, of course, technological and economic conditions are such that most transactions occur in ways and locations seemingly remote from the production of basic subsistence consumables, but in simple societies the problem is one of getting some kind of access to the sources of food.[4] The obtaining of such access requires payments or labor outputs in excess of those required of people with direct access rights. Indeed, it is precisely at this juncture that the economic phenomenon of exploitation is born as the person with impeded rights of access must buy this right with a share of his labor, perhaps a portion of his produce, from a holder of unimpeded right of access. Obviously labor exploitation can take a variety of forms, any combination of which may be found in a specific society, although there is rather strong patterning along lines of ascending socioeconomic complexity. For example, payment for access may involve personal services, military assistance, or drudge labor.

Given stratification, but holding other things constant, assuming equal energy inputs, a person enjoying unimpeded access to basic resources will end up with a larger final product under his control than will one who lacks such access. Without laboring this point let us note a relevant corollary: Some individuals without primary access rights to basic resources may actually enjoy a higher standard of living than some who have them if their capital is greater or if the amount and quality of capital is the same and energy input of the latter is very great while that of the

---

[4] Despite the complications of a highly elaborated division of labor, and even of the welfare mechanisms of diverse modern economic systems, the question of access to basic resources remains the central problem of contemporary national states, both old and new. Two examples indicate the spectrum: The problem of differential investment in agriculture and industry in Communist China immediately implies differential access; so does the character of "racial" riots in the United States, which have displayed a uniform feature in raids on food markets, among other targets. Obviously, this is a difficult question requiring lengthy analysis falling beyond the scope of the present work, which is concerned with simpler forms of society.

former is very low. In more complex social arrangements a class of highly skilled managers may stand between the owners (perhaps even the state) and the laborers and from their strategic positions derive the greatest return known in the society. In complex societies, as already indicated, the division of labor is so complex as to have a great portion of the labor force working at specialized tasks far removed from the production of subsistence. Consequently, a major portion of the population in such a society will never act in direct relation to basic resources. Their existence continues to depend on diverting great portions if not the entirety of the returns of their labor to acquiring subsistence goods. By this stage, however, there has been a dramatic increase in the kinds of things that must be considered basic resources. Not only have a variety of natural substances of no significance in simple society, like iron, lead, coal, or molybdenum, joined the things necessary to the physical support of life, but tools and factories have as well. Unlike simple cultures, where any mature person, given access to raw materials, can make usable copies of the tools of his or her own culture, in a complex civilization it is not possible for individuals to reproduce that culture's technology, even if granted access to all necessary raw materials. It is very much to the point that something like a great factory, which cannot be constructed with the labor of an individual or even a large kin group, may be held as an exclusive possession by a single person.

It is not the complex forms of stratification found in modern industrial society that lie at the core of this chapter. Our concern is with the simplest stratified societies that are known or can be sketched from available data. We are interested in the processes by which stratification emerges, and we must inquire also into the problems of social control that must accompany the emergence of stratification. This leads us to consider the means by which order is maintained in such a society. Finally, in this chapter we will investigate the internal instability of simple stratified systems and relate this to warfare and to the central theme of the next chapter, the emergence of the state.

THE ORIGINS OF STRATIFICATION

The question of the origins of stratification refers to the development of differentiated rights of access to basic resources. It is possible thus to narrow the question because pristine stratification develops in a simple technological milieu, probably equivalent to that associated with neolithic peasant villages. Appearing before the development of metallurgy and complex full-time craft specialization, there are few if any technological instruments of production which cannot be constituted anywhere in the society, provided that there is unimpeded access to basic resources. The major qualification is limited but interesting and has to do with the assembling of a work force since the manufacture of some instruments of production, for example large fishing craft, is facilitated by the coordinated labor of several individuals. As we have seen, in egalitarian societies there is little difficulty in assembling such a force when it is necessary and the product of combined labor is available to all. Rather than pursue this point here, I prefer to suggest that the blocking of access to enlarged labor groups is derived from an earlier process of blockage from basic resources.

Because the question of the origins of stratification revolves about the process by which basic resources were converted from communal to private property, it is well to grasp the bull by the horns and face the problem that has inspired so much verbiage since the eighteenth century and before, much of it by some great social commentators and all of it tendentious (just as this book is). Cutting through a voluminous literature, let us approach the matter by criticizing the work of Melville J. Herskovits, who stated his position flatly and in a highly conventional anthropological context.

Herskovits was perfectly content to make the concept of property a dependent variable but resisted any effort to view it as a causal agent vis-à-vis any other significant aspect of sociocultural process.

> Our task . . . is to obtain a sense of the variation pos-
> sible in this, as in other aspects of the economic life of
> the folk with whom we are concerned and to seek to
> determine the mechanisms operative in bringing about
> such property arrangements as exist among nonliterate
> peoples (Herskovits, 1960, p. 330).

Ridiculing as meaningless the effort to understand economic evolution as a process involving a transition from some kind of communism to private ownership, Herskovits felt that such an approach could not be divorced from biased political pamphleteering. His major reason for antipathy, however, was methodological; he flatly denied the validity of any and all types of reconstruction utilizing data from observed simple societies:

> For here, no less than in other segments of man's social
> life, to attempt to draw specifications of the first forms
> of property, to search out the dawn of a property sense
> in man through the study of forms of property in the
> "rude" civilizations of contemporary nonliterate man, is
> but an academic enterprise doomed to scientific futility
> by the simple fact that no hypothesis of this order is
> subject to the ultimate test of reference to relevant data
> (Herskovits, 1960, p. 326).

I cannot refrain from saying that the specifications for proof demanded by Herskovits cannot be met in any science that deals with the past, but would abolish much of biological science, especially almost all of evolutionary biology, and would wipe out much of astronomy in passing. Geology and some other sciences would also have to go, at least in those of their aspects that treat of the origin and development of the earth and its crust.

Actually, so demanding are Herskovits' canons that he violated them himself. In the same book previously cited, for example, he offered a refutation of "the doctrine of communal ownership of land among hunting and food-gathering peoples" (Herskovits, 1960, p. 335). He gave a number of examples, most of them shared with others, like Robert H. Lowie, who had moved along the same theoretical path somewhat earlier. It does not seem to have occurred to Herskovits that his use of these examples violates his own rule of method. Indeed, there is justification for regarding his use of this material as a particularly flagrant violation of standards of accuracy. The reason for this is simple and has to do with the quality of the data cited. In all of the cases, as it happens, the conditions described are not aboriginal but result from strong acculturative pressures emanating from much more highly organized societies. This is the case with the Eastern Algonkians (*cf.* Leacock, 1954), and there is a special rub in the case of the Ceylon Vedda, for the source Herskovits cited (Seligman, 1911) itself contains the evidence that the Veddas were living in completely nonaboriginal ways.

The position of Herskovits outlined here is completely consistent with the relativism of which he was a foremost exponent and which is manifest in his calculated use of the term "nonliterate" in the matter quoted. The despised term is "preliterate," which Herskovits found pejorative and, worse, a symbol of an evolutionary scheme that requires all nonliterates ultimately to become literate. Against this background it can be understood why Herskovits delighted in culling definitions of property that stress recognition of "the fact that in the course of its development every society has devised a special mold in which to cast its traditions of ownership" (Herskovits, 1960, p. 318). This leads inexorably to the logical relativistic conclusion: "*the ultimate determinant of what is property and what is not is to be sought in the attitude of the group from whose culture a given instance of ownership is taken*" (Herskovits, 1960, p. 326; italics in original).

Wittingly or no, by giving the anthropologist an impossible assignment, Herskovits buried the question. That he actually saw what he was doing is likely, for he followed the preceding remark with the observation that, "[i]f this makes generalization the more difficult, the difficulty must be accepted and taken into account" (Herskovits, 1960, p. 326).

If generalization built on multiplex emic ethnography is impossible, the reverse of the procedure demanded by Herskovits is simple enough to be feasible. Rather than inquire into interior understandings of property concepts held by denizens of a variety of societies, information is gathered on access, first to basic resources. Such information as we have on hand indicates that most simple societies—however they may be embedded in an ideological web of permissions, rights, obligations, reciprocations or what have you—do not interfere with the individual's access to the places where the means of subsistence may be acquired. If we study production, distribution, and consumption in such societies and do not ask selected informants to tell us what it is we are seeing, the resultant data will come much closer to substantiating the model we are offering than the antigeneralizing congeries discussed by Herskovits.

It should be added that our objections to Herskovits are aimed explicitly at the portion of the total phenomenon of "property" that relates to access to basic resources. That all societies known to ethnography permit some very close control by some individuals over the use, disposal, and destruction of some objects is patent. It is worthy of discussion only to the extent of remarking that even with regard to humble, nonbasic, nonstrategic items, the web of social relations sometimes creates such demands for exchange as to obviate most of our own culture's concepts of private property.

When it comes to the problem of the origins of private property Herskovits, as might be expected, buried the issue in a failure to make any distinctions about the kind of property involved. As far as he was concerned, "the phenomenon is a universal one, since there is no group who live so precariously that there is not some tool, some weapon, some bit of ornament or clothing that is not regarded as indisputably the possession of its maker, its user, its wearer" (Herskovits, 1960, p. 327). Believing this, and seeing no distinction between basic resources and other kinds of property, Herskovits saw the role of the anthropologist as limited to the description of the ethnographic variations in the institution and analysis of its social and economic role. As for origins:

> The ownership of wealth may have arisen from the exploitation of the weak by the strong; it may have arisen from differences in privileges possessed by the two sexes; it may be the result of differences in energy and foresight between members of the earliest human community. Or it may have been none of these; or again it may have been one of them in one part of the earth, and another in a different locality; while in still other areas it may have been any one of several combinations of these possibilities (Herskovits, 1960, pp. 326–7).

With regard to the ownership of noseplugs, penis sheaths, and even digging sticks or hand axes, I doubt that any of them arose from any of the conditions specified by Herskovits, singly or in combination, anywhere in the world. I am even more certain that none of these conditions can explain any case of the emergence of private property in respect to access to basic resources. One blanket reason should suffice although others might be given: Every condition mentioned by Herskovits is either of such antiquity as to have arisen no later than the earliest appearance of the hominids if not before, or is the other kind of anachronism. The last seems to apply to the condition of exploitation of the weak by the strong, at least in the usual economic sense of exploitation, which requires the prior existence of the phenomenon to be explained.

We have already seen that differences of energy and foresight, to attend to the only condition mentioned by

Herskovits which might have a bearing on the problem, may be assumed to be universal in man and probably extend to many other animals as well. If the assumption is correct, such differences could account for the origin of private property only if that trait were universal. It must be admitted that Herskovits is consistent, for he not only claims universality for private property but also implies that it is as old as "the earliest human community." But these contentions cannot be accepted if my analysis of egalitarian economies (see Chapter 3) is valid.

If restricted access to basic resources is not a universal characteristic of human societies and if it appeared fairly late in history and at different places at different times, what can be its initiating conditions? In juxtaposition to those conditions proposed by Herskovits, I offer the following as a provisional list: population pressure; shifts in customary postmarital residence patterns; contraction or sharp natural alteration of basic resources; shifts in subsistence patterns arising from such factors as technological change or the impingement of a market system; development of managerial roles as an aspect of maturation of a social and ceremonial system. I explicitly reject warfare and slavery as initiating conditions and turn to this question after discussing the positive conditions.

POPULATION PRESSURE

In a very well-known passage Meyer Fortes and E. E. Evans-Pritchard state flatly: "it would be incorrect to suppose that governmental institutions are found in those societies with greatest density [of population]. The opposite seems to be equally likely, judging by our material" (Fortes & Evans-Pritchard, 1940, p. 7). By government, these authors mean "centralized authority, administrative machinery, and judicial institutions" (Fortes & Evans-Pritchard, 1940, p. 5); we briefly consider their theses and this demographic generalization in particular below. At the moment, however, my interest in introducing the statement is to call attention to one instance of reluctance by anthropologists to accept demographic phenomena as causal factors in cultural development.

More recently, Robert Adams has taken a negative stand on the causal efficacy of demographic factors. Indeed, discussing the origins of the state he cuts directly across the provisional list of conditions that I see as the context for the emergence of stratification and the state as itemized just above. Adams writes: "The effect of regarding ecological response as the primary creative process . . . is to encourage the search for misleadingly self generating extracultural factors, such as population pressure, or the managerial requirements of irrigation systems, as the effectively independent causes of cultural development" (Adams, 1966, p. 15). Especially with regard to population size and density, Adams seems to hedge after his bold negative statement. We understand the reason for his negative position; indeed, we had better take note of it:

> Particularly in Mesopotamia, where the sedentary village pattern seems to have been stabilized for several millennia between the establishment of effective food production and the "take-off" into urbanism, it may be noted that there is simply no evidence for gradual population increases that might have helped to precipitate the Urban Revolution after reaching some undefined threshold (Adams, 1966, pp. 44–5).

This might be enough to frustrate my whole intention, despite my conviction that social evolution is a real process that occurs in real but shifting environments and not one of an infinite variety of games that people may choose to play with the raw materials of culture. The games are those of the analysts; most call them models. In real life there are sequences of causes and effects, and these sequences occur at real places separated by time and space. Indeed this point may be discerned as a central theme of Adams' book, for he takes full account of local differences before telling us that "the parallels in the Mesopotamian and

Mexican [political evolutions] . . . suggest that both instances are most significantly characterized by a common
core of regularly occurring features" (Adams, 1966, pp.
174–5). But, to return to the reasons for my optimism about
the possibilities of a demographic thesis for the emergence
of stratification and the state, I turn once again to Adams'
own critical description of the available and relevant archaeology:

> An increasingly serious problem in both areas is the
> disproportionately greater share of attention that the
> earliest agricultural origins are receiving than subse-
> quent phases in the consolidation of a sedentary way
> of life. Late prehistoric villages are virtually unrepre-
> sented by excavations carried out according to modern
> (post-World War II) standards. As a result, changes
> in ecological adaptations or subsistence patterns that
> might have contributed to the onset of the Urban Revo-
> lution remain on the whole hypothetical. Reconstruc-
> tions of individual settlements based on large-scale
> clearance . . . are still virtually unknown (Adams,
> 1966, pp. 26–7).

So the question is still archaeologically open, despite Adams'
general statement of position. Perhaps this is why in presenting the details of his argument he sometimes seems,
despite himself, to adopt a populationist approach (*cf.*
Adams, 1966, pp. 43, 44, 46).

When we turn from the admittedly inadequate archaeological record to the world of ethnographic observation, we discover a rich supply of data. All of it is "secondary," of course, in the sense that it derives from situations
set in motion not by indigenous forces but to some extent
by pressures released by outside influences, specifically from
other societies which had already developed more advanced
patterns of economic organization, stratification, and government. Although the definition of a secondary situation
is extremely simple, the actual patterns it may include are
quite diverse and complex. For example, the pressures often

arise not from direct political interaction with the outside but from a number of traits accepted without awareness of their consequences. The precise combination of traits and their effects can be viewed as unique if analyzed in sufficient detail, but the forces they release and the way these play upon further developments show great regularity around the world.

Let us consider the case of Tikopia to which we have previously had recourse in other contexts and which can be used because it has been the subject of the extraordinarily competent work of Raymond Firth. It is also of great interest because it has been studied since Firth's original work in 1928–1929, not only by Firth in 1952, but also by James Spillius (*cf.* Spillius, 1957; Firth & Spillius, 1963).

Between 1929 and 1952 the population of Tikopia increased by about 35 per cent, until it was in the throes of famine (Firth, 1959, p. 53). To be sure, this was not the first time famine had occurred, but this time one of the major restraints on overpopulation, the organization of the society to inhibit marriage and conception, was greatly weakened if not destroyed by exposure to the outside world. To the extent that famines occurred in the past—and this is somewhat speculative, as put by Firth (1959, p. 52)—the solutions seem to have developed along the lines of warfare and "expulsion of some section of the people." These solutions have been eliminated by the encroachments of European society in the form of more frequent colonial government visits and interference and more particularly by an established branch of the Melanesian Mission. Firth believes that the sum total of outside forces offsets the "pendulum" rhythm in Tikopia demography. His succeeding conclusion is most appropriate to the present argument: "In my opinion, such changes in demographic pressure on subsistence are far more responsible for much of the structure of primitive societies than anthropologists have generally allowed" (Firth, 1959, p. 54).

When we inquire explicitly into the consequences of population expansion for the native system of land tenure and access in Tikopia, we discover:

> The results included a division of land holdings by married brothers, a tendency to restrict the interests of married women in their lineage land, and a sharper definition of personal rights in land as against rights of other lineage and clan members, and community members (Firth, 1959, p. 180).

More particularly, there has been mounting pressure to exclude nonaffines from easy access to lineage-held land or at least to insist that temporary access, granted, for example, to a sister's son, conferred no title. Firth offers the statement of a Tikopian informant to this effect:

> . . . If a man has had trouble with his patrilineal kin he will go and live with his mother's brother. If that family dies out then he will continue to live there . . . He himself will say, "I live on my mother's brother's lands." But should he say "My lands," then in course of time his mother's brother's clan will come to him and will chase him away because he called the lands his. But so long as he acknowledges their ownership they will allow him to stay (Firth, 1959, p. 160).

This statement takes on added significance when it is realized that:

> A "rent" (in Tikopia view, more in the nature of acknowledgement of land ownership) was paid in the form of a small proportion of the crop. By 1952, there was a definite hardening of attitude by owners, due primarily to the famine (Firth, 1959, p. 177).

Under known demographic pressure, then, Tikopia has displayed increasing narrowness in granting access to basic resources, plus the growth of invidious distinctions and new emphasis on a simple system of rent.

Before leaving the excellent Tikopia material, there is a further point made by Firth that is of great importance.

I refer to his observation that the narrowing of access rights has not yet brought about much in the way of individual rights to land; rather, there has been increasing emphasis on small-scale agnatic lineages. I raise this point because some treatments of the theme of developing stratification make an unwarranted assumption that stratification requires individual ownership. Such seems, for example, to be the view of Robert Adams in the work cited earlier. Adams, following Jacques Soustelle, sees the possibility that in Mexico, "as late as the time of the arrival of the Spaniards private property was still 'in the act of coming into existence'" (Adams, 1966, p. 64, citing Soustelle, 1962, p. 80). While the institution of individual private property is of great importance, particularly in the later evolution of economic and social systems, it is ethnocentric to view it as the only form of "private" property. In many societies the system of stratification is couched in terms of unilineal or bilateral core kin groups holding preferential rights of access to basic resources.

The thesis that stratification is related to demographic density is far from original. I am not sure how old the idea is, nor shall I attempt to pursue this matter here. It is sufficient to point out that C. K. Meek, a pioneer in the study of land tenure systems in the far-flung British colonial empire just before its collapse, has put the essential point quite succinctly:

> If land is plentiful, population sparse and the people are still content with a subsistence economy, then it is possible to practise a system of shifting cultivation without the necessity of imposing rigid rules of tenure. But when the population becomes denser, or for some reason there is a marked increase in the area of cultivated land, it may become necessary to devise more settled systems of holding land (Meek, 1946, pp. 1–2).

The point can be illustrated by many examples; I choose one in which the statement is unambiguous and based on direct observation of the reporter. In Northern Nigeria the practice some fifty or more years ago was for individuals and families to apply to a "chief" or to a family head for usufructory rights to land. Such a grant could have been without temporal limit but gave no privilege of alienation by exchange. Then in 1921 Meek himself observed:

> that in crowded areas applicants for land were inclined to offer, and chiefs to accept, more than the modest presents which are normally given, not as rent, but as an acknowledgement of the chief's political authority, which includes the authority to dispose of vacant lands. In virtue of these larger payments there was a growing tendency for the occupier to regard his farm as alienable property (Meek, 1946, pp. 149–50).

Examples such as Meek gives can be found elsewhere in Africa. M. E. Elton Mills and Monica Wilson take note of the problem in their survey of a Xhosa-Mengu district in South Africa in 1949–1950:

> The allocation of arable land and the regulation of the commonage were traditionally the business of the chief or village headman in council, which was guided by traditional law (for the system is but a modification of the traditional tribal system), but as the population is increasing and land grows scarcer and scarcer, the law is, of necessity, changing (Mills & Wilson, 1952, p. 8).

Actually, though many statements of this kind appear in the literature, and some are supported by citations of evidence, it is surprising that to my knowledge no comparative studies have been undertaken to determine empirically exactly what relationships exist between population density and forms of land tenure. My own interest in this problem has been limited to the assembly of a limited number of cases, but I have recommended the problem to someone else for more extensive search, analysis, and perhaps a dissertation.

This section may be concluded by turning back to the quotation with which it began. Fortes and Evans-Pritchard have attacked the frequently held assumption that complexity of government, specifically the emergence of the state, is related in some way to population density. Since the statement quoted was published, the question has been seriously studied by Robert F. Stevenson, who added several cases to those on which the two British social anthropologists based their conclusion. By contrast, Stevenson's findings strongly support the hypothesis of a *positive* relationship. However, he suggests:

> that the hypothesis should be modified to acknowledge that along the borders of states or within the interstices of states, formerly acephalous systems may develop or maintain quite high [population] densities in small areas, well in advance of the development of specialized political institutions of their own (R. F. Stevenson, 1965, p. 331).

This does not upset the main conclusion:

> Once this modification is made there is rather impressive support of the hypothesis. In short, analysis of both the *African Political Systems'* cases and the total picture of Tropical Africa as a whole (viewed as a general pattern) shows a pronounced general conjunction between state formation and higher population density (R. F. Stevenson, 1965, pp. 331–2).

This does not completely settle the issue. Clearly, what I have elsewhere called the "secondary" developments can, if analyzed as pristine examples, lead to the formulation of deviant models which apparently confound more basic regularities. Proper analysis reveals these for what they are: special cases referable to special rules governing secondary developments and not directly applicable to problems of pristine emergence.

Stevenson recognizes that high population density by itself does not always appear in association with state institutions. He deduces from this that such density cannot be the necessary and sufficient cause of the development of state structure. Rather, he prefers a model involving several factors, among which relatively high population density would play a very important role.

While Stevenson's analysis pertains explicitly to state formation and not to the emergence of stratification, it has obvious significance for the latter. I certainly agree, for example, that the idea of a single cause in this area is weak and untenable. On the other hand, I am inclined to believe that additional causal factors, when identified, will be difficult to isolate since I expect them to be capable, at least in part, of being represented as aspects of basic demographic problems.[5]

SHIFTS IN RESIDENCE RULES

That increasing population density may lead to stratification is a logical hypothesis capable of empirical verification and perhaps even proof. Meanwhile, a few other tasks can be essayed in the same spirit of hypothesis. In particular, we may ask for some specification of the actual mechanisms by which population pressure can lead to stratified forms of tenure.

In his analytical description of the society of the Kachin (Chingpaw) of northeastern Burma, E. R. Leach has focused attention on the institution of *mayu-dama,* a system of relations between affinally related groups, such

---

[5] One factor adduced by Stevenson is trade and its effects on social structure. The trouble with trade as a cause of stratification is that, other things being constant, the flow of goods in and out of a nonstratified society will be regulated by mechanisms neutral or more probably antipathetic to the formation of stratification. We need only refer back to earlier sections of this book which discuss economic circulation in egalitarian and rank societies to see that there are built-in devices that prevent accumulation and that dispel the possibility of using trade goods as capital or as the basis of a system of socioeconomic exploitation. Again, the situation will be markedly different between the situation in which one or more parties to that trade are already stratified or even organized as states. In the latter situation there are many possibilities for a rapid change in the constitutions of the previously nonstratified societies.

that wife takers display significant inferiority in their relations with the group that has given them women. The *mayu* are the superiors, the *dama* the inferiors. The designations are particular to the situation, especially in the form of Kachin social organization that is known as *gumlao* and may be classified as egalitarian in the terminology we are using. In other words, in the egalitarian form of Kachin society the superiority of *mayu* to *dama* is dependent upon an actual flow of marriages. What is more, the superiority of any particular *mayu* status is compromised by the fact that marriage exchanges form a circle, so that "A" may be *mayu* to "B" while "B" is *mayu* to "C" who might well be *mayu* to "A," effectively dissolving any over-all class system. What is of interest to our immediate problem is what happens when the normal viripatrilocal rule of postmarital residence is broken.

First, let us emphasize that *gumlao* Kachin tenure is egalitarian. The basic situation is one in which a differentiation is made between usufruct and something called *madu*, which Leach translates as "ownership" (1954, p. 155), but which might more appropriately be identified as "stewardship." As Leach says: "This latter kind of ownership implies claims of sovereignty over the land rather than rights over its products. The claims are of value as status symbols; from a strictly economic point of view their value is, if anything negative, since they involve the owner in expense" (Leach, 1954, p. 155). (It could be argued that gumlao Kachin society is ranked, in our terms, but the hierarchy is not clear. In any case, ranking is compatible with economic egalitarianism, and our problem is to generate stratification.) Usufruct does not involve tributary dues of any kind from villagers to headmen (Leach, 1954, p. 204). But in *gumsa* (stratified) Kachin society:

> All those who are not in a favored status and recognized lineage kinsmen of the chief must contribute to the chief a thigh . . . from every four-footed animal slain, and they must contribute free labour to the

preparation of the chief's hill field and to the building of the chief's house (Leach, 1954, pp. 204-5).

Now we are ready for the relation of stratification to residence rules in this one illustrative case:

> The formal seniority of the *mayu* to the *dama* in such cases provides the basis for claims to prior land title on the part of the *mayu*. Some affinal links are associated with land tenure while others are not, but it is always the former which are given emphasis and which are the most enduring. The basis of the *dama* inferiority seems to lie in the fact that where *mayu* and *dama* are members of one territorial unit the *dama* must, by implication, have broken the normal rule of patrilocal residence. The fact that the *dama* are settled alongside the *mayu* implies that the founder of the *dama* [lineage] must have settled matrilocally with his father-in-law, and it is thus a token of inferior status (Leach, 1954, p. 83; *cf.* p. 168).

Once more I must admit that the data are not altogether clear and tend to suggest the point I am making, rather than to prove it. Leach scarcely goes into the question of motivation for uxoripatrilocal residence. He says that such a "situation usually originates in circumstances where the bridegroom is on bad terms with his relatives or else they are very poor" (Leach, 1954, p. 169). It seems reasonable that such a phenomenon would be related to microecological variation and the fact that population may not increase uniformly even between two sites rather close to each other.

Analysis is significantly redirected to the question of population pressure. Kachin, like many other societies, makes a distinction between original settlers and later comers, with the former holding preferential rights. While I cannot pursue the point here, it can be hypothesized that some of the latecomers, especially in secondary situations such as the Kachin, which exists in a region that has long been adjacent to much more highly organized economies and polities, are not only alien to the local Kachin lineage, but are not even Kachin. Such cases are widely distributed in the ethnographic literature and bring up a matter discussed in more detail below, namely clientship and slavery and their relation to stratification. In addition to clients, Kachin are said to have slaves who occupy somewhat confusing statuses. As we show, the confusion is a structural matter, for sometimes they are treated as dama or inferior affinals, but worse, at other times they are treated as people beyond all kinship ties. Yet there is a dialectic working here, for as stratification matures, the upper group which commands privileged access to the basic resources can develop political power more rapidly by resting on a nonkin labor force and even by playing off the interests of relatives and clients who are in fact resident aliens. But I am now outrunning the original point of this section and will turn instead to the question of the growth of managerial specialization and its role in the development of stratification.

WAS THERE AN ANCIENT "MANAGERIAL REVOLUTION"?

The emergence of the giant corporation in modern capitalist society led theorists some decades ago to emphasize the distinction between ownership and management. It is common for writers who dwell on this subject to begin their analyses with a few remarks about feudal Europe, move rapidly to the Industrial Revolution and then to our own time. That is the case in the work of A. A. Berle, Jr., and Gardiner Means (1932) and James Burnham (1941). Such an approach, well fitted to the problems those authors contended with, is not appropriate for our present problem, but some of the general notions that they developed in handling problems of ownership and management are of use.

Berle and Means, for example, see that "the corporate system tends to develop a division of the functions formerly accorded to ownership" (Berle & Means, 1932, p. 119), and these functions include: having interests in an enterprise, acting with respect to it, and having power over it. The first implies that there is a socially recognized status which is entitled to whatever yields may be forthcoming. The second implies that there is a status associated with the right to make all effective decisions concerning the enterprise. The third implies that the actual function of management can be delegated, that is, dissociated from the first. Implicit in the first two functions is the concept of right to commit energy to the enterprise thus obtaining a yield. This point is made explicitly, although without emphasis, in Burnham (1941, p. 81). But Burnham, like Berle and Means, neglects almost everything that happened in Europe before feudalism, and none of them have any place at all for events occurring outside of Europe (or modern America) at any time. Fortunately, there is at least one other strong managerial theory covering a wider range than the foregoing. I refer, of course, to the so-called hydraulic theory presently associated with the name of Karl Wittfogel (1955, pp. 43–54), but, as Wittfogel himself has shown, it is a theme in the work of many outstanding classical economists. At the heart of the thesis is a distinction between rainfall agriculture and any system of farming that either requires a significant amount of irrigation or special drainage. As Wittfogel explains it, water for crops may be inadequate, untimely, or in too great abundance. The first two require some means of getting moisture to the soil, and the last requires a means of rapidly getting rid of excess water or preventing floods. Wittfogel then argues that irrigation and drainage works are likely to extend beyond and crosscut small-scale interests so that nothing less than a community, if not several communities, is involved. What is more, the labor required for such enterprises is likely to exceed the potential of small groups, requiring some regular system of labor recruitment on a community or even wider basis. This need for labor, in turn, soon establishes an additional requirement for managerial organization of this labor force. Meanwhile, there are also managerial requisites connected with disbursing the water in the irrigation system and with the adjudication of disputes concerning water use.

With special regard to property, Wittfogel has suggested distinguishing three grades of hydraulic society. Given other aspects of hydraulic farming, "[w]hen independent active property plays a subordinate role both in its mobile and immobile forms, we are faced with a relatively simple pattern of property. We shall call the thus structured conformation a simple hydraulic society" (Wittfogel, 1955, p. 46; 1957, pp. 230–1). A semicomplex hydraulic society is then defined in terms of the development of independent active property in industry and commerce but not in agriculture, and a complex hydraulic society in terms of strong independent active property in agriculture as well as industry and commerce (Wittfogel, 1955, p. 46; 1957, p. 231; see his explanation of "strong" and "active").

Actually, Wittfogel has displayed only passing interest in the problem we are now confronting. Though he has intense concern for the relations between hydraulic agriculture and the emergence of formal political power and the state, he passes off the problem of the relation between hydraulic farming and the emergence of stratification with a few highly generalized statements. Indeed, he sees no necessary special relationship: "Agricultural tribes handle their property in many different ways; and this is as true for hydraulic as for non-hydraulic communities" (Wittfogel, 1955, p. 48; 1957, p. 232). He documents this statement with a reference to George P. Murdock (1949, p. 38 ff.) that proves less than enlightening because Murdock is discussing inheritance rules without making any distinctions as to type of property involved or the level of the society in which the variations appear. Returning to Wittfogel, his most comprehensive statement is that "in both nonhydraulic and hydraulic small farming communities the forms of land tenure vary; and the tendency toward communal control is strong but not universal" (Wittfogel, 1955, pp. 48–9;

1957, p. 233). Yet Wittfogel does expose a possible difference, although he views it as the earliest form of the
process whereby governmental power in a hydraulic situation tends to undermine private property rights:

> In the sphere of hydraulic works . . . antiproprietary
> forces appear regularly. A primitive peasant, using his
> own tools, cultivates land that may or may not be
> communally regulated, and the seeds for his crops may
> belong to him personally or to his kin group. Under
> nonhydraulic conditions this is the whole story. In a
> hydraulic setting cultivation proper follows a similar
> pattern; but the "preparatory" operations do not. The
> tools are privately owned, but the raw materials for
> making the hydraulic installations (earth, stone, and
> perhaps timber) either are communal property—that
> is, owned by nobody or everybody—or, if they are
> found on land held by a particular individual, family,
> or clan, are taken over by the community. And the end
> products of the community's coordinated effort, the
> ditches or canals, do not become the property of the
> individual farmers or farming families that participate
> in the work, but, like the water which they carry to
> the individual fields, they are controlled ("owned") by
> the community's governing agency (Wittfogel, 1957,
> p. 234).

Note that Wittfogel adds the following comment: "small
ditches that require the labor of only a few individuals or
a kin group are the property of those who make them"
(Wittfogel, 1957, p. 234).

A critical article by Leach has taken Wittfogel to task
because of asserted comparative irregularities drawn from
Ceylon. That is to say, Leach argues that Ceylon, although
hydraulic, deviates significantly from the Wittfogel model.
Actually, Leach's evidence may be read to confirm or at
least support Wittfogel's position. At any rate, Leach contributes a concise statement of the issue that is central to
the argument raised here: "the key element . . . [is] the

existence of a self-perpetuating bureaucracy which ruled by owning the rights to power and office rather than by owning rights to property" (Leach, 1954, p. 4).

This formulation raises two problems: Can a complex polity arise in the absence of stratification, as I have defined it? Can stratification emerge out of a system of differential access to political power?

To offer a brief but tendentious response to the first question, it can be said that there is a gap of great magnitude between the concept of "weak property," Wittfogel's device for minimizing the role of property in the political structure of hydraulic society, and the absence of stratification. As a matter of fact, in China, a major stage for Wittfogel's thesis, the archaeological evidence for stratification appears to be much earlier than the earliest signs of large-scale irrigation (*cf.* Chang, 1963, pp. 92–3, 171–3). A similar order of events has also been suggested for the New World. Presumptive evidence of stratification (for example, burials showing marked wealth differences; housetypes ranging from small to grand; sumptuary goods, and so on) may actually relate to situations closer to ranking as the term is used in this book. Conversely, the absence of clear evidence of major irrigation or drainage projects does not necessarily convey a total lack of hydraulic or hydroagricultural concerns. That simple irrigation construction may go hand in hand with the emergence of stratification is suggested by what is known about the modern Kalinga of the northern Philippines. Among the Kalinga "ownership" of a source of irrigation water went to the person placing under cultivation the first field to use it. Subsequent users, presumably lower on the watercourse, are required to pay for water, although the price may be waived for close relatives. The "owner" of the watersource has significant restraints on his control. Like users farther down the drainage system, he has responsibilities to let the water through, to facilitate its passage and, in a dry spell, he may not hoard or use up all the water. Furthermore, the "owner" has no vested right to the water beyond a fair share for his original plot. This is shown by the fact that such an owner, should he prepare a new field along the lower course of the water supply, requires the permission of all his partners in the existing canal system. Clearly underlying this requirement is the work situation—irrigation ditches and canals are the product of collective labor, as is the continual task of cleaning the watercourses (Barton, 1949, pp. 103–6).

One fairly obvious means by which managerial roles in an irrigation situation may logically give rise to a form of stratification is by relieving the manager from drudge labor, or by requiring lesser members of the team to work for him, or both. None of these things occurs in Kalinga, but in the eastern Pueblo area in the United States the chief's fields were cultivated, at least in part, with the labor of the villagers (Wittfogel, 1955, pp. 50–1; 1957, p. 235). At the level of Hawaii the system was much more complicated and formalized; what is more, control over water resources in Hawaii was used to bolster control over land. This was achieved by using the sanction of restricting access to irrigation water rather than to land (Sahlins, 1958, 15–6). Once again, however, the indications are that some form of stratification, defined as differential access to basic resources, precedes the emergence and certainly the crystallization of sophisticated political institutions. It is perhaps worthwhile to note that once emergent stratification has precipitated more complex political forms there is strong probability that the new and burgeoning political roles will afford new paths of development for stratification. Indeed, it is precisely when such a situation is created that war and conquest as social institutions begin to play their most significant role in the maturation of the state. We return to this matter later.

The speculative nature of this section is not relieved by the difficulties that hamper research into these problems. Where there are good possibilities for investigating relations between population density and forms of land tenure, for example, there is no place where a field worker can investigate questions of pristine stratification. Not one of the simple irrigation societies now extant is free of substantial economic and political interference from one or more more complexly organized alien societies. It is reasonable to suppose, however, that some valuable work may be done on the kinds of tensions and conflicts that arise in such societies; the more valuable knowledge of the means by which these difficulties are overcome seems unlikely to be forthcoming except by logical construction and extrapolation.

WAR

It was a widely held idea in the nineteenth century that the root of the state was firmly planted in war. Herbert Spencer, for example, wrote:

> Everywhere the wars between societies originate governmental structures, and are causes of all such improvements in those structures as increase the efficiency of corporate action against environing societies (H. Spencer, 1896, p. 520).

> This development of simple headship in a tribe by conflict with other tribes, we find advancing into compound headship along with larger antagonisms of race with race (H. Spencer, 1896, p. 523).

> As this differentiation by which there arises first a temporary military head, who passes insensibly into a political head, is initiated by conflict with adjacent societies, it naturally happens that his political power increases as military activity continues (H. Spencer, 1896, p. 524).

Proponents of the theory that war was the precipitating cause of complex political organization also quite generally held that stratification originated in military action and conquest. Here is Ludwig Gumplowicz on this point:

. . . we first recognize the beginnings of separate immovable property when one horde has overpowered another and uses its labor force. As soon as there are subjects who are excluded from the enjoyment of certain goods which their own labor contributed to produce, in favor of the ruling class, and when the members of the ruling class are protected in their enjoyment of them by the well-organized whole, then there arises separate or private property in immovable goods . . . The primitive horde emerges from [the] condition of . . . [equality] . . . only when a strange horde comes within its reach as the result generally of migration or a plundering raid. If it subjects the strangers its wants are more easily satisfied and its economic life is raised above the primitive condition. The "extra" labor of some for others begins (Gumplowicz, 1899, pp. 116, 125).

The American anthropologist Otis T. Mason joined the chorus, insisting that, "In the fourth period, the ownership of land, still respecting natural boundaries, began to assume a more artificial form by reason of improvements in the apparatus of war" (Mason, 1892, p. 120).

I doubt that we can ever know with complete certainty, for the simplest societies now verge on extinction or live in vastly different physical and cultural environments, but I defend on the basis of available ethnographic data and on the basis of logic the proposition that warfare increases in frequency as societies become more complex. As I have elsewhere stated (Fried, 1961, pp. 134–47), warfare increases in rank society over egalitarian society, increases still more in stratified society over rank society, and crests after the appearance of the state. Furthermore, it seems to me that warfare serves to institutionalize stratification only when the social orders of one or more parties to the warfare are already stratified.

While it is a matter of ethnographic record that some rank societies have engaged in warfare for explicit goals of territorial expansion, pressure to engage in such warfare has every reason to be less in a rank than a stratified society. With specific reference to economic motives for war, there is substantially less occasion for these in rank than in stratified society. This is a consequence of the economic egalitarianism of rank society; since all members have access to basic resources, consumption of subsistence goods will show a high degree of uniformity and this is reinforced by the operation of various systems of redistribution as already sketched in the previous chapter. Contrast this with the situation in stratified societies where whole sectors of the population have precarious relations to subsistence while other sectors are not only free to accumulate surpluses of both productive and consumption goods, but are encouraged to do so by the very structure of their society and the ideology which supports it. In such societies the noneconomic motives for war are also likely to be much enhanced. What is more, the cultural development of warfare is more likely to receive special attention in a stratified society as owners can make economically rational decisions to divert resources and labor into military activities. For example, in stratified society there is much more opportunity to establish a professional military force. Obviously, it is not the earliest form of society that can achieve such organization; an arrangement of age grades can achieve something of professionalism in this respect even in an egalitarian setting. It seems unlikely, however, that such societies would themselves manage to develop the specialized technology of war that has grown parallel with the flourishing of stratification and the state.

There remains the question of a special relationship between military status and the basic resources of society. Could the holding of a special martial role be the foundation of stratification? On empirical grounds the answer to this seems to be in the negative, despite the seeming attractiveness of an argument that applies to our own cultural experience in which military success is readily translated into economic advantage. But in rank societies military statuses tend to be ephemeral, and, even more, they are contained within the patterns of kinship that are the main coordinates of group formation. In such groups military pre-eminence is usually segregated from other socioeconomic functions. Referring to war and peace among the Nootka, Philip Drucker tells us that "the two fields of activity and the attitudes and values that went with them were sharply compartmented off from each other" (Drucker, 1951, p. 343). He also says flatly that "war chiefs . . . did not use their strength nor their reputations as killers to bully their fellows" (Drucker, 1951, p. 343). Rather than war and military roles being the source of stratification, it seems that stratification is a provoker of war and an enhancer of military status.

SLAVERY

Slavery, being a form of stratification, cannot be its root or cause. The phenomenon of slavery is worth discussing in the context of this chapter for at least three reasons. For one thing, a natural inclination to take and hold slaves has sometimes been pronounced a fundamental trait of human psychology. More seriously—as few who read this book will react to the previous statement with anything but amusement or irritation—slavery has been asserted to exist in societies otherwise described as egalitarian. If so, this might indicate that slavery was one of the initial forms of stratification, perhaps the very first. Whatever the truth about this, the incidence of slavery does require some of our attention. A third problem therefore arises from this and the fact that slavery is polytypic. We are therefore inquiring into some of its main forms and especially into its relations with other forms of stratification.

Like most words in the lexicon of social science, "slavery" is not easy to define once for all in a manner subsuming all possible treatments. My purposes are best served by a definition given more than half a century ago by H. J. Nieboer; his definition was not original, but I spare myself and the reader further elaboration of this point. More significant to the present argument is Nieboer's awareness of the difficulties which are described at the outset of his work on the subject (Nieboer, 1900, p. 1 ff.). The problems still existed a third of a century later; covering the subject for the first edition of the *Encyclopedia of Social Sciences,* Bernhard J. Stern was of the opinion that "It is frequently difficult . . . to distinguish with any precision between such categories as slaves, serfs, subjects, submerged classes and low castes" (Stern, 1934, p. 73). It was a simple step, after thus setting the stage for further confusion, for Stern to replace the useful Nieboer definition with something quite amorphous: "the ownership of persons outside of family relations whereby the owners control the lives of their slaves, often sanction their use in ritual sacrifice and frequently subject them to compulsory labor" (Stern, 1934, p. 73).

It is perhaps unfair to criticize Stern too much for this formulation; after all, Nieboer did try to simplify his own definition to: *"slavery is the fact that one man is the property or possession of another"* (Nieboer, 1900, p. 7; italics in original). In Nieboer's case, however, "property or possession" implied without exception that some kind of compulsory labor was being performed (Nieboer, 1900, p. 8). So as to make this feature an explicit feature of the institution I prefer his fuller statement. A slave is *"a man who is the property or possession of another man, and forced to work for him"* (Nieboer, 1900, p. 7; italics in original. Obviously the use of masculine nouns and pronouns introduces an unnecessary limitation, which we can simply ignore).

Concern for the definition of slavery is not merely a matter of sociological pedantry or hairsplitting. Considering the question of the existence of slavery in otherwise egalitarian societies, it is of prime importance to determine if the person asserted to be a slave indeed is required to act as one. An example may clarify my intention. Alfred

Métraux has written about so-called slavery among the Mbayá of the South American Chaco: "The most severe punishment that a *Mbayá* could inflict on an unruly slave was to threaten to take back the horses and other things he had given him and refuse to employ him any longer" (Métraux, 1946, p. 309). If the criterion of compulsion be applied to the Mbayá, their alleged institution of slavery evaporates. Slaves may be beaten or bartered, slain or sold, they may be manhandled or even manumitted, but they cannot be fired. More precisely, even though there may be something of a voluntary element in some means by which some slaves enter the status, there is nothing properly called voluntary in the subsequent performance of their assigned tasks. Any weakening of the principle of involuntary servitude is a reduction of the degree of slavery. Where there are such reductions, and many kinds of cases can be cited, it is preferable to employ some other word, like "prisoner," "indentured laborer," "peon," "serf," "bondman," or other. Such usage will not totally eliminate cases of ambiguity but should reduce them to a manageable minimum; the relative simplicity of applying the criterion of involuntary servitude also commends this usage.

Although his concentration was on the means of subsistence, the sample of societies labeled "hunters and fishers" by Nieboer comes close to overlapping my category of egalitarians; in any event, though some of his sample societies, like those from the Northwest Coast, are rank societies, none is stratified by my criteria. It is interesting to note, then, that of Nieboer's eighty-two hunting and fishing tribes eighteen were reported to keep slaves. This amounts to 22 per cent and might suggest the strong possibility that slavery paves the way for a more general stratification of society were it not for certain critical deficiencies in the picture presented by these data. There is not sufficient space in the present book to attempt a full treatment of this subject, but the main points can be indicated. First, there remains, even after Nieboer's refreshing skepticism, considerable doubt of the aboriginality of several cases in his sample, such as Abipone and Tehuelche. Second, there is much value in raising the question of whether the institution reported is indeed to be considered slavery. Third, the greatest portion of hunting and fishing societies asserted by Nieboer to have slavery were located in the Northwest Coast area.

Before taking a slightly closer look at Northwest Coast slavery, a couple of methodological points should be made. Nieboer was working with available ethnographic data of mixed quality, to say the least. Some world areas, like New Guinea, were very poorly known, and the accounts from many other areas lacked any claim to rigor or precision. Unfortunately, though many of the ethnographies in question relate to societies which underwent irreversible change a century or longer ago, the same criticism can be applied to present treatments, as I interpret statements from the old works. In our favor, however, is a much heightened awareness of culture change that informs more recent analyses. Similarly, although the point was first made long ago, there is less inclination in modern anthropology to accept at face value the formula that one "tribe" equals one statistical case in a sample. Unfortunately, no simple alternative has replaced this formula. As it happens, however, the value of the number of cases is insignificant when compared with the value of more critical analysis of the structure and internal coherence of those cases or of a smaller number of them for which the data are relatively clear.

Perhaps the most positive statement concerning the magnitude of aboriginal Northwest Coast slavery was made by W. C. MacLeod: "slavery on the northwest coast among the natives was of nearly as much economic importance to them as was slavery to the plantation regions of the United States before the Civil War" (MacLeod, 1928, p. 649). This contrasts sharply with a more recent overview of the situation by a specialist in Northwest Coast culture: "It is difficult to estimate the slave population of the area, but it was certainly never very large, for slave mortality was high.

Slaves' economic utility was negligible. They gathered fire-wood, dug clams, and fished, but so did their masters" (Drucker, 1965, p. 52).

The over-all picture I would like to present of Northwest Coast slavery can be sketched briefly, although I cannot properly defend it in the present short treatment. I believe that "slaves" should be better referred to as "captives" and that their numbers, as Drucker says, must have been small at almost all times, although the general situation probably varied. (Compare this treatment of Northwest Coast "slavery" with that in Leslie White [1959, pp. 200–3].) It is likely that in pre-European times, before the end of the eighteenth century, captives must have been quite few and comprised, with negligible exceptions, women and children. With the growth of certain aspects of Northwest Coast economy triggered by developing trade, much stimulated and multiplied by exchange with Europeans, and with elaboration of political structure stimulated by European contact and the technological facilitation of warfare (also a product of the heightened emphasis on ranking which fed back from the previous influences and others we cannot here detail), the social and to a lesser extent the economic value of captives increased. This led to a peak population in this status and also to the closest approximation that was to be achieved between the Northwest Coast status of captive and that of slave as earlier defined. The latter phenomenon may also be attributable, at least in part, to increased knowledge of slavery practiced elsewhere in the United States, although I must admit that this is merely a speculation on my part. At any rate, the peaking of slavery came shortly before its decline, which was the result of a battery of causes, including outright prohibition by newly imposed superordinate authority (the Canadian and United States governments), of war by the same superordinate colonial power, and transformation of aboriginal economy, again largely through suppression of the rank-bestowing and rank-validating potlatches and other giveaways.

One difficulty in this hypothesis arises from a lack of reliable first-hand accounts of the progress of slavery in the Northwest Coast area. Those references which I have seen, although admittedly only a small portion of the relevant literature, are alike in attributing a prevalence of slaves to an earlier period. It was never the generation being observed that possessed a lot of slaves and only rarely even the generation of their fathers. Usually the holding of large numbers of slaves was projected into a shady and remote past.

It would not be proper to turn this section into a full-scale inquiry into Northwest Coast slavery despite the interest and significance of the subject. We must conclude, therefore, with a brief consideration of certain salient points having to do with the social status of slaves and their relation to Northwest Coast economy and ideology.

Aurel Krause, writing in 1885 on the basis of an extended trip to the Northwest Coast including a stay among the Tlingit, had little to say about the contemporary slavery and placed the holding of larger numbers further in the past (Krause, 1956, pp. 105, 111–2). Consulting earlier travelers' accounts he presents a picture of the institution that is not altogether clear. Some of the earlier accounts indicate that the lot of slaves was not severe, but other statements stress their condition as "a very sad one." Few of the accounts throw any light on the status of the slave as laborer. Such remarks on this topic as I have seen tend to be along the lines of this statement by Edward S. Curtis:

> Slavery was firmly established among the coast Salish. But the harrowing pictures which that word brings before our mind have little connection with the institution as it existed among the Indians of this region. Slaves were captives taken in war and traded from tribe to tribe, and almost always the prisoners were

women or children. They wielded paddles in their masters' canoes, fished, gathered wood, cooked, and made baskets and other utensils, but they labored no more strenuously than the free members of the lower class, and in return they were well treated as members of the household . . . As concerns his labor the slave was no great asset, and the principal reason for the existence of the institution of slavery was that the possession of captives reflected honor and dignity upon their owners (Curtis, 1913, p. 74).

It is my impression, subject to correction, that though chiefly status may have depended on "slaves," this dependence was not on labor power. That is, slaves did not spend their time producing commodities to enhance their master's wealth and improve his position as the giver of potlatches. It is explicitly stated that the highest value of a captive was as a sacrifice; he might be killed at the climax of various rituals, and it was for this potential moment he was kept.

One hypothesis about the nature of Northwest Coast slavery advanced some time ago by Drucker suggests that the slaves' "principal significance was to serve as foils for the high and mighty, impressing the inequality of status on the native consciousness" (Drucker, 1939, p. 55). It is easy to agree with the first part of his assertion; not only could a captive be murdered during various ceremonies, but he could also be killed at what seems a whim of his master, perhaps as an object for venting anger. That slaves functioned as a means of reinforcing native concepts of status is less certain. The logic of society is not necessarily that of Occam's razor, but the ranking system of the Northwest Coast was quite coherent in the absence of a slave stratum. Indeed, one of the most commonly encountered remarks about Northwest Coast slavery is that the members of these societies did not regard the slaves as a part of the social system (Boas, 1897, p. 338; Drucker, 1939, p. 55; and so on).

Actually, the question of the role of captives in Northwest Coast society is a confused one. Whatever statements may have been collected purporting to represent the cognitive attitudes toward slaves, the empirical data reveal a contradictory picture. Take the Bella Coola, for example:

> In former times it probably would have been difficult for a stranger to tell married slaves from members of the Bella Coola community until he had been long in the country to understand more than appeared on the surface. . . . Marriages between Bella Coola men and slave women were not infrequent, while like partnerships between slave men and even the daughters of chiefs were not unknown. The slave might become an influential member of the community, though the fact that he was not free was never forgotten. . . . [T]he public life of the village, where all lived and ate together, tended to break down the unsystematically enforced differences of rank (McIlwraith, 1948, pp. 160, 161, 162).

This might be compared with the situation reported among the Owikeno Kwakiutl:

> Low class or ne'er-do-wells are called xa'mala . . . and are just above slaves. The latter are called k!a'ku and are usually war captives. If slaves are freed, they are then classed as xamala . . . Even a person born of xamala parents could rise above his station. In other words, caste is neither rigid nor dependent solely on birth (Olson, 1954, p. 220).

It should be clear by now that the status called "slavery" in the Northwest Coast cultures bears little resemblance to that associated with stratified societies. It is also difficult to see how such captive statuses might have developed into a generalized system of stratification. Clearly being a captive or a descendant of captives was a matter that could be used to one's disadvantage within the ranking game played by the society, but in the societies this did not seriously engage any question of access to basic resources.

THE STRATIFIED SOCIETY

Having inquired into a few of the things that may have been conducive to emergence of a stratified society and having rejected still others, we still must say something about stratified society as a political field. At this point our treatment becomes even briefer and more programmatic. This stems from the empirical condition previously mentioned: Societies that are stratified but lack state institutions are not known to the ethnographer. Indeed, as argued elsewhere, pristine examples of such societies have probably not existed on our planet for 2,000 years or more. It is doubly unfortunate that the invention of writing occurred no earlier than at the time of the emergence of the most ancient states. There are no authentic written records from which the development of a pristine state can be directly read.

As a methodological consequence, it is necessary to reconstruct a probabilistic model of a stratified, nonstate society by extrapolating from what is known about the earliest states, by constructing a logical model which bridges the gap between the most complex rank societies known and the simplest states, and by cautiously drawing upon data supplied by modern secondary (perhaps "tertiary" or "quaternary" would be more appropriate terminology) states. With apologies I must admit that I am not going to attempt such a reconstruction here, although I look forward to making the attempt in a future publication. For the most part, I shall rely in this book on the brief analysis of the state in the next and final chapter, hoping that the reader is stimulated to supply his own intermediate model. It is necessary, however, to make a few minimal comments.

While a model of stratified nonstate society can be built within the confines of a congruent model of kin relations, the probability is slight that the kin model will in fact contain it. This ties in the first instance to the association we have tried to find between the emergence of the state and the growth of population both in total size and density. It also has to do with the emergence of genuine socioeconomic classes associated with markedly contrasted standards of living, security, and even life expectancy. Even the most marked differences of rank in a rank society do not, as we have tried to indicate, lay any basis for a comparable division of the population. I assume that as a consequence of these differences the stratified society will face a magnitude of internal disputes, pressures, conflicts, such as is unknown and inconceivable in rank society. If there is a partially congruent kin-organized system of restraints and balances, it is doomed to increasing incidence of failure if relied on to maintain the political integration of the society. (Despite this recurrent failure, there is no dearth of effort in stratified and state societies to use whatever is available of kin systems to maintain order.) Limited successes to one side, a kind of Liebig's Law of the Minimum comes into play and increasing emphasis is placed on non-kinship mechanisms of political and economic power. It is precisely these mechanisms that mature, coalesce, and form the state.

Note that such a picture does not present the emergence of the state as a simple event. The state forms in embryo in the stratified society, which, by this reasoning, must be one of the least stable models of organization that has ever existed. The stratified society is torn between two possibilities: It builds within itself great pressures for its own dissolution and for a return to a simpler kind of organization, either of ranking or egalitarian kind, but lacking differential access to basic resources. It is likely, as a matter of fact, that such a process goes on within small enclaves even after a state has been formed. That is my interpretation, for example, of what goes on in what Eric Wolf has called the "corporate peasant community" (Wolf, 1955, p. 456 ff.). On the other side, the stratified community, to maintain itself, must evolve more powerful institutions of political control than ever were called upon to maintain a system of differential ranking. To be sure, many of the specific institutions are essentially ideological and amount to internalization of norms, which requires the identification of the unprivileged with such political slogans as "the sanctity of private property" or "the good of the state." It must be underlined, despite some recent work by behavioral political scientists, that the acceptance of such slogans and the concurrent behavior it induces is invariably backed by a variety of forms of naked power. It is possible for such applications of power to be made in the context of a preexisting set of kin relations, but it is not likely that this will long remain the case. We are aware that some of the most repressive individual-to-individual relations are to be met within the framework of kinship; there is no dearth of cases of parental cruelty. Yet such cases exist within a larger frame of reference which implies that to survive is to assume ultimately the superordinate role, albeit with a victim who was not the original persecutor. In relations within stratified societies there can be no such assumption, and therefore there must be additional bolstering. Usually that bolstering involves the appearance of agents who function to maintain the economic and political system and whose position in that system has nothing to do with kinship. Indeed, that position usually represents the antithesis of kinship.

It should not be thought that the generally unhappy tone of the preceding remarks indicates any feeling on my part that the state as a form of political and economic organization would have been better avoided. My view is that it could not be avoided. No individual choices in the matter were ever presented in any significant sense. Just as stratification grew within unstratified societies without the conscious awareness of the members of the affected societies, so the state emerged and was hard at work concentrating its power on specific cases long before any reflective individual took the effort to isolate and identify the novelty.

The novelty was the state. Let us turn to it.

CHAPTER 6

The State

For some time now there has been a movement to abolish the word "state," at least from the works of political scientists. David Easton (1953, p. 108) says, "The word should be abandoned entirely." He says that if the word is scrupulously avoided, "no severe hardship in expression will result. In fact, clarity of expression demands this abstinence." Gabriel Almond and James Coleman, to offer another influential example, echo and enlarge upon this point of view:

> [The] rejection of the "state and non-state" classification, which is found throughout the anthropological, sociological, and political science literature is not merely a verbal quibble. It is a matter of theoretical and operational importance. Such a dichotomous classification could come only from an approach to politics which identifies the political with the existence of a

specialized, visible structure, and which tends to restrict the political process to those functions performed by the specialized structure . . . Indeed, it is this emphasis on the specialized structures of politics which has led to the stereotyped conception of traditional and primitive systems as static systems, since the political systems most likely to be differentiated are executive-legislative and adjudicative structures. The mechanics of political choice are there as well, but in the form of *intermittent* political structures. The rule to follow which we suggest here is: If the functions are there, then the structures must be, even though we may find them tucked away, so to speak, in nooks and crannies of other social systems (Almond & Coleman, 1960, p. 12).

This strikes me as a lengthy phrasing of what the anthropologist E. Adamson Hoebel stated flatly a decade earlier: "where there is political organization there is a state. If political organization is universal, so then is the state" (Hoebel, 1949, p. 376).

The contents of the previous chapters should make it clear that I cannot agree with these distinguished social scientists. I do agree that the issue "is not merely a verbal quibble." We must not be confused by the persistence of political functions in "nooks and crannies" of social systems, that is, in other aspects or subsystems of the larger social system, even after the emergence of specialized apparatus. Appreciation of the efforts of modern political scientists to cast broader nets and catch important political processes outside the formal institutions of modern government must not lessen our dismay at the implicit emasculation of the concept of force and power as the fountainhead of those institutions designated "the state."

Furthermore, to press the "nooks and crannies" theory into the analysis of simple societies, as suggested by Almond and Coleman, can have the precise result they deplore, the obscuring of the dynamics of political development. On the other hand, recognition of the fact that there was a time, not too long ago by anthropological reckoning, when there were no states does not obscure anything. Certainly it does not necessarily encourage a static point of view; for example, the discussion of the instability of stratified society at the end of Chapter 5 shows how dynamic analysis can be if it is related to the nonstate-state dichotomy. Nor does use of this dichotomy necessarily prevent broad-gauged analysis that includes, *inter alia*, evaluation of economic, kin, ritual, or other relationships. This conclusion, too, should be obvious from the discussions in our earlier chapters.

Although the question goes beyond the simple problem of definitions, it is necessary to confront that problem at the outset. Once again it is not a matter of determining the "true" meaning of a word but of stating clearly what that word is to mean in our usage and why it is advantageous to use it that way.

Admittedly, earlier tendencies to hypostasize the state —to associate the state with some mystical concept of "people," of mass will, or of highest good—did considerable damage. It is not surprising that such usage would prompt reaction. But it would be foolhardy to dispense with a useful and necessary concept because it has been improperly refined.

A state is not simply a legislature, an executive body, a judiciary system, an administrative bureaucracy, or even a government. From the point of view developed in earlier chapters, a state is better viewed as the complex of institutions by means of which the power of the society is organized on a basis superior to kinship. Note that all the power available in a society does not necessarily become pre-empted by the state. Of course, the state may be involved in a number of contests for major and minor sources of power and it may even temporarily lose some of those contests, although to lose too big a one, or too often, will invariably lead to a shift in the *de facto* power-holding group.

When I say that the state is an organization of the power of society I refer to many different things. Of great importance is the claim of the state to paramountcy in the application of naked force to social problems. Frequently this means that warfare and killing become monopolies of the state and may only be carried out at times, in places, and under the specific conditions set by the state. Other episodes involving killing will draw the punitive reaction of the organized state force. Sometimes this concern for the control of violence invades the narrowest of kin groups and even extends to the individual's rights to his own person as in the frequent prohibition of suicide.

In the final analysis the power of a state can be manifested in a real physical force, an army, a militia, a police force, a constabulary, with specialized weaponry, drill, conscription, a hierarchy of command, and the other paraphernalia of structured control. How different from what we encountered in exploring political control in egalitarian and rank society. To the extent that a stratified society lacks formal and specialized mechanisms of control it courts disaster, for in the face of weakening bonds of kinship, in face of the commonplace realization that the web of kin cannot contain the enlarged population or the increasing numbers of others, of non-kinsmen in the society, it becomes a question of developing formal, specialized instruments of coercion or reverting to a more easily maintained system of access rights to basic resources. It is the task of maintaining general social order that stands at the heart of the development of the state. And at the heart of the problem of maintaining general order is the need to defend the central order of stratification—the differentiation of categories of population in terms of access to basic resources. Undoubtedly, as already indicated, one means of doing this is to indoctrinate all members of society with the belief that the social order is right or good or simply inevitable. But there has never been a state which survived on this basis alone. Every state known to history has had a physical apparatus for removing or otherwise dealing with those who failed to get the message.

PRISTINE STATES

All contemporary states, even those that seem to be lineally descended from the states of high antiquity, like China, are really secondary states; the pristine states perished long ago. The word "perished" is unfortunate. States, despite several efforts to deal with them as organic entities, are not organic at all, and although they may come to an end, they certainly do not "die" in anything but an analogical sense. Indeed, few and legendary have been the states which came to termination by the extinction of their populations; usually a rather large body of survivors has carried on under a new political system. Perhaps it would be more appropriate to consider the end of a state to be a process more like dismantling or disassembling, as the component institutions and their related social groups or associations break apart and fall individually, or, more significantly, fall *collectively* into disuse.

At any rate, there once were states that emerged from stratified societies and experienced the slow, autochthonous growth of the specialized formal instruments of social control out of their own needs for these institutions. Through time the institutions coalesce and with this unification emerges a power, held and manipulated perhaps by a priest, a warrior, a manager, or a charismatic madman who just happens to be the genealogical leader of the largest kin group in the now heterogeneous social fabric. The power itself represents a quantum leap over anything previously wielded, but it is a long time before the wielders of the new power realize its full extent and possibilities. Far from being a conscious creation of naturally power-hungry psychological types, it is at least as probable that the power develops more rapidly than the abilities of its handlers. It takes time for a king to become a god.

When a pristine state emerges it does so in a political

vacuum. That is, there is no other more highly developed state present that might help it toward stateship. A pristine state does not appear as a reaction to colonial pressures. No outside society is manipulating the economy, drawing off or developing resources, putting in money, drawing off labor, or even supplying a flow of goods, the motion of which might call forth a new group of entrepreneurs either native to the society or drawn from abroad. The pristine state does not have models available to build on or to reject. There are no constitutions, legislatures, bureaucracies, armies, commissariats, or police departments to copy. There are not even full-scale kings but only lineage heads, temporary war chiefs, or big-men—the private redistributors whose power is as fragile as their last successful party.

It is not the case, however, that pristine states grew without company. By the very nature of the population distribution in late Neolithic times, the stratified-society-going-pristine-state was surrounded by other societies, some of these, also agricultural, developing in tandem. This development is helped by rivalry, trade, warfare, and communication in sharpening needs for more political specialization, for more professional organization, and for tighter internal control. There is one thing, however, that such a society can do in such an environment that is not possible in a ranking society, much less an egalitarian one. It can overrun less well-organized neighbors and incorporate them within its own system as an inferior social stratum. This is the developmental juncture where conquest theories of the state fit. The state is virtually born, and stratification is well established as a fully functioning system; then warfare can lead to conquest and the emergence of superstratification on the basis of an already well-elaborated system of stratification.

To discuss fully the identity of the pristine states and to attempt to describe the precise nature of their emergence is not possible in these pages. It may be that the task is ultimately impossible in any context for the reasons alluded to earlier: Literacy appears only with the emergence of the earliest states, and recorded history is much younger. The kinds of evidence we have are essentially archaeological and inferential. Although the general patterns of emergence may be discerned, details are fragmentary at best.

How many pristine states have been known? Note first the phrasing of the question, which deliberately implies that some pristine states may have flourished at least briefly without leaving behind any clues to their existence. It may well be, for example, that one or more pristine states may have appeared in Africa south of the Sahara three or more millenniums ago. As knowledge of Africa is enriched and more and more archaeology is undertaken, it may be possible to detect remnant influences that will enhance the probability that one or more such states existed, only to disappear from sight and memory.

In terms of actual empirical evidence the problem of the number of pristine states remains complex. Should all known examples of pristine state formation be contracted to two, one center in the Old World and the other in the New? If so, what are the candidates for the primary initiating centers? In the Old World, to take the earliest known appearances of state organization, the contest for priority seems in the studies of recent years to have tipped in favor of Mesopotamia rather than Egypt. Yet to what extent in this very first situation does the juxtaposition of two centers figure as a crucial aspect of the situation. That is, it must be asked whether this matter of juxtaposition was itself a necessary ingredient in the rise of the state in the Near East. Beyond the immediate realm of Mesopotamia and Egypt, cases can be made for the pristine emergence of the state in the Indus and Yellow River Valleys. Yet both of these cases, particularly the latter, are weakened by the relative lateness of state development vis-à-vis the sequence of events in the Middle East. Furthermore, the archaeology of the early Indus civilization reveals elements that certainly originated farther west, suggesting that some influences were felt from more complex societies that already existed. In China too there is some debate about the independence of its Neolithic foundations and also of its subsequent development.

Although the question is partly an empirical one that must await further archaeological contributions, it has substantial theoretical aspects that I apologize for raising without being able to settle. Once pristine states are well developed and actively pushing out the limits of their populations and areas, the relations between such states and their less well-organized hinterlands are relatively simple to follow. But what of the earliest periods? Central to the matter is the question of how much or how little pressure or stimulation of a higher center on a lower one constitutes a case of secondary development? Skipping over the Indus situation, the problem is most clearly presented in the Chinese data. At the time of emergence of the earliest known Chinese state, perhaps 3,500 years ago, the Near East had already known some 1,500 years of state organization. Furthermore, as Chang Kwang-chih, among others, has noted: "many essential elements of Chinese civilization, such as bronze metallurgy, writing, the horse chariot, human sacrifice, and so forth, had appeared earlier in Mesopotamia" (Chang, 1963, p. 136). The conclusion was quick to follow: "Many scholars argue that civilization came to China as a result of stimulus diffusion from the Near East . . ." (Chang, 1963, p. 136). Chang himself does not think that the question can yet be resolved, with regard to Chinese civilization, but he obviously favors the opposite interpretation, that many of these developments were convergent. Part of his case rests on the demonstration that if Chinese civilization did arise "suddenly," it did not arise without substantial previous foundation. But even accepting the older hypothesis of stimulus diffusion, can such a theory be extended to embrace the origins of the state? Really there are two questions here. It is one thing to imagine or find examples of the stimulus diffusion of an object or a technique. The idea of cultivating plants, of making ceramics, or of using a certain kind of tool can be envisaged as spreading over vast distances, largely through the actual transport of the end products or the spread of information about them. It is not so easy to envisage the spread of a collection of institutions comprising a particular form of the state unless at the same time there is some substantial ongoing revision of the society that prepares a climate receptive to the new institutions. It is just such preparation that is lacking in China, except as a normal indigenous process that is almost completely contained within the core area of Chinese culture. In the face of such considerations, then, I personally lean to interpreting China as a case of pristine state formation, and for similar reasons I consider the earlier Indus valley state (or states?) in the same way. Not so, however, the growth of the states that appear in so many nineteenth-century treatments of the origin of the state. Without going into detail here, I simply state that it seems to me that such famous states of antiquity as those of Crete, Greece, Troy, and Persia—and certainly Rome and all the states of western and northern Europe—are secondary.

THE BASIC NATURE OF THE STATE

The state, then, is a collection of specialized institutions and agencies, some formal and others informal, that maintains an order of stratification. Usually its point of concentration is on the basic principles of organization: hierarchy, differential degrees of access to basic resources, obedience to officials, and defense of the area. The state must maintain itself externally as well as internally, and it attempts this by both physical and ideological means, by supporting military forces and by establishing an identity among other similar units.

The primary functions of the state, internal and external maintenance of a specific order of stratification, give rise immediately to a number of characteristic institutions. Here, of course, there is much more latitude in what any particular state may develop. The situation can be analyzed in terms of Marshall Sahlins and Elman R. Service's general and specific evolution: The leap to the state is of general evolutionary status and all states, both pristine and secondary, have a core of features in common. But the subsequent development of particular states, even of particular pristine states, is specific, hence essentially local-adaptive and divergent. Nonetheless, all must have dealt or must continue to deal with some combination of the following: Population must be controlled in a number of senses. The state should have some means of identifying its own subjects or citizens, of distinguishing members and nonmembers. This is often accomplished by setting boundaries, but it can be done through birth and parentage. In either case it is necessary to define the unit and, beyond this, to have individuals identify themselves with this unit. Sometimes this also involves the construction of a variety of categories of membership or it may require effective limitation on the physical mobility of the members or of nonmembers, the latter being forbidden to enter, or admitted in small numbers under special restrictions. Sooner or later most states are concerned about the size of their membership, and censuses are run to discover this. Censuses, of course, relate to another common attribute of states to which we shall turn very shortly; they tax or otherwise make levies upon their memberships, for the activities that the state carries out must be subsidized.

The state must deal with trouble cases. Quite early there appears some statement of norms associated with sanctions. Customary handling of disputes does not automatically disappear, but customary rules and procedures are reinforced by formal iteration and application. Rules that might have applied between kin groups are now applied within kin groups by an external force. With the state comes the possibility that members of a common kin group can accuse one another, sue one another, and betray one another to a larger society that stands beyond kin. If the emergent state defines the limits of interpersonal injury and aggression, it also is soon required to handle disputes over things and over agreements. Beyond the growth of law in this sense, there is the necessary growth of procedure, of courts or their equivalents, of officers of adjudication, officers of punishment, record keepers and communicators, and varieties of functionaries that differ from system to system.

The state must establish and maintain sovereignty, which may be considered the identification and monopoly of paramount control over a population and an area. When the state is defined as in this chapter, it follows that its structure must be in a sense cellular, that is, made up of a variety of different kinds of components, with these components being joined into subsystems that articulate with the whole, with the larger structure of government, only at higher levels. Examples of component cellular subsystems include family and kin groups, communities and regions, offices and bureaus, clubs and gangs, and even layers and levels of the administrative apparatus itself. In the communications among these sometimes disparate entities there is always an understood priority of arrangement of orders and coercive inducements to decisions, the level of highest ultimate priority is equivalent to the internal concept of sovereignty. There is also an external aspect of sovereignty as discrete political units recognize or dispute each other's autonomy. It is not necessary, however, to go more deeply into these difficult matters in the present discussion (*cf.* Fried, *n.d.*).

Externally oriented maintenance of sovereignty has through most of history rested in the final analysis on military activities. Yet a moment's pause and reflection will bring many questions about this sweeping statement. A military establishment is always dependent upon the general economy of the state which supports it. It also is liable to ideological pressures on its morale, and these relate to larger aspects of the society. It is also evident that history has known many small states, militarily weak, that have endured for relatively long periods amidst more powerful neighbors. Thus weak sovereignties may be protected by concatenations having little to do with the small state in question, as when Thailand remained sovereign between French and British colonial expansions. Still, the fact has been that even the smallest states have had some military sting, and this they frequently maximize through combinations established by treaties that retain their sovereignty while promising broader military support.

It is in the maintenance of internal sovereignty, however, that some of the most fascinating questions about political organization lie. As discussed in Chapter 1, sovereignty is tied to legitimacy and that in turn requires more than naked power. No state known has ever been devoid of an ideology that consecrated its power and sanctioned its use. Many states, however, have undergone situations in which, to use the familiar Chinese phrase, the mandate of heaven has been lost by a ruling group. Where this has happened within a social system, or even as the result of violent overthrow attendant upon invasion, the basic principles of the previous order of stratification have rarely been seriously altered. Instead, a new portion of the population assumes the vacated roles and statuses, and the old order is resumed with minor alterations.

That analysis of the concept of legitimacy is an ultimate problem for the social scientist is patent from the nature of the phenomenon. As indicated in our first chapter, even such a crusty proponent of positive polity as John Austin recognized that physical power alone was not sufficient to integrate a state. Yet growing sophistication brings the realization that power lies not merely in the ability to direct police or other military force at a specific social object, but in such things as control of sources of information and the means of communication. From what we know of the ancient pristine states, these were matters of great significance from the outset. That early ruling elites sometimes appeared in priestly guise, making the specialized business of government and management an esoteric art, or that some nonpriestly ruling classes achieved the same end by controlling literacy and making recorded history their personal tool is evidence of this.

A very early complication in the rise of states is the development of a social sector that stands beneath the rulers but acts as the agency of control. Here is the inevitable bureaucracy that in some states burgeons and seems to overwhelm all other aspects of administration. Elsewhere a military establishment may play the central role, or it may be the ritualists, or a group whose power stems from crucial roles in the system whereby goods are produced or otherwise obtained and circulated. Often there is a combination of these, varying through time and with other factors that affect the society at large. Analogists, who detect the functions underlying these roles in simpler societies, often jump to the conclusion that the state is omnipresent or, what is much the same thing, that there is no distinctive thing as a state. To the extent that such a view encourages understanding of the means by which even the simplest societies are articulated and integrated it may be tolerated. But such a view has its cost, that is, the obscuring of great regularities in the evolution of society and of the central and recurrent role of the limitation of rights of access to basic resources in the quantum leap in social structure that has attended the emergence of the state.

We may conclude this brief consideration of the nature of the state by briefly noting one function that begins as a derived need and soon contends for dominance among all the functions. To carry out all the other functions, the specialized apparatuses of the state must have means of transforming basic resources into more fluid kinds of wealth. There must be a treasury or bursary which can support and underwrite the activities of state minions whose efforts are far removed from the daily tasks of subsistence. It is not necessary at the outset that this wealth be in the form of media of exchange, but the efficiency of the state is so much increased by the invention of all-purpose money that few experiments in stateship have long endured without it. But, whether a state has adopted all-purpose money or not, it must have means of separating the producers of raw wealth from a greater or lesser portion of the output. Taxation has many forms. One of the most interesting is the conscription of labor which, for all its crudeness, has the advantage of flexibility, enabling the rulers to concentrate effort on tasks in their own order of priority.

At this juncture the involuted character of the state becomes predominant. Operation of the fiscal apparatus, though almost an end in itself, feeds back into every other function already mentioned and creates additional ones. More and more specialists are needed to operate the system. More and more devices are needed to maintain increasing exploitation of the population. More than any other form of human association, the state is devoted to expansion—of its population, of its territory, of its physical and ideological power. Small wonder that there have been so few pristine states in history for when such a state appears in a given area of the world it quickly sets about converting its environing societies into parts or counterparts of itself. The appearance of a pristine state, then, is the trigger of a usually vast movement toward state formation. States that arise due to such a process, however, do not repeat the steps which the original state experienced. These are the secondary states.

SECONDARY STATES

There is an interesting theory that the evolution of air-breathing life transformed the earth and paradoxically created conditions under which further appearances of such life from nonliving matter could no longer take place as a spontaneous phenomenon on this planet. Whether or not this is a valid picture of an event in biochemical evolution, something much like it took place when pristine states appeared in a few places between about 5,000 and 3,000 years ago in the Old World and the New. While such states did not succeed in transforming all other societies into parts or counterparts of themselves, they did begin a process of penetration that seems to be culminating in our own time. More to the point, the appearance of a pristine state in an area frequently precludes further spontaneous pristine development as adjacent societies are forced into secondary molds.

If the analysis of the previous pages and of the previous chapter is essentially correct, the appearance of a pristine state is not a random process but is determined by the presence of certain finite conditions. It follows from this that those areas in which the state has appeared most recently, and of course always through secondary processes, are areas where deficiencies in local conditions have to be made up by pressures and models and stimuli originating from already established states. In our own contemporary world colonialism has played this role. It can be shown, for example, that states that in their expansion, overrun simpler societies have grave problems in effectively exploiting the areas occupied by those societies, or their labor potential, unless they make far reaching changes in the social organizations they encounter. Because the basic institutions of stateship are lacking in the invaded societies, there is no means by which the intruder can obtain the compulsive holds it requires. The natives are described as lazy and shiftless, disorganized, undisciplined and uncooperative. One solution, much favored in the past, is the extirpation of the entire population. If pressure to occupy the area is not so great, other means are employed, and first among these is the imposition of external organization, a chain of command. Where no chiefs exist, chiefs are found, usually created by fiat. Such political reformation of simple societies never goes on in a vacuum. Simultaneously, the native economy is undermined and transformed by the introduction of money, new commodities, wage labor or slavery, and a more or less subtle erosion of older patterns of access to basic resources. At the same time new ideologies are introduced and despite varying amounts of syncretic maintenance of older belief systems, new religions bring new ideas of hierarchy and subordination, a new view of labor, and altered ideas of interpersonal relations.

Secondary states emerge through processes quite different from those that give rise to the pristine states. It is unfortunate that all real examples of state formation available for first-hand investigation are of secondary type. All too often, students of such state formation have assumed that, except for the inevitable unique elements that mark any particular case, the process of developing stateship they observe is the one that must always transpire. The present book has been an attempt to controvert that view, and attempt also to sketch a theory of the evolution of ranking, social stratification, and the state compatible with the information presently on hand and in the spirit of contemporary political anthropology.

BIBLIOGRAPHY

Aberle, David F. 1952. "'Arctic Hysteria' and Latah in Mongolia," *Transactions of the New York Academy of Sciences,* Series 11, 22:291–7.

Aberle, David F., A. K. Cohen, A. K. Davis, M. J. Levy, Jr., and F. X. Sutton. 1950. "The Functional Prerequisites of a Society," *Ethics,* 60:2.

Adams, Robert M. 1966. *The Evolution of Urban Society.* Chicago: Aldine.

Aginsky, Burt W. 1949. *This Man-Made World.* New York: Rinehart (preliminary edition).

Almond, Gabriel A., and James S. Coleman (eds.). 1960. *The Politics of Developing Areas.* Princeton: Princeton University Press.

Anderson, Paul K., and James L. Hill. 1965. *"Mus musculus:* Experimental Introduction of Territory Formation," *Science,* 148:1753–5.

Austin, John. 1954. *The Province of Jurisprudence Determined* and the Uses of the Study of Jurisprudence. New York: Noonday. First published 1832 and 1863.

Balikci, Asen. 1964. Development of Basic Socio-Economic Units in Two Eskimo Communities. Ottawa: National Museum of Canada Bulletin 202.

Barton, Roy F. 1949. The Kalingas, Their Institutions and Custom Law. Chicago: University of Chicago Press.

Beaglehole, Ernest, and Pearl Beaglehole. 1938. Ethnology of Pukapuka. Honolulu: Bishop Museum Bulletin 150.

Bentley, Arthur F. 1949. The Process of Government. Bloomington, Ind.: Principia Press. First published 1908.

Berle, A. A., Jr., and Gardiner C. Means. 1932. The Modern Corporation and Private Property. New York: Commerce Clearing House.

Berndt, C. H. 1961. "The Quest for Identity: The Case of the Australian Aborigines," Oceania, 30:81–107.

Berndt, Ronald M. 1962. Excess and Restraint: Social Control Among a New Guinea Mountain People. Chicago: University of Chicago Press.

Berndt, Ronald M., and Catherine H. Berndt. 1951. Sexual Behavior in Western Arnhem Land. New York: Viking Fund Publications in Anthropology 16.

————. 1964. The World of the First Australians. Chicago: University of Chicago Press.

Birket-Smith, Kaj. 1929. The Caribou Eskimos, Material and Social Life and their Cultural Position. Copenhagen: Gyldendal.

Blair, Archibald. 1789. "Capt. Blair's Report, Dated 9th June," in "Extracts from the Bengal Consultations of the XVIIIth Century Relating to the Andaman Islands," in R. C. Temple (ed.), The Indian Antiquary, 29 (1900): 103–16.

Boas, Franz. 1897. "The Social Organization and the Secret Societies of the Kwakiutl Indians," Annual Report of the Board of Regents of the Smithsonian Institution for the Year Ending June 30, 1895, pp. 311–738. Washington, D. C.: Government Printing Office.

Bohannan, Paul. 1957. Justice and Judgement Among the Tiv. London: Oxford.

————. 1963. Social Anthropology. New York: Holt, Rinehart & Winston.

Brown, P., and H. C. Brookfield. 1959. "Chimbu Land and Society," *Oceania*, 30:1–75.

Brown, W. Jethro. 1906. *The Austinian Theory of Law*. London: Murray.

Brownlee, Frank. 1943. "The Social Organization of the Kung (!Un) Bushmen of the North-Western Kalihari," *Africa*, 14:124–9.

Burnham, James. 1941. *The Managerial Revolution*. New York: Day.

Buxton, Jean. 1958. "The Mandari of the Southern Sudan," in John Middleton and David Tait (eds.), *Tribes Without Rulers*. London: Routledge.

California, State of. 1955. *Progress Report to the Legislature by the Senate Interim Committee on California Indian Affairs*. Sacramento: Senate of the State of California.

Cappannari, Stephen C. 1960. "The Concept of Property Among Shoshoneans," in Gertrude E. Dole and Robert L. Carneiro (eds.), *Essays in the Science of Culture in Honor of Leslie A. White*. New York: Crowell.

Carpenter, C. R. 1942. "Societies of Monkeys and Apes," *Biological Symposia*, 8: 177–204.

———. 1965. "The Howlers of Barro Colorado Island," in Irven DeVore (ed.), *Primate Behavior*, pp. 250–91. New York: Holt, Rinehart & Winston.

Chance, M. R. A. 1961. "The Nature and Special Features of the Instinctive Social Bond of Primates," in Sherwood L. Washburn (ed.), *Social Life of Early Man*, pp. 17–33. Chicago: Aldine.

Chang Kwang-chih. 1963. *The Archaeology of Ancient China*. New Haven: Yale University Press.

Codere, Helen. 1950. *Fighting with Property*. Monograph of the American Ethnological Society 18. New York: Augustin.

Cohen, Felix S. 1935. "Transcendental Nonsense and the Functionalist Approach," *Columbia Law Review*, 35:809–49.

Colson, Elizabeth. 1951. "The Plateau Tonga of Northern Rhodesia," in Elizabeth Colson and Max Gluckman (eds.), *Seven Tribes of British Central Africa*. London: Oxford.

———. 1953. *The Makah Indians*. Minneapolis: University of Minnesota Press.

Curtis, Edward S. 1913. *The North American Indian, Vol. IX:*

The Salishan Tribes of the Coast. Cambridge, Mass.: Harvard University Press.

Davie, Maurice R. 1929. *The Evolution of War*. New Haven: Yale University Press.

DeVore, Irven, and K. R. L. Hall. 1965. "Baboon Ecology," in Irven DeVore (ed.), *Primate Behavior*, pp. 20–52. New York: Holt, Rinehart & Winston.

Drucker, Philip. 1939. "Rank, Wealth and Kinship in Northwest Coast Society," *American Anthropologist*, 41:55–65.

————. 1951. *The Northern and Central Nootkan Tribes*. Bureau of American Ethnology Bulletin 144. Washington, D. C.: U. S. Government Printing Office.

————. 1965. *Cultures of the North Pacific Coast*. San Francisco: Chandler.

Easton, David. 1953. *The Political System*. New York: Knopf.

Edel, M. M. 1965. "African Tribalism: Some Reflections on Uganda," *Political Science Quarterly*, 80:357–72.

Eisenstadt, S. N. 1963. *The Political Systems of Empires*. New York: Free Press.

Elkin, A. P. 1964. *The Australian Aborigines*. Sydney: Angus & Robertson.

Epstein, A. L. 1958. *Politics in an Urban African Community*. Manchester: University of Manchester Press.

Fathauer, George H. 1961. "Trobriand," in David M. Schneider and Kathleen Gough (eds.), *Matrilineal Kinship*. Berkeley: University of California Press.

Firth, Raymond. 1926. "Proverbs in Native Life, With Special Reference to those of the Maori," *Folk-lore*, 37:134–53, 245–70.

————. 1940. *The Work of the Gods in Tikopia*. London School of Economics and Political Science Monographs on Social Anthropology 1 and 2.

————. 1956. *Human Types* (rev. ed.). London: Nelson.

————. 1957. *We, the Tikopia* (2nd ed.). London: Allen & Unwin. First ed. published 1936.

————. 1959. *Economics of the New Zealand Maori* (2nd ed.). Wellington, N. Z.: R. E. Owen, Government Printer. First ed. published 1929.

————. 1959. *Social Change in Tikopia*. New York: Macmillan.

———. 1961. *History and Traditions of Tikopia.* Wellington, N. Z.: The Polynesian Society Memoir 33.

———. 1963. "Bilateral Descent Groups: An Operational Perspective," in Isaac Schapera (ed.), *Studies in Kinship and Marriage,* pp. 22–37. Royal Anthropological Institute Occasional Paper 16.

———. 1965. *Primitive Polynesian Economy* (2nd ed.). London: Routledge. First ed. published 1939.

Firth, Raymond, and James Spillius. 1963. *A Study in Ritual Modification: The Work of the Gods in Tikopia in 1929 and 1952.* London: Royal Anthropological Institute Occasional Paper 19.

Fortes, Meyer. 1940. "The Political System of the Tallensi of the Northern Territories of the Gold Coast," in Meyer Fortes and E. E. Evans-Pritchard (eds.), *African Political Systems,* pp. 239–71. London: Oxford.

Fortes, Meyer, and E. E. Evans-Pritchard. 1940. *African Political Systems.* London: Oxford.

Fortune, R. F. 1932. *Sorcerers of Dobu.* London: Routledge.

Freeman, J. D. 1961. "On the Concept of the Kindred," *Journal of the Royal Anthropological Institute,* 91:192–220.

Freire-Marreco, B. W., and J. L. Myres. 1912. *Notes and Queries on Anthropology,* (4th ed.). London: Royal Anthropological Institute.

Fried, Morton H. 1952. "Land Tenure, Geography and Ecology in the Contact of Cultures," *The American Journal of Economics and Sociology,* 11:391–412.

———. 1957. "The Classification of Corporate Unilineal Descent Groups," *Journal of the Royal Anthropological Institute,* 87:1–29.

———. 1961. "Warfare, Military Organization, and the Evolution of Society," *Anthropologica,* 3:134–47.

———. 1964. "Ideology, Social Organization and Economic Development in China: A Living Test of Theories," in Robert A. Manners (ed.), *Process and Pattern in Culture,* pp. 47–62. Chicago: Aldine.

———. n.d. "State," in *Encyclopedia of Social Sciences,* in press.

Friedrich, Carl Joachim. 1963. *Man and His Government: An Empirical Theory of Politics.* New York: McGraw-Hill.

Gluckman, M. 1960. "Tribalism in Modern British Central Africa," *Cahiers d'Etudes Africaines,* 1:55–70.

———. 1965. *Politics, Law and Ritual in Tribal Society.* Oxford: Blackwell.

Goldenweiser, A. 1922. *Early Civilization.* New York: Knopf.

Goodall, Jane. 1965. "Chimpanzees of the Gombe Stream Reserve," in Irven DeVore (ed.), *Primate Behavior,* pp. 425–73. New York: Holt, Rinehart & Winston.

Gough, Kathleen. 1962. "Variation in Interpersonal Kinship Relations," in David M. Schneider and Kathleen Gough (eds.), *Matrilineal Kinship,* pp. 577–613. Berkeley: University of California Press.

Grote, George. 1846–1856. *History of Greece* (12 vols.). London: Murray.

Gumplowicz, Ludwig. 1899. *The Outlines of Sociology,* Frederick W. Moore (trans.). Philadelphia: American Academy of Political and Social Science.

Hall, K. R. L., and Irven DeVore. 1965. "Baboon Social Behavior," in Irven DeVore (ed.), *Primate Behavior,* pp. 53–110. New York: Holt, Rinehart & Winston.

Harris, Marvin. 1963. *The Nature of Cultural Things.* New York: Random House.

Hart, C. W. M., and Arnold R. Pilling. 1960. *The Tiwi of North Australia.* New York: Holt, Rinehart & Winston.

Hartland, E. Sidney. 1924. *Primitive Law.* London: Methuen.

Herskovits, Melville J. 1960. *Economic Anthropology.* New York: Knopf.

Hobbes, Thomas. 1929. *Hobbes's Leviathan.* Oxford: Clarendon. Reprinted from the edition of 1651.

Hobhouse, L. T. 1922. "The Historical Evolution of Property, in Fact, and in Idea," in *Property, Its Duties and Rights,* pp. 3–31. New York: Macmillan.

Hoebel, E. Adamson. 1949. *Man in the Primitive World.* New York: McGraw-Hill.

———. 1954. *The Law of Primitive Man.* Cambridge: Harvard University Press.

———. 1958. *Man in the Primitive World* (2nd ed.). New York: McGraw-Hill.

Hogbin, H. Ian. 1934. *Law and Order in Polynesia: A Study of Primitive Legal Institutions.* London: Christopher.

————. 1951. *Transformation Scene, The Changing Culture of a New Guinean Village.* London: Routledge.

Hogbin, H. Ian, and C. H. Wedgwood. 1953. "Local Grouping in Melanesia, Part 1," *Oceania,* 23:241–76.

Holmberg, Allan R. 1950. *Nomads of the Long Bow: The Siriono of Eastern Bolivia.* Smithsonian Institution Institute of Social Anthropology Publication 10. Washington, D. C.: U. S. Government Printing Office.

Imanishi, Kinji. 1963. "Social Behavior in Japanese Monkeys, *Macaca fuscata,*" in Charles H. Southwick (ed.), *Primate Social Behavior.* Princeton: Van Nostrand. Originally published in *Psychologia,* 1 (1957): 47–54.

International Labour Organization. 1953. *Indigenous Peoples.* Geneva: International Labour Office.

Jay, Phyllis. 1965. "The Common Langur of North India," in Irven DeVore (ed.), *Primate Behavior,* pp. 197–249. New York: Holt, Rinehart & Winston.

Jones, J. Walter. 1940. *Historical Introduction to the Theory of Law.* Oxford: Clarendon.

Josselin de Jong, J. P. B. de. 1948. *Customary Law (A Confusing Fiction).* Amsterdam: Koninklijke Vereeniging Indisch Instituut, Mededeling 80, *Afr. Volkenkunde* 29.

Josselin de Jong, Patrick Edward de. 1951. *Minangkabau and Negri-Sembilan, Socio-Political Structure in Indonesia.* Leiden: University of Leiden.

Jouvenal, Bertrand de. 1957. *Sovereignty, an Inquiry into the Political Good.* Chicago: University of Chicago Press.

Kardiner, Abram. 1945. *The Psychological Frontiers of Society.* New York: Columbia University Press.

Keesing, Felix. 1962. *The Ethnohistory of Northern Luzon.* Stanford: Stanford University Press.

Kelson, Hans. 1961. *General Theory of Law and State,* Anders Wedberg (trans.). New York: Russell. Originally published as Vol. 1, Twentieth Century Legal Series, Cambridge: Harvard University Press, 1945.

Kirchhoff, Paul. 1959. "The Principles of Clanship in Human Society," in M. H. Fried (ed.), *Readings in Anthropology,* II, 260–70. New York: Crowell. Originally written in 1935. First published in 1955 in *Davidson Journal of Anthropology.*

Koford, Carl B. 1963. "Group Relations in an Island Colony of Rhesus Monkeys," in C. H. Southwick (ed.), *Primate Social Behavior*, pp. 136–52. Princeton: Van Nostrand.

————. 1965. "Population Dynamics of Rhesus on Cáyo Santiago," in Irven DeVore (ed.), *Primate Behavior*, pp. 160–74. New York: Holt, Rinehart & Winston.

Kortlandt, A., and M. Kooij. 1963. "Protohominid Behavior in Primates," *Symposia of the Zoological Society of London*, No. 10, pp. 61–88.

Krause, Aurel. 1956. *The Tlingit Indians*, Erna Gunther (trans.). Seattle: University of Washington Press. First ed. published in 1885.

La Potherie, Bacqueville de. 1753. *Histoire de l'Amerique Septentrionale*, Vol. 1. Paris: Nyon.

Leach, E. R. 1954. *Political Systems of Highland Burma: A Study of Kachin Social Structure*. Cambridge: Harvard University Press.

Leacock, Eleanor. 1954. *The Montagnais "Hunting Territory" and the Fur Trade*. Menasha, Wis.: American Anthropological Association Memoir 78.

————. 1955. "Matrilocality in a Simple Hunting Economy (Montagnais-Naskapi)," *Southwestern Journal of Anthropology*, 11:31–47.

Lewis, George C. 1849. *An Essay on the Influence of Authority in Matters of Opinion*. London: Parker.

Lips, Julius E. 1938. "Government," in Franz Boas (ed.), *General Anthropology*, pp. 487–534. New York: Heath.

Lin, Yueh-hua. 1961. *The Lolo of Liang Shan*, Pan Ju-shu (trans.). New Haven: Human Relations Area Files Press.

Lowie, Robert H. 1927. *The Origin of the State*. New York: Harcourt.

McIlwraith, T. F. 1948. *The Bella Coola Indians* (2 vols.). Toronto: University of Toronto Press.

MacLeod, William Christie. 1928. "Economic Aspects of Indigenous American Slavery," *American Anthropologist*, 30:632–50.

Mair, Lucy. 1962. *Primitive Government*. London: Pelican.

Malinowski, Bronislaw. 1926. *Crime and Custom in Savage Society*. London: Routledge.

————. 1934. "Introduction," in H. Ian Hogbin, *Law and Order in Polynesia: A Study of Primitive Legal Institutions.* London: Christopher.

Marsden, Samuel. 1932. *The Letters and Journals of Samuel Marsden 1765–1838,* John Rawson Elder (ed.). Dunedin, Scot.: Coulls, Somerville, Wilkie.

Marshall, Lorna. 1959. "Marriage Among !Kung Bushmen," *Africa,* 29:335–65.

————. 1960. "!Kung African Bands," *Africa,* 30:325–55.

————. 1961. "Sharing, Talking, and Giving: Relief of Social Tensions Among !Kung Bushmen," *Africa,* 31:231–49.

Mason, Otis T. 1892. "The Land Problem," in Brooklyn Ethical Association (sponsor), *Man and the State,* pp. 111–30. New York: Appleton.

Mauss, Marcel. 1947. *Manuel d'ethnographie.* Paris: Payot.

Meek, C. K. 1946. *Land Law and Custom in the Colonies.* London: Oxford.

Meggitt, M. J. 1962a. *Desert People, A Study of the Walbiri Aborigines of Central Australia.* Sydney: Angus & Robertson.

————. 1962b. "Indigenous Forms of Government Among the Australian Aborigines." Paper presented at the Fifteenth Réunion de la Société Jean Bodin, Brussels, 1962. (mimeo.)

Métraux, Alfred. 1946. "Indians of the Gran Chaco," in Julian H. Steward (ed.). *Handbook of South American Indians,* 1:197–370. Washington, D. C.: U. S. Government Printing Office.

Michelson, Truman. 1932. *Notes on the Fox Wapanowiweni.* Washington, D. C.: The Smithsonian Institution, Bureau of American Ethnology, Bulletin 105.

Mills, M. E. Elton, and Monica Wilson. 1952. *Land Tenure.* Pietermaritzburg: Shuter & Shooter.

Mitchell, J. C. 1956. *The Kalela Dance.* Rhodes Livingstone Papers 27. Manchester: Manchester University Press.

Moerman, Michael. 1965. "Ethnic Identification in a Complex Civilization: Who Are the Lue?" *American Anthropologist,* 67:1215–30.

Moore, Stanley. 1960. "Marxian Theories of Law in Primitive Society," in Stanley Diamond (ed.). *Culture in History: Essays in Honor of Paul Radin.* New York: Columbia University Press.

Morgan, Lewis. 1878. *Ancient Society*. New York: Holt, Rinehart & Winston.

———. 1922. *League of the Ho-Dé-No-Sau-Nee or Iroquois*. New York: Dodd Mead. First published in 1851.

Murdock, George P. 1949. *Social Structure*. New York: Macmillan.

———. 1960. "Cognatic Forms of Social Organization," in G. P. Murdock (ed.), *Social Structure in Southeast Asia*. Chicago: Viking Fund Publications in Anthropology 29. Quadrangle.

Murphy, Robert F., and Julian H. Steward. 1956. "Tappers and Trappers: Parallel Processes in Acculturation," *Economic Development and Cultural Change*, 4:335–55.

Naroll, Raoul. 1964. "On Ethnic Unit Classification," *Current Anthropology*, 5:283–91, 306–12.

Newman, Philip L. 1965. *Knowing the Gururumba*. New York: Holt, Rinehart & Winston.

Nieboer, H. J. 1900. *Slavery as an Industrial System*. The Hague: Nijhoff.

Oberg, Kalervo. 1953. *Indian Tribes of Northern Mato Grosso, Brazil*. Smithsonian Institution, Institute of Social Anthropology, Publication 15. Washington, D. C.: U. S. Government Printing Office.

Okada, Ferdinand E. 1954. *A Comparative Study of Marginal Societies*. Unpublished Ph.D. dissertation, Columbia University.

Oliver, Douglas. 1955. *A Solomon Island Society*. Cambridge, Mass.: Harvard University Press.

Olson, Ronald L. 1954. *Social Life of the Owikeno Kwakiutl*. Anthropological Records, Vol. 14. Berkeley: University of California Press.

Parsons, Talcott. 1961. "An Outline of the Social System," in Talcott Parsons, Edward Shils, Kaspar D. Naegele, and Jesse R. Pitts (eds.), *Theories of Society*, pp. 30–79. New York: Free Press.

Petrullo, Vencenzo. 1939. *The Yaruros of the Capanaparo River, Venezuela. Bureau of American Ethnology Bulletin No. 123*, pp. 163–290. Washington, D. C.: U. S. Government Printing Office.

Polanyi, Karl. 1953. *Semantics of General Economic History*.

New York: Columbia University Council for Research in the Social Sciences. Reprinted in M. H. Fried (ed.), 1959, *Readings in Anthropology*, 2:162–84. New York: Crowell.

Pospisil, Leopold. 1958. *Kapauku Papuans and their Law*. New Haven: Yale University Publications in Anthropology 54.

————. 1963. *Kapauku Papuan Economy*. New Haven: Yale University Publications in Anthropology 67.

Putnam, Patrick. 1948. "The Pygmies of the Ituri Forest," in Carleton S. Coon (ed.), *A Reader in General Anthropology*, pp. 322–41. New York: Holt, Rinehart & Winston.

Radcliffe-Brown, A. R. 1930. "Former Numbers and Distribution of the Australian Aborigines," *Official Yearbook of the Commonwealth of Australia*, 23. Canberra: Commonwealth Bureau of Census and Statistics.

————. 1933. "Sanction, Social," in *Encyclopedia of the Social Sciences*, 18:531–4. New York: Macmillan. Reprinted in A. R. Radcliffe-Brown, *Structure and Function in Primitive Society*. New York: Free Press, 1952.

————. 1948. *The Andaman Islanders*. New York: Free Press.

Rasmussen, Knud. 1931. *The Netsilik Eskimos, Social Life and Spiritual Culture*. Copenhagen: Gyldendal.

Ratner, Stanley C., and M. Ray Denny. 1964. *Comparative Psychology: Research in Animal Behavior*. Homewood, Ill.: Dorsey.

Reynolds, Vernon, and Frances Reynolds. 1965. "Chimpanzees of the Budongo Forest," in Irven DeVore (ed.), *Primate Behavior*, pp. 368–424. New York: Holt, Rinehart & Winston.

Richardson, Jane. 1940. *Law and Status among the Kiowa Indians*. Monographs of the American Ethnological Society 1. New York: Augustin.

Rivers, W. H. R. 1906. *The Todas*. New York: Macmillan.

Robertson, Edmund. 1911. "Jurisprudence," in *Encyclopaedia Britannica* (11th ed.), 15:571–9. Substantially reprinted from the 9th ed. of 1875–1889.

Royal Anthropological Institute. 1951. *Notes and Queries in Anthropology* (6th ed.). London: Routledge.

Sahlins, Marshall. 1958. *Social Stratification in Polynesia*. Seattle: University of Washington Press.

————. 1959. "The Social Life of Monkeys, Apes and Primitive

Men," in M. H. Fried (ed.), *Readings in Anthropology*, 2:186–99. Also printed in *Human Biology*, 31 (1959): 1.

————. 1961. "Segmentary Lineage: An Organization of Predatory Expansion," *American Anthropologist*, 63:322–45.

————. 1962. *Moala: Culture and Nature on a Fijian Island*. Ann Arbor: University of Michigan Press.

————. 1963. "Poor Man, Rich Man, Big Man, Chief: Political Types in Melanesia and Polynesia," *Comparative Studies in Society and History*, 5:285–303.

————. 1965. "On the Sociology of Primitive Exchange," in *The Relevance of Models for Social Anthropology*. Association for Social Anthropologists Monograph 1. New York: Praeger.

Sait, Edward McChesney. 1938. *Political Institutions, A Preface*. New York: Appleton.

Schaller, George B. 1963. *The Mountain Gorilla: Ecology and Behavior*. Chicago: University of Chicago Press.

————. 1965. "The Behavior of the Mountain Gorilla," in Irven DeVore (ed.), *Primate Behavior*, pp. 324–67. Princeton: Van Nostrand.

Schapera, Isaac. 1956. *Government and Politics in Tribal Societies*. London: Watts.

Schebesta, Paul. 1929. *Among the Forest Dwarfs of Malaya*. London: Hutchinson.

Scheffler, Harold W. 1965. *Choiseul Island Social Structure*. Berkeley: University of California Press.

Schneider, Joseph. 1950. "Primitive Warfare: A Methodological Note," *American Sociological Review*, 15:772–7. Reprinted in Leon Bramson and George W. Goethals (eds.), *War: Studies from Psychology, Sociology, Anthropology*, pp. 275–83. New York: Basic Books.

Scott, John Paul. 1958. *Aggression*. Chicago: University of Chicago Press.

Seagle, William. 1941. *The Quest for Law*. New York: Knopf.

Seebohm, Frederic. 1883. *The English Village Community*. London: Longmans.

Seligman, C. G., and B. Z. Seligman. 1911. *The Veddas*. Cambridge, Eng.: Cambridge University Press.

Service, Elman R. 1960a. "Kinship Terminology and Evolution," *American Anthropologist*, 62:747–63.

————. 1960b. "Sociocentric Relationship Terms and the Australian Class System," in Gertrude E. Dole and Robert L. Carneiro (eds.), *Essays in the Science of Culture in Honor of Leslie A. White.* New York: Crowell.

————. 1962. *Primitive Social Organization: An Evolutionary Perspective.* New York: Random House.

Shils, E. A., and Henry A. Finch. 1949. *The Methodology of the Social Sciences.* [by Max Weber] New York: Free Press.

Shirokogoroff, S. M. 1929. *Social Organization of the Northern Tungus.* Shanghai: Commercial Press.

Smith, Marian W. 1940. *The Puyallup-Nisqually.* New York: Columbia University Press.

Sorokin, Pitirim. 1959. *Social and Cultural Mobility,* pp. 11–70. New York: Free Press. Reprinted in Talcott Parsons, et al., (eds.), 1961, *Theories of Society,* pp. 570–3.

Soustelle, Jacques. 1962. *The Daily Life of the Aztecs on the Eve of the Spanish Conquest,* Patrick O'Brian, trans. New York: Macmillan.

Southwick, Charles H., Azhar Beg, and M. Raffiq Siddiqi. 1965. "Rhesus Monkeys in North India," in Irven DeVore (ed.), *Primate Behavior,* pp. 111–59. New York: Holt, Rinehart & Winston.

Speck, Frank G. 1915. *Family Hunting Territories and Social Life of Various Algonkian Bands of the Ottawa Valley.* Canada, Geological Survey Memoir 70 (Anthropology Series). Ottawa: Government Printing Bureau.

————. 1926. "Land Ownership Among Hunting Peoples in Primitive America and the World's Marginal Areas," *Twelfth International Congress of Americanists,* 2: 323–32. Rome: Garroni.

Spencer, Baldwin, and F. J. Gillen. 1904. *The Northern Tribes of Central Australia.* London: Macmillan.

————. 1912. *Across Australia,* Vol. 1. London: Macmillan.

Spencer, Herbert. 1893. *The Principles of Sociology,* Vol. 2. New York: Appleton.

————. 1896. *The Principles of Sociology,* Vol. 1. New York: Appleton.

Spencer, Robert F. 1959. *The North Alaskan Eskimo.* Bureau of American Ethnology, Bulletin 171. Washington, D. C.: U. S. Government Printing Office.

Spillius, James. 1957. "Natural Disaster and Political Crisis in a Polynesian Society: An Exploration of Operational Research," *Human Relations*, 10:3–28, 113–26.

———. 1957. "Polynesian Experiment: Tikopian Islanders as Plantation Labour," *Progress*, 46:91–6.

Steenhoven, Geert vanden. 1956. *Research Report on Caribou Eskimo Law*. Ottawa: Canadian Department of Northern Affairs.

———. 1962. *Leadership and Law among the Eskimos of the Keewatin District, Northwest Territories*. The Hague: Nitgeverij Excelsior.

Stefansson, Vilhjamur. 1919. *My Life with the Eskimos*. New York: Macmillan.

Stern, Bernhard J. 1934. "Slavery, Primitive," in *Encyclopedia of the Social Sciences*, 14:73–4. New York: Macmillan.

Stevenson, H. N. C. 1943. *The Economics of the Central Chin Tribes*. Bombay: The Times of India Press.

Stevenson, Robert F. 1968. *Population and Political Systems in Tropical Africa*. New York: Columbia University Press.

Steward, Julian. 1938. *Basin-Plateau Aboriginal Sociopolitical Groups*. Bureau of American Ethnology, Bulletin 120. Washington, D. C.: U. S. Government Printing Office.

———. 1955. *Theory of Culture Change*. Urbana: University of Illinois Press.

Strong, William Duncan. 1929. "Cross-Cousin Marriage and the Culture of the Northeastern Algonkian," *American Anthropologist*, 31:277–88.

Swanton, John R. 1943. *Are Wars Inevitable?* Smithsonian Institute War Background Studies 12. Washington, D. C.: U. S. Government Printing Office.

Teicher, Morton I. 1960. "Windigo Psychosis," in Verne F. Ray (ed.), *Proceedings of the 1960 Annual Spring Meeting of the American Ethnological Society*, pp. 1–129. Seattle: University of Washington Press.

Thomas, Elizabeth Marshall. 1959. *The Harmless People*. New York: Knopf.

Turney-High, Harry Holbert. 1949. *Primitive War, Its Practice and Concepts*. Columbia: University of South Carolina Press.

Tylor, Edward B. 1888. "On a Method of Investigating the Development of Institutions: Applied to Laws of Marriage and Descent," *Journal of the Royal Anthropological Institute*, 18:245–69.

Vanoverbergh, Morice. 1925. "Negritos of Northern Luzon," *Anthropos*, 20:148–99, 399–443.

Vayda, Andrew P. 1956. *Maori Warfare*. Manuscript Ph.D. dissertation, Columbia University.

———. 1960. *Maori Warfare*. Wellington, N. Z.: Polynesian Society Monographs 2.

Vayda, Andrew P., Anthony Leeds, and David Smith. 1961. "The Place of Pigs in Melanesian Subsistence," in Viola E. Garfield (ed.), *Proceedings of the 1961 Annual Spring Meeting of the American Ethnological Society*, pp. 69–77. Seattle: University of Washington Press.

Vinogradoff, Paul. 1920. *Outlines of Historical Jurisprudence*, Vol. 1. London: Oxford.

Vos, A. de. 1965. "Territorial Behavior Among Puku in Zambia," *Science*, 148:1752–3.

Vreeland, H. H. 1958. "The Concept of Ethnic Groups as Related to Whole Societies," in W. M. Austin (ed.), *Report of the Ninth Annual Round Table Meeting on Linguistics and Language Studies*, pp. 81–8. Monograph Series on Languages and Linguistics 11. Washington, D. C.: Georgetown University Press.

Wagley, Charles. 1940. "The Effects of Depopulation Upon Social Organization; as Illustrated by the Tapirape Indians," *Transactions of the New York Academy of Sciences*, 3: 12–16.

Warner, W. Lloyd. 1958. *A Black Civilization* (rev. ed.). New York: Harper.

Weber, Max. 1947. *The Theory of Social and Economic Organization*, A. M. Henderson and Talcott Parsons (trans.), Talcott Parsons (ed.).

———. 1954. *Max Weber on Law in Economy and Society*, Edward Shils and Max Rheinstein (trans.), edited and annotated by Max Rheinstein, Twentieth Century Legal Series, Vol. 6. Cambridge, Mass.: Harvard University Press.

———. 1962. *Basic Concepts in Sociology*, H. P. Secher (trans.). New York: Citadel.

White, Leslie A. 1959. *The Evolution of Culture.* New York: McGraw-Hill.

Wittfogel, Karl A. 1955. "Private Property in Simpler Hydraulic ('Oriental') Societies," *Sociologus,* 5:43–54.

———. 1957. *Oriental Despotism.* New Haven: Yale University Press.

Wolf, Eric R. 1955. "Types of Latin American Peasantry: A Preliminary Discussion," *American Anthropologist,* 57:452–71.

Wright, Quincy. 1942. *A Study of War,* Vol. 1. Chicago: University of Chicago Press.

INDEX

Aberle, David F., 8, 82
Abipone, 219
acculturation, 55, 193
accumulation, 187–8
Adams, Robert, 197–8, 201
administrative functions, 21
adultery, 78
African Bushmen, 12, 54, 75, 91,
    172; interpersonal conflict in,
    77–8; sharing and, 98; terri-
    toriality of, 95
African Pygmies, 54, 68
age, 28; division of labor and,
    129; status and, 32–3
aggression, 42, 80, 147–8, 237;
    see also conflict; war
Aginsky, Burt, 86
agriculture, 53, 112, 119, 130,
    168; hydraulic, 208–12; women
    in, 129
Algonkians, Eastern, 193; social
    organization of, 60–1
Almond, Gabriel, 227–8
altruism, 35
"amok," 80
ancestor worship, 138, 140
Ancient Society (Morgan), 162
Andaman Islanders, 55, 86, 91,
    104
Anderson, Paul K., 46 *n.*
animal (noncultural) societies,
    38–49, 57; boundaries of,
    95–6; see also primate societies
anomie, 56
Apayao, 61

"Arctic hysteria," 82
"aristoi," 127
Aristotle, 83
association, basis of, 45–6
Austin, John, 11 *n.*, 16, 17–9,
    23–5, 145, 151–2, 238
Australian aborigines, 54, 82, 85;
    group affiliation of, 98–9; kin-
    ship ties of, 120; law among,
    91–3; marriage among, 127;
    population of, 55–6; territori-
    ality in, 95–8
authoritarianism, 13 *n.*
authority: defined, 13; internali-
    zation of, 23; law and, 90;
    leadership and, 83, 88–9,
    133–4; power and, 11–4; *vs.*
    prestige, 43; in rank society,
    134, 146–7, 150

baboon, 39, 47, 48; role prescrip-
    tion in, 42
Balikci, Asen, 59, 87
band, 55; composite, 69, 99; con-
    flict in, 70–82; defined, 67;
    division of labor in, 70; ecol-
    ogy and, 56–7; exogamy in,
    69–70; external relations of,
    94–107; kinship in, 68, 69,
    120–1, 124; law in, 90–4;
    leadership in, 83–9, 98–9; mem-
    bership in, 83–9; military or-
    ganization in, 104; ownership
    in, 130–1, 136, 142–3, 188;